Unfinished Projects

Unfinished Projects

Decolonization and the Philosophy of Jean-Paul Sartre

Paige Arthur

VERSO

London • New York

First published by Verso 2010
Copyright © Paige Arthur
All rights reserved
(Chapter 10 first appeared in Jonathan Judaken, ed.,
Race After Sartre (Buffalo: SUNY Press, 2008))

The moral rights of the author have been asserted

1 3 5 7 9 10 8 6 4 2

Verso
UK: 6 Meard Street, London W1F 0EG
US: 20 Jay Street, Suite 1010, Brooklyn, NY 11201
www.versobooks.com

Verso is the imprint of New Left Books

ISBN-13: 978-1-84467-398-8 (hbk)
ISBN-13: 978-1-84467-399-5 (pbk)

British Library Cataloguing in Publication Data
A catalogue record for this book is available from the British Library

Library of Congress Cataloging-in-Publication Data
A catalog record for this book is available from the Library of Congress

Typeset by MJ Gavan, Truro, Cornwall
Printed in the United States by Worldcolor/Fairfield

Contents

Acknowledgements

Though it is difficult to know where to start in thanking the many people who have influenced the course of this book, I wish to begin with the professors who inspired me and taught me so much. A wonderful teacher named Vernon Lidtke sparked my interest in intellectual history when I was an undergraduate at Johns Hopkins. At UC Berkeley, Martin Jay was a perspicacious reader whose comments and direction were crucial at all stages—especially finishing. His patience, support, and wry sense of humor humanized the writing process. Tyler Stovall's wise guidance and encouragement helped me enormously. Carla Hesse was an invaluable mentor to me over the years. I give thanks also to Loïc Wacquant, whose intensity and ludic manner mark all of his students.

There are many others who have helped this project along, either through conversation, reading drafts, friendship, general encouragement, or renting me an apartment in Paris. They are Julianne Gilland, Julian Bourg, Tina Sessa, Ania Wertz, Joel Revill, Jenelle Troxell, Brett Wheeler, Judith Surkis, Sarah Kennel, Chris Otter, Rebecca Wittmann, Dirk Moses, Andrew Jainchill, Jonathan Judaken, Jay Winter, Richard Wolin, Jerrold Seigel, and the late Martin Malia. I want to make special mention of Sam Moyn, who connected me with Verso Books, and whose suggestion many years ago that I look into the origins of the idea of the "cultural Other" set me on the path of writing this book (though he may not remember it). Thanks are also owed to Christian Barry and Joel Rosenthal at the Carnegie Council for Ethics in International Affairs and Carlene Bauer at *Elle* magazine for being understanding bosses and coworkers, as well as interested parties, as I finished writing this book.

Finally, I give greatest thanks to my partner, Josh, and my parents, Dave and Tam.

Introduction:
Sartre, the Intellectual Left, and the Emergence of the "Cultural" Other

> You did not have to be that bright to realize, right from the first revolts, that we were witnessing the beginning of what was to be the most significant event of the second half of the century: the awakening of nationalism among the Afro-Asian peoples.[1]

"He was my master," wrote Gilles Deleuze of Sartre—a master, but not in the typical sense of a philosophy professor guiding his students along a path of academic wisdom. The year was 1964, and Sartre had just declined the Nobel Prize for literature, citing his unwillingness to become an institution. For Deleuze, the act was purely Sartrean; it emphasized both the refusal to represent any one thing—indeed, the philosophical will to "contest the notion of *representation*, the very *order* of representation"—and the constant impulsion toward being different from public impressions of him, from his past works, and even from himself. Deleuze called Sartre his master because, for him, Sartre represented the "modern" projects of revolutionizing every aspect of his work and his person, generating "radical novelty," and making genuine "events" of his acts and utterances. He admired Sartre's new and aggressive manner of posing problems and polemicizing them; he marked the recently ended war in Algeria as the crucial source for reinflating Sartre's hope for a politics of freedom, which had been let down after the Liberation. "We speak of Sartre as if he belongs to an outmoded epoch," Deleuze noted. "Alas! It is rather we who are already outmoded in the contemporary conformist moral order. At least Sartre allows us to wait vaguely for future moments, for reprises in which thought will reconstitute itself."[2]

---

1 Jean-Paul Sartre, "The Frogs Who Demand a King," in *Colonialism and Neocolonialism*, trans. Azzedine Haddour, Steve Brewer, and Terry McWilliams (New York: Routledge, 2001), 102; first published in *L'Express*, September 25, 1958.

2 Gilles Deleuze, " 'Il a été mon maître,' " *L'île déserte et autres textes: textes et entretiens, 1953–1974*, ed. David Lapoujade (Paris: Editions de Minuit, 2002), 112, 110. The essay originally appeared in *Arts*, November 28, 1964, 8–9. Deleuze also wrote two reviews of Sartre-related texts early in his career. See his review of Régis Jolivet's *Le problème de la mort chez M. Heidegger et J.-P. Sartre* in *Revue philosophique de la France et de l'étranger* 143 (January–

Deleuze was not the only poststructuralist philosopher to note the weight and significance of Jean-Paul Sartre for the generation that succeeded him.[3] Jacques Derrida, making reference to Sartre's famous statement that Marxism was the untranscendable horizon of his time, once claimed that "in the end, it was Sartre who was the 'untranscendable horizon.' "[4] This fascination extended to Michel Foucault, who had hoped to rival Sartre's popular success, and who, along with Deleuze, established an activist relationship with the older philosopher in the early 1970s. There is, however, a palpable ambivalence concerning these attitudes. Not only had Sartre tried to adapt his philosophy of freedom to Marxism—a social theory criticized by Deleuze, Derrida, and Foucault, as well as by many French intellectuals by the late 1970s—but he had also been a fellow-traveler of the French Communist Party (PCF) from 1952 to 1956.[5] From these engagements issued a set of texts defending the Soviet Union that have come under sharp criticism from intellectuals who began to gain prominence in the late 1970s, "The Communists and the Peace" most famous among them. Bernard-Henri Lévy, the chief "New Philosopher" of that era, signaled the general tone of these critics, writing, "These texts can and must be condemned. It can and must be found shocking that the author of *Being and Nothingness* lent his support to a politics that was the living denial of everything he had said and thought until then."[6]

As Deleuze's evocation of the French-Algerian War suggests, however, there is another view to take of Sartre's trajectory, one that would align it with the history of decolonization alongside the history of communism. While Marxist political movements had suffered major losses in France by the end of the 1970s, the effects of colonialism were still alive and kicking. If Deleuze was right that "Sartre allows us to wait vaguely for future moments," perhaps one of those moments appeared in 1996, at a conference on *postcolonialisme*—a term

---

March 1953), 108–9; and his review of Sartre's *Materialismus und Revolution* (German-language edition) in *Revue philosophique de la France et de l'étranger* 145 (April–June 1955), 237.

3   For a re-evaluation of Sartre's significance for the next generation, see Nik Farrell Fox, *The New Sartre: Explorations in Postmodernism* (New York: Continuum, 2003); and Tilottama Rajan, *Deconstruction and the Remainders of Phenomenology* (Stanford: Stanford University Press, 2002).

4   Interview with Jacques Derrida in 1983, reprinted in *De Sartre à Foucault: Vingt ans de grands entretiens dans* Le Nouvel Observateur (Paris: Hachette, 1984), 371–2.

5   Foucault had briefly joined the PCF, a fact he did not like avowing publicly. Michel Foucault (interview), "Foucault répond à Sartre," *La Quinzaine littéraire* 46 (March 1–15, 1968), 20–2.

6   Bernard-Henri Lévy, *Sartre: The Philosopher of the Twentieth Century*, trans. Andrew Brown (Malden, Mass.: Polity, 2003), 356.

that did not yet share the heavy theoretical baggage of its Anglophone cognate. In the opening article of the issue of *Dédale* dedicated to the conference, French political scientist Sami Naïr discussed the "two looks" that still hold North and South in reciprocal relations of both conflict and exchange.[7] The North, according to Naïr, still too often views the South with the assimilating gaze of the Orientalist. The South, "facing the objectivizing enterprise of the North," still too often constitutes its elites (like technocrats, businessmen, and intellectuals both secular and religious) as modes of being primarily in relation to the West. What is particularly striking about this contribution to the nascent debate on postcolonialism—what, if anything, it means in France—is the author's use of various discourses that define the way the French talk about relations between the West and the non-West. There is, first, the language of the French Revolution and a broad republicanism: democracy, individual liberty, universal inclusion, juridical equality, and human rights. There is, second, the postwar language of economic and social transformation and its attendant concerns: globalization, immigration, host societies, development, identity, minorities.

And there is, third, framing the myriad of questions concerning the meaning of postcolonialism according to Naïr, the language of Sartre's existential phenomenology: *l'altérité, la mauvaise foi, autrui, l'authenticité, l'être-pour-autrui*[8]—and, of course, the dueling looks made famous in his discussion of the for-itself's encounter with the Other in *Being and Nothingness*, but used, more pertinently for postcolonialism, to political ends in his famed essay on negritude, "Black Orpheus." In the opening paragraph of that essay, written in 1948 as the preface to Léopold Sedar Senghor's *Anthologie de la nouvelle poésie nègre et malgache*, Sartre, like Naïr decades later, wrote of the conflicting but mutually reinforcing looks of two unequal collectivities: "The white man has enjoyed for three thousand years the privilege of seeing without being seen … Today, these black men have fixed their look upon us and our look is thrown back in our eyes."[9]

The turn that Sartre took in "Black Orpheus," and earlier in *Anti-Semite and Jew*, toward describing the situation of individuals in terms of their perceived membership in collectivities of race and religion marked a departure from his fixation on the absolute freedom of the individual. Though Sartre noted toward the end of *Being and Nothingness* the many aspects of the

---

7   Sami Naïr, "Les deux regards," *Dédale* 5 and 6 (Spring 1997), 17–30.

8   Ibid., 17, 17, 18, 26, 26.

9   Jean-Paul Sartre, *Black Orpheus*, trans. S. W. Allen (Paris: Gallimard, 1963), 7–8 (translation modified).

contingent situation into which any individual might be thrown, including racial and religious affiliation, in that work he nonetheless held tenaciously to the view that those characteristics—a person's facticity—cannot dampen the free spontaneity of consciousness, which can ultimately choose itself no matter its lot.

This postwar turn toward a centering of situation, collectivities, and the mediation of human freedom in Sartre's philosophical concerns was contemporaneous with the beginning of his two great political engagements, the first with Marxism and communism, the second with Third World independence movements. In his philosophical works, Sartre's interest shifted from discussions of the phenomenology of consciousness, elaborated in *The Transcendence of the Ego* and *Being and Nothingness*, toward a phenomenology and sociology of social being. There are ongoing debates about whether or not this shift constituted a "break," as Lévy would have it, or whether there are significant continuities between the "early" and the "late" Sartre. In a recent contribution to this debate, Sam Coombes argues that the Sartrean notion of bad faith, for example, overlaps with Marxist conceptions of false consciousness.[10] A primary difference between the two, however, concerns who (or what) is responsible for each of these states. For the early Sartre, the fact of individual freedom meant that, ultimately, each one of us is responsible for choosing to adopt the position of bad faith. Though Sartre never renounced his idea of the freedom of individuals to choose both how they make (transcend) their own surroundings and how they give meaning to them, by the time of the *Critique of Dialectical Reason*, Vol. I (1960), Sartre made it clear that he believed that that freedom is often severely circumscribed.[11]

In his explicitly political, nonartistic works, which are mostly occasional pieces including articles in *Les Temps Modernes* and other publications, prefaces to works by non-Western, non-French, and/or non-white writers, and speeches and manifestos, Sartre's engagements were clear, even blunt. Often written in a muckraking and deliberately provocative style, these works repeated almost inevitably the Manichean view of a hierarchical world divided between forces of revolution and counterrevolution for which Sartre was famous. The accuracy of these characterizations of the conflicts of Sartre's

---

10   Sam Coombes, *The Early Sartre and Marxism* (New York: Peter Lang, 2008).

11   Sartre says in the 1976 documentary, *Sartre par lui-même*, that he would never have been able to join the French Communist Party because it would have forced him to recant his notion of free, spontaneous consciousness. He cites Georg Lukács's fate in renouncing *History and Class Consciousness* as one to be avoided. Alexandre Astruc and Michel Contat, *Sartre par lui-même* (Paris: Institut national de l'audiovisuel and Sodaperaga, 1976).

time—although accuracy, it must be admitted, may not have been a necessary part of these texts' rhetorical strategies—was always deeply contested, and it was left to Sartre's more rigorous works either to argue for their plausibility or to give a richer, more nuanced picture.

In the end, however, this need for rigor and justification led to Sartre's own undoing. A life-long disbeliever in any form of redemption, personal or collective, Sartre was unable in his final philosophical work to deliver what he had promised for so many years: a grounding for the view that the actions of individuals would lead to the creation of a single meaningful history. The projected work that would address this task, *Critique of Dialectical Reason*, Vol. II, was not published in Sartre's lifetime. The unfinished, labyrinthine manuscript that appeared after his death only served to emphasize the scope of its failure—in this and the first volume, which are comprised of hundreds of thousands of words, Sartre showed his self-appointed task to have been ultimately a Quixotic undertaking. On the ashes of this failed project lay the dialectic, History, Marxism, and, indeed, Sartre himself as an intellectual institution.

ANOTHER SARTRE

But was this really the end of Sartre? Did his failure to give Marxism a philosophical ground—which itself could be (and was) interpreted as a reflection of the inherent incapacity of Marxist regimes to harmonize human freedom with socialism—ultimately render his thinking obsolete, even during his own lifetime? The answer to these questions was yes, according to his many French detractors. This backlash against Sartre did not abate, however, even after his passing in 1980. Lévy tells us that the invective directed at Sartre was evidence of

a total hatred. It was a hatred which included every shade of opinion and pursued him to the grave. And it was a hatred which, above all, was expressed with a violence at once scatological and murderous, which I am not sure one can find many other examples of.[12]

It is important to keep in mind the intensity of many French intellectuals' reaction to Sartre—or, perhaps more to the point, his dominance—and it would seem that, as much as they would like to be rid of him once and for all, he is in

---

12 Lévy, *Sartre*, 34. Lévy devotes a section of the first chapter to the hatred of Sartre (33–8). Sartre sympathizer William McBride writes of the "phenomenon of Sartre-rejection or Sartre-dismissal" (82) in his essay, "Sartre and His Successors: Existential Marxism and Postmodernism at Our *Fin de Siècle*," *Praxis International* 11, no. 1 (April 1991), 78–92. Also on this theme, see the work of official biographer John Gerassi, *Jean-Paul Sartre: Hated Conscience of His Century* (Chicago: University of Chicago Press, 1984).

some sense still impossible to escape. Indeed, in the past ten years, there has been evidence of a rise in interest in Sartre—if only as a negative pole. Alain Renaut, one of the academic philosophers associated with the New Philosophy of the late 1970s, published *Sartre: Le dernier philosophe* in 1993, a book devoted to describing Sartre's irrelevance to contemporary philosophy.[13] Bernard-Henri Lévy, for his part, finds Sartre to be a suitable measure for the twentieth century. In *Sartre: The Philosopher of the Twentieth Century*, Lévy divides Sartre's life and work into phases of good and bad: an early, libertarian, "good" phase associated with his unengaged philosophy and creative works of the 1930s and early 1940s, and a later, communist, "bad" phase associated with *The Communists and the Peace*, Stalinism, Maoism, engaged theater, and a whole host of political "errors."[14]

The most pertinent fact concerning this global critique of Sartre's politics is that has focused almost exclusively on his Marxism and his political choices in support of Soviet communism in the mid 1950s and, later, French Maoists. The so-called New Philosophers made their careers on quasi-obsessive critiques of Marxism and those who made the "political error" (strangely, Lévy himself often uses this Marxist concept) of believing in its political promise. In the post–Cold War era, this particular critique has only gained in legitimacy in the French intellectual field, which is now dominated by liberal thinkers who are in the process of recuperating the neglected work of Sartre's contemporary Raymond Aron, and elevating Albert Camus to the 1950s' chief moralist.[15] An exclusive focus on this aspect of Sartre's work and politics, however, has hindered the study of Sartre's second great political engagement: that as a critic

---

13   Alain Renaut, *Sartre, le dernier philosophe* (Paris: Grasset, 1993). For a defense of Sartre's continuing relevance, see Juliette Simont, "The Last Picture Show (à propos du livre d'Alain Renaut, *Sartre, le dernier philosophe*)," *Les Temps Modernes* 574 (May 1994), 111–45.

14   See also Annie Cohen-Solal, *Sartre: A Life*, trans. Anna Cancogni (New York: Pantheon, 1987); and Tony Judt, *Past Imperfect: French Intellectuals, 1944–1956* (Berkeley: University of California Press, 1992).

15   For an American version of the phenomenon, see Tony Judt, *The Burden of Responsibility: Blum, Camus, Aron and the French Twentieth Century* (Chicago: Chicago University Press, 1998). It is odd that in discussing Camus the anti-communist moralist who argued for principled rather than revolutionary justice, Judt does not treat the development of Camus's ideas in relation to his own membership in the Communist Party (1935–37)—in fact, he does not even mention it. Camus had been dismissed from the party in 1937 after criticizing its accommodation with colonialism during the Popular Front. Addressing this rejection might have given more insight into the strong turn against communism that Camus took in the postwar era, and also might have complicated even more the already complicated picture of his views on Algeria. For a discussion of Camus's membership in the Communist Party, see Ronald Aronson, *Camus and Sartre: The Story of a Friendship and the Quarrel That Ended It* (Chicago: University of Chicago Press, 2003), 25.

of colonialism and neocolonialism.[16] Even Lévy acknowledges that, in spite of Sartre's universally "wrong" choices in favor of communism, he was often "right" in his choices in favor of decolonization, particularly in the case of Algeria where, as Lévy says, Sartre was "right" and Camus was "wrong"— the strong exception being his support of violence and terrorism to win that liberation.[17]

Right or wrong, Sartre's seemingly unconditional support for liberation movements around the world, what would come to be called his "Third Worldism," was a fact that, although related to his engagement with communism, cannot be reduced to it—particularly since this support often set him at odds with the Communist Party line. It was a political engagement that aided his turn toward stressing situation, collectivities, and the mediation of human freedom in his philosophical work, which was reflected in his choice of subjects and examples in his writing. Ultimately, his thinking on colonialism, decolonization, and neocolonialism supplied ambiguous concepts and a vocabulary for approaching what has come to be known as the "cultural" Other.

Moreover, Sartre's enduring significance among non-European intellectuals belies the assertions of irrelevance so strongly advanced by their French counterparts since 1980. After all, Sartre was the world's most famous intellectual, and his recognition of the seriousness and legitimacy of non-European intellectuals and their claims against European economic and cultural dominance lent symbolic credence both to them and their political causes. This relationship with non-European intellectuals was not an uncomplicated one, however. V.Y. Mudimbe has noted in his path-breaking book on the Africanist discourses of Europeans, *The Invention of Africa: Gnosis, Philosophy, and Knowledge*, that Sartre did not, of course, create the philosophical critique of colonialism ex nihilo. "The Indian criticism of colonialism," Mudimbe writes, "beginning in the 1920s, and the growing influence of Marxism from the 1930s onwards opened a new era and made way for the possibility of new types of discourses, which from the colonial perspective were both absurd and abhorrent."[18] However, Sartre, who was in the process of creating and occupying the dominant position in the postwar French intellectual field, was uniquely capable of focusing attention on his pet issues.[19] And, with the publication of

---

16   This fact is noted by Nourredine Lamouchi in his *Jean-Paul Sartre et le tiers monde: Rhétorique d'un discours anticolonialiste* (Paris: L'Harmattan, 1996).

17   See Lévy, *Sartre*, 346. For Lévy's discussion of the political error, see 355–80.

18   V.Y. Mudimbe, *The Invention of Africa: Gnosis, Philosophy, and the Order of Knowledge* (Bloomington: Indiana University Press, 1988), 83.

19   For a discussion of Sartre's achievement of dominating the postwar French intellectual field by synthesizing the social roles of the creator and the professor, see Anna

"Black Orpheus," Sartre "transformed negritude into a major political event and a philosophical criticism of colonialism."[20] It is this relationship with Senghor and the other writers of negritude that forms the basis for Mudimbe's suggestion that Sartre might be considered "an African Philosopher" of his time, and, further, that Sartre's interest in and support for the negritude movement as a moment in the dialectical movement of history was reflected in a shift in his work:

> A substantial part of *Being and Nothingness* is devoted to the tension between the *for itself* (*pour-soi*) and *for others* (*pour autrui*). Now Sartre dedicated himself to the analysis of the concrete consequences of this dialectic as illustrated by colonial systems.[21]

Though Mudimbe registers some ambivalence concerning the meaning of Sartre as an African philosopher, the literary critic and well-known participant in Anglo-American debates on postcolonialism Robert J. C. Young picks up the idea and runs with it in his preface to the English-language translation of Sartre's *Colonialism and Neocolonialism* (*Situations V* in French).[22] Young had previously written about Sartre as one of many demystifiers of the "white mythology" of European history in his monograph of that title.[23] In that book, Young's evaluation of Sartre's significance to this project is negative—he agrees fully with Claude Lévi-Strauss's claim that Sartre's understanding of history in the *Critique* is irremediably ethnocentric, because it still presumes the West as its meta-subject, and he concludes, "Sartre's courageous intervention against French and other colonialisms could not have a corresponding theoretical impact so long as he retained his historicist Marxist framework."[24] In his more recent preface, however, Young takes a different position: he argues that Sartre

---

Boschetti, *The Intellectual Enterprise: Sartre and Les Temps Modernes*, trans. Richard C. McCleary (Evanston, Ill.: Northwestern University Press, 1988).

20   Mudimbe, *The Invention of Africa*, 83.

21   Ibid., 83, 85. It is unclear how seriously Mudimbe takes this first suggestion. The chapter sub-section devoted to a discussion of Sartre is entitled, "J.-P. Sartre as an African Philosopher." Later on, however, Mudimbe exclaims, "But what an ambiguity in raising the French existentialist to the rank of philosopher of negritude!" (84). Mudimbe then argues that Senghor's choice of Sartre to write the foreword meant, ultimately, a "subjugat[ion of] the militants' generosity of heart and mind to the fervour of a political philosophy" and that Senghor "had asked Sartre for a cloak to celebrate negritude; he was given a shroud" (84, 85).

22   Robert J.C. Young, "Sartre: The 'African Philosopher,' " preface to Sartre, *Colonialism and Neocolonialism*. Young takes the title of his essay from Mudimbe's book.

23   Robert J.C. Young, "Sartre's Extravagances," in *White Mythologies: Writing History and the West* (New York: Routledge, 1990).

24   Ibid., 47.

has been unfairly ignored in postcolonial studies and that he might make an important contribution. Young says that the project behind bringing this particular volume of Sartre's essays to the English-speaking academic audience is to offer a correction.

Indeed, if Young's more recent assessment of Sartre reflects a dramatic reversal from *White Mythologies*, this may be a result of the fact that, in looking more closely at Sartre's work, it is clear that there is little that is simple or orthodox about his "historicist Marxist framework" (as Young himself knows). Young rightly focuses attention on the content of Sartre's *Critique*, which was written in the middle of the French-Algerian War and which bears the undeniable imprint of that conflict. Though the main project of the *Critique* is to account for the relationship between revolution and Stalinism, Sartre also devoted significant attention to colonialism—which he considered a system of institutions, practices, and attitudes—and the inherent (and justified) violence of decolonization. In fact, for Sartre, colonialism and anticolonialism represented the clearest and most powerful examples of his theory of praxis and struggle, and he used them to emphasize the "importance of substituting History for economic and sociological interpretations, or generally for all determinisms."[25]

Sartre's unique marriage of existentialism and Marxism in the *Critique*, and his steadfast refusal of determinism, lend themselves, in Young's opinion, quite readily to the needs of postcolonial discourse, even though Sartre has long been out of fashion as a philosopher in France. "Since the Althusserian attack on Sartre," he notes, "so rigorously and effectively deployed with respect to his Hegelianism, only anti- and postcolonial theory have continued to bring together this impossible but necessary articulation of the right to subjectivity with assimilation into the objectivity of history."[26] Though this would seem to skirt the issue—raised by Young himself in *White Mythologies*—of the relationship between History and ethnocentrism in Sartre's work, and hence of its utility for a discourse such as postcolonialism that tends to create local, plural histories, Young is right to highlight this particular legacy (or missed legacy, as the case may be) of Sartre's thinking. Though anticolonialism and post-colonialism are both heterogeneous discourses that cannot be reduced to a few

---

25   Jean-Paul Sartre, *Critique of Dialectical Reason*, Vol. I, *Theory of Practical Ensembles*, trans. Alan Sheridan-Smith (London: NLB, 1976), 720.

26   Young, "Sartre: The 'African Philosopher,'" xx. Young also writes, "Sartre's profound relation to postcolonial theory begins with his important demonstration of the possibility of bringing Marxism into a productive, new relation with different systems, forms of thought, and experience" (xvii).

common predicates, it is fair enough to say that both are politically engaged, and thus ill-served by the turn toward structuralism and the so-called death of the subject in the 1960s.

Interestingly enough, it would seem that a similar move to reread the later Sartre and shift his current historical significance is underway among some feminists—for many of the same reasons Young gives.[27] Sonia Kruks argues that Sartre has a bad reputation among feminists because he is associated primarily with what some take to be the masculinist Cartesianism of *Being and Nothingness* (and this in spite of that work's radical anti-essentialism, which might otherwise be attractive); they ignore later works, in particular the *Critique*. For Kruks, Sartre's "theory of situated, practical subjectivity" in the *Critique* is interesting because Sartre "defend[ed] particularity and difference while still exploring, at least as a heuristic device, the universalistic emancipatory vision of Marx."[28] She cites, in particular, "Sartre's account of collectives and of the serial relations of their members" as useful conceptual tools, arguing,

> The identities of individual women ... are constituted in large measure "in exteriority," as members of multiple collectives (for example, as objects of male sexual desire, as consumers of particular kinds of products, as members of ethnic collectives, as pregnant females, as workers in a segmented labor market). Moreover, the relationship between women and feminism ... can be clarified using Sartre's distinction between collectives and groups, that is, between passively mediated ensembles and intentionally created ones.[29]

Iris Marion Young strongly seconds Kruks's recuperation of the Sartre of the *Critique* in her essay, "Gender as Seriality: Thinking about Women as a Social Collective."[30] Like Robert J.C. Young, Kruks and Iris Marion Young emphasize both an active subjectivity—necessary to politics—and the necessary mediation of that subjectivity theorized at length in the *Critique*.

These concerns of postcolonialism and feminism provide the frame for new avenues of research into the emergence of some of Sartre's key concepts, and also into the dissemination of those concepts. These two discourses intersect, perhaps not coincidentally, at the notion of collective otherness—and, in

---

27   See Julien S. Murphy, ed., *Feminist Interpretations of Jean-Paul Sartre* (University Park: Pennsylvania State University Press, 1999).
28   Sonia Kruks, "Identity Politics and Dialectical Reason: Beyond an Epistemology of Provenance," in Murphy, ed., *Feminist Interpretations of Jean-Paul Sartre*, 240.
29   Ibid., 245.
30   Iris Marion Young, "Gender as Seriality: Thinking about Women as a Social Collective," in Murphy, ed., *Feminist Interpretations of Jean-Paul Sartre*.

particular, the otherness of marginal collectivities—and both take a keen interest in *Critique of Dialectical Reason* instead of *Being and Nothingness*.

ANOTHER FRANCE

The story I tell of Jean-Paul Sartre is not confined to the man and his work; it is also a story of France, of the relationship between France and its colonies, and of globalization more generally. It is a history of intellectual anticolonial protest and its legacy. Through Sartre, I try to grasp the profound transformations engendered by decolonization and, in particular, the Left's responses to them.

I begin by establishing Sartre's interest in colonialism and the struggle against it in the immediate postwar era in places like Indochina and Madagascar—that is, before the war in Algeria. In Part I, I take a close look at how Sartre's concerns with racism, anti-Semitism, and colonialism influenced the development of his philosophy from the 1940s to 1954. I examine Sartre's engagement with the negritude literary movement, the early mobilization of his journal, *Les Temps Modernes*, on behalf of Indochinese and Algerian nationalism, and his classic definition of anti-Semitism as a "hatred of humanity" as aspects of a shift away from a radical conception of individual human freedom toward a recognition of the force of collectively created bonds.

The movement toward decolonization in the 1940s and 1950s serves as a determining background for this intellectual trend. At work was a profound decentering of the European grounds of history, knowledge, and conceptions of the self—a process of which Sartre was but a very famous symptom. Nonetheless, it was Sartre's global fame and his willingness to use it in the service of non-Europeans that was important. Sartre wielded his symbolic capital strategically to lend support to causes created in the periphery. Unlike the anticolonialism of André Gide, which focused on reforming colonialism to make the European tutelage of non-European peoples more effective, Sartre's anticolonialism recognized outright the legitimate subjectivity of colonized peoples—not as potential, but as fact. His arguments in support of their right to self-determination were analogous to existentialist arguments concerning individual freedom: each person is responsible for her own acts, and evading such responsibility is to live in bad faith.

To what extent is such an analogy persuasive, however? Peoples are not persons. And even in Sartre's most advanced and rigorous discussion of the creation and functioning of collectivities, he does not grant them that status. One of the oddities of postwar French intellectual discourse has been the collapse of this very distinction through a shift in the meaning of the term, the

"Other." This term, which in phenomenological discourse designated the structure of *interpersonal* relationships, has now come to be identified as well with the structure of *intercultural* relationships. This oddity is directly traceable back to the influence of Sartre's *Being and Nothingness*, in particular his section on the "look" of the Other, as well as his essay "Black Orpheus," on Frantz Fanon's *Black Skin, White Masks* (1952). Here, Fanon dissected the meaning of a particular event: a white child pointing at him while saying to her mother, "Look, a Negro!"[31]

On what grounds might the analogy between the interpersonal and the intercultural Other hold, and can one find those grounds in Sartre's work? This is the task I turn toward in Part II, whose chapters focus on Sartre's arguments concerning the creation of "subhuman" groups in the colonial situation, the function of colonialism and racism in the *Critique of Dialectical Reason*, and, finally, that work's reception and significance in the wake of the French-Algerian War. Covering the period from 1954 to 1962—also the years of the war in Algeria—I explore further the shift in focus in Sartre's philosophy from radical freedom to objective constraints by paying particularly close attention to the way that Sartre applied his theories concerning such constraints to contemporary events. In my discussion of Sartre's social phenomenology of racism and the colonial situation, I show that he does not rely on a notion of "the Other" in order to describe relations between collectivities. I argue that, in fact, his work makes clear that the analogy in question is incoherent—that cultural or any other differences defined in terms of collective identity must be approached through an examination of social relationships, and not through an application of existential or psychological categories. That is, it calls into question the validity of the paradigm of "the Other" in describing and accounting for intercultural relationships.

In these chapters, I also discuss the most famous—and scandalous—of Sartre's applications of theory to event in this era, his preface to Frantz Fanon's

---

31   Frantz Fanon, *Black Skin, White Masks*, trans. Charles Lam Markmann (New York: Grove Press, 1967), 109. See David Macey's criticisms of the English translation of this book as well as his remarks on the influence of *Being and Nothingness* in "Fanon, phenomenology, and race," *Radical Philosophy* 95 (May/June 1999), 8–14. Macey also points out other important influences, including Maurice Merleau-Ponty and Jean Lhermitte. For other comments on the relationship between Sartre and Fanon, see Ranjana Khanna, *Dark Continents: Psychoanalysis and Colonialism* (Durham, N.C.: Duke University Press, 2003); Timothy J. Reiss, "Mapping Identities: Literature, Nationalism, Colonialism," in Christopher Prendergast, ed., *Debating World Literature* (New York: Verso, 2004), 110–47, esp. 143–6; and Patrick Williams, " 'Faire peau neuve'—Césaire, Fanon, Memmi, Sartre and Senghor," in Charles Forsdick, ed., *Francophone Postcolonial Studies* (London: Arnold, 2003), 181–91.

The Wretched of the Earth, in which he asserted that the violence of decolonization would produce new human beings and values, both in the colonies and the metropole. I argue, however, that this text is not exemplary of Sartre's thinking on colonialism, even though it is often taken to be. Indeed, without contextualizing the preface within the more meticulous argumentation of the *Critique*, the ambivalence of Sartre's attitude toward the outcomes of revolutionary movements and his explanations for their violence are lost.

The preface was, however, an important indication of the general radicalization of the French-Algerian War, which had begun in 1954, when the Front de Libération Nationale (FLN) launched a military campaign against the French army, with independence as its goal. In 1956, the socialist Left had broken apart, literally, over the Section Française de l'Internationale Ouvrière's (SFIO) support for giving the army "special powers" in Algeria—a move that led to the Battle of Algiers, famously captured in the 1966 film of that name. By 1958, the party only existed in truncated form, and the Left was splintered. With limited electoral success during the 1960s—the exception being François Mitterrand's challenge of de Gaulle for the presidency in 1965—it was not until the reconstitution of the socialists under the Parti Socialiste in 1972 that the Left once again became a significant electoral force on its own. The Parti Communiste Français (PCF)—which had also supported granting the special powers—was being bled of intellectual support not only for its ambivalent attitude toward Third World nationalist movements, but also for the continuing Stalinism of the party's leadership after Khrushchev's secret speech and the Soviet repression in Hungary.

With the divisions over the war in Algeria escalating, in May 1958, a constitutional crisis engulfed the country, provoked by the threat of revolt within the army by elements supporting the settler lobby in Algeria. It led to the collapse of the constitution and the end of the Fourth Republic. Charles de Gaulle stepped into power, only serving to deepen the fears of many on the Left that France was turning inexorably toward fascism. Sartre and the team at *Les Temps Modernes* viewed it as a coup; the militarization of French society, combined with the claims of the right-wing *pied noir* activists, evoked fears that the maintenance of colonialism was bolstering anti-democratic forces in France. Military exigency—and, in fact, the army itself—was making political decisions in the place of the people. De Gaulle had come to power, Sartre pointed out, because the majority of the army supported him. Thus, he concluded, de Gaulle had, objectively, been imposed on France by the army.[32]

---

32   Sartre, "The Frogs Who Demand a King," 118.

Meanwhile, ex–*Temps Modernes* editor Francis Jeanson established a network of *porteurs de valise* ("suitcase carriers") to carry money clandestinely to the FLN. In 1960, Sartre and other leading intellectuals threw down the gauntlet to the regime, publishing their Manifesto of the 121, which recognized the justice of the FLN's cause and called on people (especially soldiers) not to participate in French repression. The Manifesto was immediately censored, and Sartre (among others) was targeted for assassination by the right-wing Organisation armée secrète (OAS).

No one was more disbelieving than Sartre when it was de Gaulle who brokered the peace deal giving independence to Algeria in 1962. In Part III, which treats the period from 1962 to 1968, I discuss the continuing political impotence on the Left in the aftermath of the war in Algeria, as de Gaulle claimed credit for mastering the colonialist lobby—thus stealing the Left's most powerful political chip, as most every observer recognized at the time. Still, I argue that intellectual anticolonial protest during the French-Algerian War provided a set of engagements that would strongly influence the politics of the Left to 1968 and beyond. Rather than seeing these years as a moment of quiet before the storm of 1968, I see them instead as years of activity that served to firm up left-wing commitments against imperialism and colonialism in all of its forms, as intellectuals such as Sartre found enormous prestige *outside* of France as a mode of compensation for their political weakness at home. Thus, I trace the well-known criticism of American "imperialism" and of the Vietnam War associated with the events of May 1968 back to intellectual anticolonial protest during the war in Algeria. I point out that an important model for left-wing intellectual activity and argumentation for the rest of the decade was the infamous petition, the Manifesto of the 121.

I am particularly concerned with this development of a global under-standing of personal responsibility in this period, which I examine through an analysis of three moments in Sartre's work in the 1960s: his 1963 eulogy of Patrice Lumumba, the leader of the newly independent Congo who had been assassinated in 1961; his "Rome Lecture" on ethics, which he delivered at the Gramsci Institute in 1964, but which was never published; and his participation in the 1967 Russell Tribunal, which was created to determine whether the United States was open to charges of war crimes in Vietnam. In these three cases, I show that the critique of colonialism and neocolonialism went hand-in-hand both with the development of an understanding of justice that was not confined to national communities, but rather defined across borders, and with the elaboration of an ethics that prioritized the needs of the "least favored" among humans, no matter where they exist. Finally, though, I point out that there was one clear engagement in which Sartre's call to prioritize the needs of the least favored did not yield clear ideas (at least in his own eyes) about which side merited greater support. This is the case with the Arab-Israeli conflict, which Sartre struggled with particularly in the later years of his life.

In Part IV, which treats the period from 1968 to 1980, the year of Sartre's death, I continue to trace the influence of intellectual anticolonial protest on left-wing politics, especially on the politics of the noncommunist Left. Specifically, I show how a postcolonial discourse on colonialism infected and shaped left-wing politics in the 1970s in the forms of anti-racist action in favor of immigrant rights, regionalist movements, and the left-wing turn away from Third Worldism and toward human rights concerns. Critiques of colonialism, I argue, provided both the primary basis for left-wing claims and a handy repository of easy-to-apply analogies concerning the injustice of the systems of exploitation that relied upon racial or ethnic divisions in the metropole. Immigration from the former colonies was cast as the importation of "colonialism" to France, with all of its attendant economic structures (Malthusianism, low wages, lack of sanitary living conditions), social stratification (de facto segregation), and patterns of thinking (racism). Regionalist movements, such as those in Brittany and Occitanie, employed the terms of both cultural and economic critiques of colonialism to justify their claims for autonomy or independence—that is, their wish to "decolonize" France itself.[33] Having allied himself in 1970 with the Maoist group Gauche Prolétarienne—whose newspaper, *La Cause du Peuple*, used the star power of his name on the masthead as a magical talisman to ward off state suppression of its views—Sartre contributed directly and indirectly to each of these causes, which were staples of Maoist activism in the early 1970s.

Finally, I argue in these chapters that the legitimacy of radical critiques of colonialism came under attack toward the mid 1970s. The story of intellectual anticolonial protest began with the idea, advanced by many on the Left in France in the 1950s, that human rights were best guaranteed when peoples were able to decide their own political fates—that is, when they gained independence. This idea was born out of the struggle against colonialism, a regime under which basic human rights were denied. The central tenet of the right of self-determination of peoples had been rejected, however, by large segments of the intellectual Left by the end of the 1970s.

---

33 See, for example, Robert Lafont, *Décoloniser en France: Les régions face à l'Europe* (Paris: Gallimard, 1971).

This turn was directly related to a rise in the fortunes of the critique of "totalitarianism" (pursuant to the publication of Alexander Solzhenitsyn's *The Gulag Archipelago* in France in 1974), which, aside from being applied to Nazi fascism and Soviet communism, came to be associated with all manner of undemocratic regimes that emerged in the wake of decolonization. As Michael Scott Christofferson has shown, the emergence of "totalitarianism" as a key term of political debate in France was intimately tied to the battle between communists and anticommunist socialists for hegemony on the Left; ultimately, it was the socialists who won, putting their leader François Mitterrand into power in 1981.[34] The ideological war these two sides waged gathered the Third Worldist critique of colonialism and neocolonialism in its wake. Although the very definition of *Third* Worldism had been nonalignment with either of the two superpower blocs, the undemocratic outcomes of many Third World revolutions made them easy targets for the "totalitarianism" label— which the noncommunist Left was quick to hang on them, thus associating them with the totalitarian regimes in Eastern Europe and their French representative, the Communist Party. In a complex and often confused debate that took place under the auspices of left-leaning *Le Nouvel Observateur* in the late 1970s, noncommunist intellectuals renounced the hopes many of them had placed in the Third World. Calling for the protection of the rights of individuals against predatory, "totalitarian" Third World governments, these intellectuals breathed new life into the rhetoric of European civilization versus non-European barbarism, effectively reanimating the moral discourse of France's *mission civilisatrice*, according to the debate's observers.

Along with this recasting of Third Worldism as a totalitarian strangling of individual liberty came a recasting of the figure of Jean-Paul Sartre in French intellectual life. No longer viewed as the staunch defender of the rights of the powerless, their inherent human dignity and freedom, and their subjectivity, Sartre has come under attack as a persistently misguided supporter of regimes that have stifled those very people. His failure (in the eyes of many) to evince a sufficient amount of public sympathy for the victims of the Soviet regime as he criticized the excesses of Western governments had rendered suspect all of his judgments—or, at least, cast a long shadow over them. The shadow of totalitarianism in French intellectual discourse reduced Sartre's support for Third World liberation movements to support for totalitarianism—even though he

---

34 See Michael Scott Christofferson, *French Intellectuals Against the Left: The Antitotalitarian Moment of the 1970s* (New York: Berghahn Books, 2004).

criticized and even rejected the repressive outcomes in many of these countries, including (to take two famous examples) Cuba and the Congo.[35]

What was at stake, however, were not the particulars of the positions Sartre took, which were varied and often context-dependent, but rather the perceived "utopianism" of his outlook—that is, his strong desire for radical political change, which by the late 1970s was no longer in fashion on the Left. The philosopher Alain Badiou described the general result of this transformation in his 1994 book, *Ethics: An Essay on the Understanding of Evil*, writing,

> Such is the accusation so often repeated over the last fifteen years: every revolutionary project stigmatized as "utopian" turns, we are told, into totalitarian nightmare. Every will to inscribe an idea of justice or equality turns bad. Every collective will to the Good creates Evil.

Sartre, the originator of the postwar conception of intellectual engagement, the defender of violence in many cases as a means of political change, the tireless agitator for innumerable causes and the assumption of these causes to the point of his own ridiculousness, could be taken as the primary target of this discourse on totalitarianism. For Badiou, such a discourse "is sophistry at its most devastating."[36]

---

35   Although Lévy claims to agree that Sartre's anticolonialism and his support for Third World liberation generally were not among his political "errors," these points of accord are overwhelmingly negated in his ceaseless evocation of the pathological positions of the "totalitarian Sartre" in his *Sartre*. The main focus of discussion when it comes to politics in the book is Sartre's lack of criticism of the Soviet Union and failure to ally himself with Alexander Solzhenitsyn. As examples, Lévy argues that even though Sartre had written an important philosophical work on the imagination, his own failed when it came to imagining suffering under communism, and even though Sartre was, on all accounts, incredibly generous, that generosity "dried up … when he was made aware … of the image, or the spectre, or simply the words of the victims of communism." Lévy, *Sartre*, 348, 334, 339, 337. There is no serious discussion of Sartre's anticolonialism, only passing references. And though Lévy admires Sartre's early anti-racism, he inexplicably decries Sartre's views on colonialism and race expressed in the *Critique*, calling them a betrayal of this anti-racism. He gives no grounds for this criticism, and nowhere discusses this section of the *Critique*. Ibid., 301.

36   Alain Badiou, *Ethics: An Essay on the Understanding of Evil*, trans. Peter Hallward (New York: Verso, 2001), 13–14. On Sartre's indifference to appearing ridiculous when it came to a cause he believed in, see the exchange between Deleuze and Claude Mauriac regarding their mutual admiration of this quality. Claude Mauriac, *Et comme l'espérance est violente* (Paris: Grasset, 1976), 355–6.

THE PROBLEM OF THE "OTHER"

In *Ethics*, Badiou also turned to the puzzle of the "cultural"—rather than inter-personal—Other as an important term in intellectual debates in postcolonial France. How and why was it that a concept originally defined solely in terms of interpersonal relationships became so attractive in terms of describing rela-tionships between groups—so much so that, in public discourse, when "the Other" is invoked, it almost always refers to a cultural Other, and not just to another person? And what are the consequences of describing the relationships between groups using this language?

As we shall see, Sartre and others did sometimes use the word in the sense of collective difference; in general, however, the Other typically was not used in this way. Though it is difficult to pinpoint an exact date for the shift in the meaning of this term, it appears to have been related to two important trends of the 1970s and 1980s: first, there was the emergence of Emmanual Levinas's ethics of alterity as an important influence on a variety of thinkers who inter-vened in the public domain in the 1970s, 1980s, and 1990s (including Jacques Derrida, Bernard-Henri Lévy, Tzvetan Todorov, Pascal Bruckner, and many others). The depth of this influence was not uniform—some thinkers were strongly marked (Derrida); some appeared to adopt a Levinasian idiom more for effect than for rigor (Bruckner); and some noted the influence in passing (Todorov). The point, however, is that the focus on "the Other" as the central category of ethical reflection passed into public discourse through these intel-lectual vectors. One work that signified this trend was Tzvetan Todorov's 1982 book on the early modern encounter of Europeans and non-Europeans, *The Conquest of America: The Question of the Other*, which was one of the first major publications to have the word "Other"—defined as the cultural Other—in its title.[37]

---

37   Tzvetan Todorov, *The Conquest of America: The Question of the Other*, trans. Richard Howard (New York: Harper & Row, 1984); see also his 1988 work whose title in French, *Nous et les autres*, also refers to a cultural Other, *On Human Diversity: Nationalism, Racism, and Exoticism in French Thought*, trans. Catherine Porter (Cambridge: Harvard University Press, 1993). There are some earlier, though less well-known, examples of this shift in usage. See, for example, Anne Marguerite Nouailhac, *La Peur de l'autre, les préjugés: racisme, antisémitisme, xénophobie* (Paris: Editions Fleurus, 1972); Georges Balandier et al., *L'autre et l'ailleurs: Homage à Roger Bastide* (Paris: Berger-Levrault, 1977); Georges Balandier, *Histoire d'Autres* (Paris: Stock, 1977); Henry Méchoulan, *Le sang de l'autre ou l'honneur de Dieu: indiens, juifs, morisques dans l'Espagne du Siècle d'or* (Paris: Fayard, 1979); Jean-Pierre Charnay, *Les contre-Orients, ou comment penser l'autre selon soi* (Paris: Sindbad, 1980); François Hartog, *Le miroir d'Hérodote: essai sur la représentation de l'autre* (Paris: Gallimard, 1980).

Second, the turn on the Left toward a concern for human rights and a stress on the universalism of some human values provided new situations in which to apply the term. Dealing with the very real particularity of cultural differences within French society itself—in particular, the large Muslim population from the former colonies—made the question of how to live with the "Other," now defined as a cultural Other, a burning issue. There have been strong calls for respect for or tolerance of France's racial and religious Others, particularly in the 1980s, when Harlem Désir founded the anti-racist organization SOS Racisme, and as the electoral success of the right-wing Front National party forced the issues of cultural difference and modus vivendi to the center of French political concerns.

As Badiou effectively pointed out, however, employing the language of Otherness in these debates is paradoxical at best and misleadingly euphemistic at worst. He devoted a chapter of *Ethics* to the question, "Is There an Other?"—concluding that if there is, it is not what the "apostles of ethics" claim it to be. Since, he argued, Levinasian ethics is necessarily theological, Badiou condemned in advance any application of such an ethics to an analysis of political action. "What," he asked, "then becomes of this category if we claim to suppress, or mask, its religious character, all the while preserving the abstract arrangement of its apparent constitution (recognition of the other, etc.)? … We are left with a pious discourse without piety."[38] The result, he continued, was to confuse a commonsensical discourse claiming "respect for difference" and "tolerance of the Other" with a religious discourse that presupposes the "ethical dominance of the Other" over the same—a confusion that "betrays" Levinas's own thinking. For Badiou, this is because "Levinas's enterprise serves to remind us, with extraordinary insistence, that every effort to turn ethics into the principle of thought and action is essentially religious."[39]

Indeed, Badiou argued, ethics simply has nothing to do with the contemporary discourse concerning "respect for the Other." Firstly, as he points out, differences among people are infinite. Secondly, and as a consequence, "No light is shed on any concrete situation by the notion of the 'recognition of the other.' Every modern collective configuration involves people from everywhere." So what did he believe this discourse was really driving at? Rather than a respect for differences, he thought its proponents actually desired its opposite: an imposition of the same. "The 'respect for differences' and the ethics of human rights do seem to define an *identity*!" he argued. "Even immigrants in

---

38   Badiou, *Ethics*, 23.
39   Ibid.

this country [France], as seen by the partisans of ethics, are acceptably different only when they are 'integrated,' only if they seek integration." He continued, in an even more forceful vein,

> Our suspicions are first aroused when we see that the self-declared apostles of ethics and of the "right to difference" are clearly *horrified by any vigorously sustained difference*. For them, African customs are barbaric, Muslims are dreadful, the Chinese are totalitarian, and so on. As a matter of fact, this celebrated "other" is acceptable only if he is a *good* other—which is to say what, exactly, if not *the same as us?* ... To prove the point, just consider the obsessive resentment expressed by the partisans of ethics regarding anything that resembles an Islamic "fundamentalist."

Badiou concluded that, in a secular, democratic society, the "whole ethical predication based upon recognition of the other should be purely and simply abandoned." This was not a plea on his part for cultural relativism, however, but for a nuanced understanding of what people do share that eschews the language of ethics. For Badiou, "the real question—and it is an extraordinarily difficult one—is much more that of *recognizing the Same*."[40]

Whether or not Badiou himself had arrived at a plausible method for "recognizing the Same" in all people, he astutely observed that the emergence of the discourse on a cultural Other was intimately tied to the unresolved dilemmas of decolonization. Evoking the theme of the subhuman made famous by Sartre in the 1950s, he wrote,

> The reign of "ethics" coincides, after decades of courageous critiques of colonialism and imperialism, with today's sordid self-satisfaction in the "West," with the insistent argument according to which the misery of the Third World is the result of its own incompetence, its own inanity—in short, of its *subhumanity*.[41]

The difficulty of sorting out these dilemmas is what gave rise to the title of this book, *Unfinished Projects*. The granting (or winning) of independence shifted the terms of debate concerning France's relationships with its former colonies, but did not eliminate many of the most vexing questions concerning the justice of economic arrangements, the legitimacy of the laws and institutions that shape an increasingly global interdependence, and how a republican political culture ought to deal with religious and cultural differences.

---

40   Ibid., 27, 24–5.
41   Ibid., 13.

The reason that I have joined decolonization with Sartre in this set of "unfinished projects" is because his work and his politics were so intimately involved in it. Sartre cannot be identified with decolonization, for decolonization has many histories, and I do not mean to suggest, against Deleuze, that Sartre "represents" it. In a Deleuzian spirit, however, I will suggest that the unfinished nature of so many of Sartre's great works (his ethics, his autobiography, his "Flaubert," and, of course, the *Critique*) parallels, if it does not represent, the process of decolonization and the condition of the postcolonial era in France. Lévy has noted, "Of this Sartrean incompleteness it is tempting to say what Spinoza said of the infinite: that the prefix 'in' is here no mark of lack but an extreme openness, a richness."[42] I hope to do this claim justice in the chapters that follow.

---

42 Lévy, *Sartre*, 220.

PART I

POLITICIZATION: SARTRE AND POSTWAR

ANTICOLONIALISM, 1945–1954

CHAPTER ONE

Putting Constraints on Freedom:
A Philosophy of Marginal Groups

> A certain newspaper in which someone wrote a rather brilliant article saying that it was necessary to refuse any complicity with violence wherever it came from had to announce the following day the first skirmishes of the Indo-Chinese war. I should like to ask this writer today how we can refuse to participate indirectly in all violence.[1]

By the end of summer in 1944, France had been liberated from German occupation; by the summer of 1945, liberation struggles in the colonies had just begun. After the failure of peace talks in 1946, Ho Chi Minh and his followers in Indochina would, over the next nine years, force the withdrawal of French forces from that area of the world following their defeat at Dien Bien Phu; in Algeria and Madagascar, attacks on settlers in 1945 and 1947 led to collective reprisals by the French army, the death tolls of which still remain in question, but which seem to have been in the tens of thousands; and revelations of torture by French and Senegalese forces placed that issue on the political agenda just a few years after the defeat of the Nazis.[2]

Intellectual anticolonialism was not invented after the war, and the editors of *Les Temps Modernes* and *Esprit* were not the first to espouse it—though they were among the first to make it a serious issue in intellectual debates.[3] André Gide had famously described the inhuman practices of plantation owners in *Travels in the Congo* (1927). The surrealists had denounced the 1925 Rif War

---

1   Jean-Paul Sartre, *What Is Literature?* trans. Bernard Frechtman (New York: Harper Colophon Books, 1965), 283. The author of the "brilliant article" was almost certainly Albert Camus, and the newspaper *Combat*. See Chapter 3 of this book, as well as Aronson, *Camus and Sartre*, 96–7.

2   On the origins of the war in Indochina, see D. Bruce Marshall, *The French Colonial Myth and Constitution-Making in the Fourth Republic* (New Haven: Yale University Press, 1973), 189–207; see also Herbert Tint, *French Foreign Policy Since the Second World War* (London: Weidenfeld & Nicolson, 1972).

3   See Alain Ruscio, "Les intellectuels français et la guerre d'Indochine: une répétition générale?" *Les cahiers de l'institut d'histoire du temps présent* 34, special issue, Charles-Robert Ageron and Philippe Devillers, eds, "Les guerres d'Indochine de 1945 à 1975" (June 1996), 113–32; and Paul Clay Sorum, *Intellectuals and Decolonization in France* (Chapel Hill: University of North Carolina Press, 1977), ch. 1.

in Morocco as well as the 1931 Colonial Exposition, and Daniel Guérin's travels in Libya and Indochina from 1927 to 1930 led him to become one of the Left's most enduring anticolonialist figures. A then-unknown Albert Camus had also exposed the injustices that had led to famine in Kabylia in his 1939 articles for *Alger-Républicain*. Many others—though less illustrious figures—made their contributions: Roland Dorgelès, *Sur la Route Mandarine* (1925); Paul Monet, *Les Jauniers: histoire vraie* (1930); Louis Roubaud, *Viet-nam, la tragédie indo-chinoise* (1931); and Andrée Viollis, *Indochine S.O.S.* (1935), which included a preface by André Malraux, for example.[4]

During the Third Republic, however, those who criticized the colonial system typically did not seek to dismantle it, but rather to reform it to help it better serve the interests of subject peoples.[5] It was this idea that animated Charles de Gaulle's speech at the 1944 Brazzaville conference, in which he declared his desire to reform the system through the establishment a new insti-tutional framework. The system, it was proposed, would grant some measure of representation to local elites both in the making of colonial policy and in political institutions in the metropole, while maintaining firm French control and denying any claim to potential political autonomy. The reforms were made with strategic aims in mind: as D. Bruce Marshall has noted, "The Brazzaville Conference assumed that by encouraging the political development of the colonies, those indigenous forces working for political change could be controlled and channeled into constructive economic and social fields."[6] As subsequent events have shown, this was a miscalculation. Indeed, after World War II, the ideas of self-determination and political independence began to take root—ideas that were driven by elites in the colonies, such as Ho Chi Minh and Habib Bourguiba, and to which left-wing elites in the metropole responded,[7] often with the direct comparison of occupation by Nazi Germany in mind.[8]

---

4   For more on interwar anticolonialism, see Daniel Guérin, *Ci-gît le colonialisme: Algérie, Inde, Indochine, Madagascar, Maroc, Palestine, Polynésie, Tunisie* (The Hague: Mouton, 1973).

5   See Raoul Girardet, *L'idée coloniale en France de 1871 à 1962* (Paris: Table Ronde, 1972).

6   Marshall, *French Colonial Myth*, 110; on the Brazzaville conference, see ibid., 102–114.

7   Elite status did not automatically confer enlightenment on this question. Sorum concluded from an examination of polling data that "people of higher income, education, and social status tended to be the strongest believers that the empire should be preserved." See Sorum, *Intellectuals and Decolonization in France*, 11.

8   *Les Temps Modernes* made this direct comparison in its first editorial on the war in Indochina. T.M. [Jean Pouillon], "Et bourreaux et victimes," *Les Temps Modernes* 12 (December 1946), i–ii.

They bore fruit in the years from the end of the war to 1962, by which time most of the colonial territories had become independent nations.[9]

The comparison to German occupation is an important one, as it linked together the events in the colonies with those in the metropole. As French intellectuals were sorting out their views on the purges, revising their positions with respect to both the United States and the Soviet Union, and dealing with the sudden and overwhelming public take-off of "existentialism" as a philosophy of radical freedom and responsibility, the intellectual field began to polarize, with certain issues becoming key factors in ordering it. Certainly, beginning especially in 1947, one's position with respect to Soviet communism and the French Communist Party (PCF) was of prime importance. It was not, however, the only factor.[10] Position-taking on the war in Indochina, and on colonialism in general, was already causing divisions among intellectuals that cannot be reduced to the emerging Cold War split, especially since many intellectuals— Sartre for example—were still attempting to find a "third way" between the two blocs, while also evincing grave concern about colonial war and the abuses and secrecy it entailed.[11] Moreover, the PCF's own position on national liberation movements had long been consistently inconsistent—shaped to fit the concerns of the Communist International—and thus shifted from support to ambivalence as its own role in domestic politics changed.[12] In contrast, as early as December 1946, with the outbreak of armed hostilities in Indochina, *Les Temps Modernes* announced its clear opposition to the war in Indochina—in a direct rebuke to Camus (discussed in Chapter 3).[13] This opposition remained

---

9   Tint, *French Foreign Policy Since the Second World War*, 199.

10   Indeed, so focused on the emerging Cold War is much of the literature on intellectuals in this era that, reading it, one would perhaps not be aware that France possessed any colonies. See, for example, Herbert R. Lottman, *Left Bank: Writers, Artists, and Politics from the Popular Front to the Cold War* (San Francisco: Halo Books, 1991); Antony Beevor, *Paris After the Liberation, 1944–1949* (Paris: Doubleday, 1994); Michel Winock, *Le Siècle des intellectuels* (Paris: Editions du Seuil, 1997); Pascal Ory and Jean-François Sirinelli, *Les Intellectuels en France, de l'affaire Dreyfus à nos jours* (Paris: Armand Colin, 1992); and Tony Judt, *Past Imperfect: French Intellectuals, 1944–1956* (Berkeley: University of California Press, 1992). One exception to this trend is David Drake, *Intellectuals and Politics in Post-War France* (New York: Palgrave, 2002).

11   For example, the "generals affair" of 1949 and the "leakages affair" of 1953–54. See Philip M. Williams, *Wars, Plots and Scandals in Post-War France* (Cambridge: Cambridge University Press, 1970), esp. Chs 3 and 4.

12   On the PCF's shifting positions in the interwar era, see Marshall, *The French Colonial Myth*, 60–1, 98; on its shifts in the immediate postwar era, see ibid., 281–2, 305; and Drake, *Intellectuals and Politics in Post-War France*, 101.

13   T.M. [Pouillon], "Et bourreaux et victimes."

constant through the vagaries of Sartre's—and the journal's—relationship to the French Communist Party.

Colonialism was clearly on the map, and Sartre did not wait until the war in Algeria to address it, as I aim to show in this and the following two chapters. While his immediate attention in the years after the war was on establishing his journal, his growing celebrity, and founding a political party called the Rassemblement Démocratique Révolutionnaire—a short-lived and not particularly successful experiment that tried to create a third force on the socialist Left, alongside the PCF and the SFIO—Sartre nonetheless evinced a consistent interest in marginalized groups that fed the subsequent denunciations of the French-Algerian War.

His opposition to colonialism, though still in development and thus not always well defined, dovetailed not only with his political concerns, but also with his definition of the writer's endeavor. In 1947, across six issues, *Les Temps Modernes* published Sartre's lengthy statement on the necessity for writers of literature to engage the important issues of their day, *What Is Literature?* At stake in every literary work, Sartre boldly declared, was nothing short of the freedom of all human beings. On his account, literary works were the ultimate proof that people are free, though they might well be unaware of it. As an emanation of the imagination, literature negates the real—it is, indeed, the activity of negating the world as it exists that is the definition of freedom for Sartre. Moreover, not only does literature represent the freedom of the person producing it, but it also implies the freedom of its readers: "The essence of the literary work," Sartre wrote, "is freedom totally disclosing and willing itself as an appeal to the freedom of other men."[14]

It was thus that Sartre explained his famous call for engagement—and, as this term implies, the mediation between literature and freedom was not to be made in the abstract. "*Being situated* is an essential and necessary characteristic of freedom," he averred, and he made repeated reference to what he considered to be the key issues of his time and place. There was the developing antagonism between the United States and the Soviet Union and the condition of the French working class, certainly; these issues were at the forefront of the *Rassemblement*'s platform and were mainstays of Sartre's political concerns. But there was also, according to the text, racism, anti-Semitism, and colonialism.[15] It is noteworthy that *What Is Literature?* appeared in the same issues of *Les Temps Modernes* as Richard Wright's *Black Boy*; a soldier's testimony

---

14   Sartre, *What Is Literature?* 145; originally serialized in *Les Temps Modernes* 17–22 (February–July 1947).

15   Sartre, *What Is Literature?* esp. 57–8, 241, 259, 269, 281.

concerning the war in Indochina; and the important dossier of articles on the war, "Indochina S.O.S.," which included articles by Claude Lefort and Tran Duc Thao.[16]

One of the ways that Sartre broached the questions of racism and colonialism in *What Is Literature?* was through invoking the concept of the "Other" —here, seemingly defined in a collective rather than interpersonal way. Reflecting on Wright's position as a black writer with both black and white readerships, Sartre averred,

> Whatever the good-will of the white readers may be, for a negro author they represent the *Other*. They have not lived through what he has lived through. They can understand the negro's condition only by an extreme stretch of the imagination and by relying upon analogies which at any moment may deceive them.[17]

This reference is puzzling and unexpected, and it provides the basis for inquiry in this and the following two chapters. The central questions I pose are how and why Sartre made the move from a theorization of interpersonal otherness to the constitution of alterity in and among collectivities. If, as *Being and Nothingness* makes clear, each of us is always an Other whose subjectivity is hidden from and unknowable by others, then what status may be granted a new category of Other that is conceived in terms of the ascription of group characteristics (white, black, Jew, woman) that are created in *history*—and, hence, knowable through dialectical procedures? Or, to put it in different terms, how does a methodological individualist like Sartre, who granted no ontological status to groups, recognize and account for collective identities? What are the properties of this collective "otherness," according to Sartre, and what role does it play in his work?

I aim to tackle these questions by viewing them through the lens of Sartre's engagement with a broad range of issues related to the critique of Western economic and cultural dominance: the poetry of negritude and his work with *Présence Africaine*; his criticism of US–style racism and the influence of Richard Wright; protest against the wars in Indochina, Algeria, and Vietnam; the

---

16   For *Black Boy*, see *Les Temps Modernes* 16–21 (January–June 1947). See also J.-B. Pontalis, "Un soldat français en Indochine," *Les Temps Modernes* 17 (February 1947); and the special section "Indochine S.O.S.," in *Les Temps Modernes* 18 (March 1947), 1039–149. The title "Indochine S.O.S." is an apparent reference to an earlier anticolonialist book, Andrée Viollis, *Indochine S.O.S.* (Paris: Gallimard, 1935).

17   Sartre, *What Is Literature?* 73. Sartre makes one other reference to a collective Other, briefly applying his theory of the "look" developed in *Being and Nothingness* to groups of peasants and workers in eighteenth-century France. See ibid., 89.

elaboration of theories of racism and other forms of group discrimination; and his reference to the imagination in "Black Orpheus," as a form of anti-racist and anticolonialist practice available to writers such as himself. Finally, I argue not only that Sartre's politicization in this era was strongly marked by anticolonialism, but also that his and *Les Temps Modernes*'s anticolonialism, which emphasized the immediate and irrevocable subjectivity of all peoples, became an alternative to the reformist version of it that had been dominant among intellectuals such as André Gide in the interwar era.

THE INESSENTIALITY OF BEING AN OBJECT FOR OTHERS: *BEING AND NOTHINGNESS*

"We become what we are only by a profound and radical negation of what others have made of us"—Sartre wrote these words in 1961, in support of Fanon's inflammatory critique of European colonialism.[18] He might have written them, however, in *Being and Nothingness*, in which one of his concerns is to argue that part of a person's being is given through the objectifying look of the Other.[19] Revealing an objectivity at the very heart of the self's subjectivity, the look of the Other signals that the self's freedom—hitherto autonomous—is at the mercy of a heteronomous power, in the form of another free self. This realization, according to Sartre, induces certain affective reactions:

> fear (the feeling of being in danger before the Other's freedom), pride, or shame (the feeling of being finally what I am but elsewhere, over there for the Other), the recognition of my slavery (the feeling of the alienation of all my possibilities).[20]

At the same time, the fact of human freedom means that each person can continually choose herself; a person who lives in good faith is one who engages in a constant process of attempting to negate the objectifying gaze that the Other incessantly turns upon her.

---

18   Sartre, "Preface," in Frantz Fanon, *The Wretched of the Earth*, trans. Constance Farrington (New York: Grove Press, 1963), 144.

19   For a discussion of the function of vision in Sartre's work, see Martin Jay, "Sartre, Merleau-Ponty, and the Search for a New Ontology of Sight," in *Downcast Eyes: The Denigration of Vision in Twentieth-Century French Thought* (Berkeley: University of California Press, 1994); for a discussion of the distinction between vision and touching in *Being and Nothingness* and its significance for the development of the notion of the Other, see Renaud Barbaras, "Le Corps et la chair dans la troisième partie de L'Être et le Néant," in Jean-Marc Moillie, ed., *Sartre et la phénoménologie* (Paris: ENS Editions, 2000).

20   Jean-Paul Sartre, *Being and Nothingness: A Phenomenological Essay on Ontology*, trans. Hazel E. Barnes (New York: Washington Square Press, 1984 [1956]), 358.

Sartre's discussion of the look of the Other is justly famous, particularly for the richness of its psychological descriptions. But it is also highly abstract: there is no world in which only two people exist, and it would be difficult to imagine what such a world would be like (or, on Sartre's view, whether beings in such a world would even be human). But Sartre used this discussion to drive home the central point he wished to defend in *Being and Nothingness*: that even this objectifying look does not impinge upon the free spontaneity of a consciousness constantly in the process of negating the world in the pursuit of a future-oriented project. Though we are always, and without any hope of escape, in situations of dominating the Other and being dominated by him, we choose our attitude toward those situations. In short, Sartre told us in this book, it is our freely chosen project that determines the meaning of any given situation, no matter how extreme, limiting, or degrading that situation may be.

Thus it may seem odd to begin an examination of the possibility of collective otherness with this massive treatise on the radical freedom of individual consciousness that was written during World War II—that is, before Sartre's move toward a theorization of intellectual engagement and, in particular, its relationship to the phenomenon of decolonization. Sartre demonstrated here nonetheless a marked concern for the possibility that group identification or any other external force (such as death) might impinge upon that freedom, devoting nearly one hundred pages to the topic in his eventual refutation of the possibility that our concrete situations or our bodily facticity—or the facticity of others—shape our freely chosen projects.[21] Sartre entertained the notion that

> much more than he appears 'to make himself,' man appears 'to be made' by climate and earth, race and class, language, the history of the collectivity of which he is a part, heredity, the individual circumstances of his childhood, acquired habits.[22]

Acknowledging that others bring a factual limit to a person's freedom—by imprisoning her, for example, or by submitting her to an exploitative economic system—Sartre exhaustively detailed these limits in terms of "my place," "my past," "my environment," "my fellowman," and "my death." "By means of the upsurge of the Other," Sartre wrote,

---

21 See the section "Freedom and Facticity: The Situation" in Sartre, *Being and Nothingness*, 619–707.

22 Ibid., 619.

> there appear certain determinations which I *am* without having chosen them.
> Here I am—Jew or Aryan, handsome or ugly, one-armed, *etc.* All this I am *for*
> *the Other* with no hope of apprehending this meaning which I have *outside*
> and, still more important, with no hope of changing it.[23]

He recognized that these are real limits, not "collective fictions" that might
simply be dismissed.

This is important, since Sartre was not defending the view that humans are
free to choose any action whatsoever at any time, as if they were gods who
create the world ex nihilo—though this may be what they aspire to do. This was
not Sartre's view, as he made clear in his discussion of what it means to
"choose," which he summarized in the section on "Freedom and Facticity,"
and which is intimately bound to his idea of authenticity. Indeed, there is a
world, and it places real limits—a "coefficient of adversity," in his terms—on
our freedom:

> Although brute things (what Heidegger called 'brute existents') can from the
> start limit our freedom of action, it is our freedom itself which must first
> constitute the framework, the technique, and the ends in relation to which
> they will manifest themselves as limits.[24]

Being free, however, does not mean getting whatever you might wish for, and it
certainly does not refer to conscious deliberation on a set of available choices
(although Sartre's notion is often caricatured as such). The freedom Sartre
intended here rests on the pre-reflective level of consciousness; it means " 'by
oneself to determine oneself to wish' (in the broad sense of choosing)."[25] That
is, it may seem as though circumstances like racism, anti-Semitism, colonialism, and so on, present coefficients of adversity that guide a person's
choices for her, but even allowing the inertia of the world to guide action is
itself a prior choice—the choice of living inauthentically (or, in bad faith).[26]

What, then, is the significance of these limits of identity, history, and fini-
tude; what force do they bring to bear? Ultimately, for Sartre, the answer is
none, and on this point he returned to two previously established arguments to
defend his claim of radical freedom. The first is that no matter how a person is
defined by others he can only grasp these characteristics in light of his own

---

23   Ibid., 671. Unless otherwise indicated, all italics are in the original text.

24   Ibid., 620.

25   Ibid., 621.

26   For a cogent discussion of Sartre's notion of choice, see Thomas R. Flynn, *Sartre
and Marxist Existentialism: The Test Case of Collective Responsibility* (Chicago: University of
Chicago Press, 1984), 7–9.

ends; the meaning they have for him can only appear in the context of the meaning his freedom has conferred upon them. Sartre had already given a stark illustration of his intent here earlier in *Being and Nothingness*, in a discussion of a passage from William Faulkner's *A Light in August*. In the story, set in the Jim Crow South, a black man is tortured at the hands of white racists. As Faulkner describes the scene, the man, though near death, does not give in to the sadism of his executioners. Instead, his composure and his peaceful gaze transcend their hatred, making their project of turning him into pure objectivity collapse. In Sartre's reading of the passage, Faulkner had demonstrated how a man is always free to create the meaning of his own situations, since, for Sartre, "Even torture does not dispossess us of our freedom; when we give in, we do so *freely*."[27] For example, a person may choose suicide over torture, and that would be his free choice. Thus, though we may not choose our situations, and in this sense our freedom is "bounded," we choose the meaning of them and, included in that, the definitions others give of us.

The second argument he employed is that "being-for-others," which is objective, represents an alienation that can never be redeemed by the self—this alienation is a necessary consequence of the fact that human beings only exist in particular situations. But this alienation is not, for Sartre, a modification of the self; in fact, the self can never encounter or really understand what he is for others. Therefore, it cannot impinge upon the self's free choice to live authentically or inauthentically. It always exists "outside"—hence the cryptic proposition, "Everything which is alienated exists only *for the Other*."[28] This assertion is in keeping with his general views on the body. According to Sartre, a person does not normally experience his own body as an object, and, hence, whatever knowledge he has about it is always in question: "Myself-as-object is neither knowledge nor a unity of knowledge but an uneasiness, a lived wrenching away from the ecstatic unity of the for-itself, a limit which I can not reach and which yet I am."[29] It is the existence of the Other that induces this uneasiness, this perpetual feeling of being in danger. It is unclear, however, whether the affective reactions that the appearance of the Other (in the inter-personal sense) induces, such as pride, shame or fear, also characterize our reactions to the other in his specific capacity as a Jew, an African, a worker, and so on. On this matter, Sartre here is silent.[30]

---

27   Sartre, *Being and Nothingness*, 672.

28   Ibid., 674. For an astute discussion of Sartre's treatment of torture, see Simont, "The Last Picture Show (à propos du livre d'Alain Renaut, *Sartre, le dernier philosophe*)," 127–8.

29   Ibid., 367.

30   There is a contentious debate, however, on Sartre's depiction of the feminine

In the course of this lengthy discussion—which in the main introduces no new philosophical arguments—Sartre set forth a curious idea concerning a person's being-for-others: that it is always "unrealizable" for himself.[31] This idea is noteworthy for two reasons. First, it provides a transition to a text that appeared in 1946, *Anti-Semite and Jew*. Second, it seems to contradict one of the central premises of *Being and Nothingness*, which is that it is through negation—not affirmation—of the Other's objectification that we become who we are. Concerning the first point, although Sartre did not use the word "unrealizable" in either *Anti-Semite and Jew* or "Black Orpheus," he did value positively the notion that Jews or Africans should take on—make their own, so to speak—the objectivity that others make of them. In a world in which discrimination exists, not to acknowledge it would be to deny one's historical condition, and thus to participate in a mystified (hence erroneous) notion of the liberal abstraction of the human being.

One wonders how these characteristics can be both a matter of facticity and unrealizable at the same time, but Sartre's point seems to have been that, since a for-itself cannot "be" anything, as it is negation by definition, it certainly cannot "be" these things that it is for others. What is particularly interesting about this discussion is the way these unrealizables appear to function as regulative ideals for Sartre—and thereby as the rudimentary beginnings of an ethics—but with a twist in the sense that they are immanent to facticity rather than given by a transcendent entity. Thus, he wrote,

> The unrealizable is an *a priori* which requires my engagement in order to be, while depending only on this engagement and while placing itself at the start beyond any attempt to realize it. What then is this if not precisely an *imperative*?[32]

What then is this if not also a reason for a person who is Jewish, for example, to choose to live her Jewishness as it has been defined by others? This is precisely the argument Sartre advanced in *Anti-Semite and Jew*, in his picture of the "authentic Jew." But Sartre had already said as much in *Being and Nothingness*:

"Other." For an overview, see Sartre's English-language translator and commentator, Hazel E. Barnes, "Sartre and Feminism: Aside from *The Second Sex* and All That," in Greene, ed., *Feminist Interpretations of Jean-Paul Sartre*. As for psychological reactions to racial or cultural otherness, it is Fanon who makes this decisive leap in *Black Skin, White Masks*, trans. Charles Lam Markmann (New York: Grove Press, 1967).

31   Sartre seems to have derived the idea of "unrealizables" during the "phony war" in 1939–40, while reflecting on a draft novel Beauvoir had sent him. See Jean-Paul Sartre, *War Diaries: Notebooks from a Phoney War*, trans. Quintin Hoare (London: Verso, 1999), 197–9.

32   Ibid., 678. For a related discussion of regulative ideals and facticity in Sartre's work, see Simont, "The Last Picture Show," esp. 123–7.

I do not choose to be for the Other what I am, but I can try to be for myself what I am for the Other, by choosing myself such as I appear to the Other—i.e., by elective assumption. A Jew is not a Jew *first* in order to be *subsequently* ashamed or proud; it is his pride of being a Jew, his shame, or his indifference which will reveal to him his being-a-Jew; and this being-a-Jew is nothing outside the free manner of adopting it.[33]

Presumably this being-a-Jew is unrealizable for the for-itself, even as it is a fact for others. This points up an interesting issue raised by *Being and Nothingness*, but that does not get fully addressed in that work. Sartre believed that our bodies are always marked: these markings are contingent upon our situations, not a matter of biology,[34] and they are given by the world as we "exist" it, in his terms, through our bodies. Thus, for example, racialized bodies exist, but race does not. Sartre's anti-essentialism extends quite explicitly and logically to a specific critique of racism: one that does not blithely ignore real differences lived by human beings, but at the same time does not allow any imputation whatsoever that those differences are a matter of essence. "Face, sense organs, presence," he wrote, "all that is nothing but the contingent form of the Other's necessity to *exist himself* belonging to a race, a class, an environment, etc."[35] The upshot is that *Being and Nothingness* could be viewed not just as a defense of an abstract human liberty, but also as a concrete defense of the liberty of *specific* humans who are objectively classed into different groups and who therefore experience the world differently.[36]

It must be noted, however, that this exhortation to actively take on one's being-for-others suggests something about authenticity that is quite different from Sartre's earlier definition of it: it is directly related to a person's facticity, to those characteristics that are given by others, but that do not touch the for-itself. This problem is but one of many that result from Sartre's strict dualist ontology, and it is one that his attention to collectivities and social being after *Being and Nothingness* tries to resolve.[37] Sartre's discussion of the relationship between freedom and facticity demonstrates that conceptualizing collective Otherness will be a thorny—and perhaps impossible—task that is complicated

---

33   Ibid., 677.

34   There is, however, a long-running debate on whether Sartre's depiction of women either implies or explicitly relies upon a biological determinism.

35   Ibid., 451.

36   This is one of the ways that Fanon uses Sartrean existentialism in *Black Skin, White Masks*.

37   The criticisms of this ontology are too numerous to cite here, but for a short summary, see Vincent Descombes, *Modern French Philosophy*, trans. L. Scott-Fox and J.M. Harding (New York: Cambridge University Press, 1980).

by the terms of his phenomenology itself. One solution might be simply to try to ascribe to groups as a whole the same agency and structural relations that obtain between for-itselfs. This is what Alexandre Kojève did in adapting Hegel's master-slave dialectic to groups. Such a strategy was not, however, a temptation for Sartre, who always kept his attention squarely trained on the person as the primary element and the only agent. *Being and Nothingness* is a wholly pessimistic vision of the world in which every for-itself is potentially or actually in conflict with every other for-itself. Every relationship is a relationship of domination or submission, whether the Other is a French man like Sartre or an Algerian resistance fighter. So why should *Sartre* have anything special to say about—or even wish to acknowledge—collective Otherness? To put the question another way, can the interpersonal Other come to be the racial Other, the Jewish Other, the feminine Other, the colonial Other, the cultural Other? And do these terms have any meaning in the vocabulary of phenomenology, or will new terms be needed?

Sartre would in fact have to devise a new language to describe the concrete relations between any two individuals who are members of different groups, but he did not supply it until he published the *Critique of Dialectical Reason.* Between the end of the war and 1960, then, Sartre's increased activity on behalf of marginal collectivities represented a unique and powerful merging of philosophical and political concerns.

THE PROBLEM OF DEFINING COLLECTIVITIES: *ANTI-SEMITE AND JEW* AND *THE SECOND SEX*

The fact that his language does not help to describe collective Otherness is apparent in *Anti-Semite and Jew* (1946), Sartre's first non-literary attempt at reorienting existentialism to address the problem of a passion (hatred, in this case) whose object is not an individual, but a group. *Anti-Semite and Jew* was a landmark text that remains relevant today. It should be read partly, however, as a more thorough analytical examination of ideas expressed in his 1938 novella, "Childhood of a Leader." In that story, Sartre traced the path of Lucien Fleurier, a self-searching French high school student from a middle-class family recently migrated to Paris from the provincial town of Férolles. The story follows Lucien as he tries to answer the question, "Who am I?" "My name is Lucien Fleurier but that's just a name," Sartre writes. "I don't give a damn about anything. I'll never be a leader."[38] As he explores his identity through

---

38   Jean-Paul Sartre, "Childhood of a Leader" in *The Wall*, trans. Andrew Brown (London: Hesperus Press, 2005), 139.

taking on the beliefs and values of those he admires, Lucien becomes increasingly disdainful toward Jews and women, and increasingly oriented toward anti-democratic politics. He commits to his new beliefs by joining the Camelots du Roi, a youth movement associated with the right-wing Action Française that was active in street skirmishes in the 1930s. Like the anti-Semite that Sartre would later describe in *Anti-Semite and Jew*, Lucien chooses hatred of Jews as a means of grounding his own identity. By the end of the story, Lucien has become "a leader"—in his own mind, at least—through his will to treat others (especially women and Jews) as objects, and hence among his possessions and under his command.

Sartre effectively rewrote and expanded aspects of this story in *Anti-Semite and Jew*. The biggest difference was the addition of a portrait of Jews in this text, and the prescriptions he offers. The structure of Sartre's argument in *Anti-Semite and Jew* is unsurprising: he begins with the anti-Semite because she affords an examination of the passion of an individual consciousness that had been discussed only two years before in *Being and Nothingness*, and also prefigured in "Childhood of a Leader." The problem, then, is why a certain person (an anti-Semite) has a particular passion (hatred of Jews). But the problem could not be solved simply by applying Sartre's descriptions of the fundamental attitudes toward others without modification, described in *Being and Nothingness*, since what is hated in this case must be a group. Thus, Sartre had to say how it is that an other can affect us not in his capacity as an abstract interpersonal Other (which he no doubt is), but in his capacity as a specific, Jewish other. In the end, however, Sartre was unable to do this. Instead, he proposed two arguments to account for anti-Semitism that contradict one another, demonstrating that the conceptual tension between "freedom and facticity" was still alive and well.

Nonetheless, this highlighting of the specificity of the Other, and the influence this specificity may or may not have on our attitudes toward him, is a definite turn in Sartre's work, and it is one that cannot be reduced to a single causal explanation. The most compelling and oft-cited argument is that World War II and Sartre's involvement (however great or small) in resistance to the Nazi occupation were the key factors in his turn toward theorizing not just human freedom in the abstract, but also the freedom of particular humans in particular situations of oppression. There is also, however, strong reason to see Sartre's turn in relation to the work (and persistent prodding) of Beauvoir, whose classic treatise, *The Second Sex* (1949), exceeded Sartre's attempts in this period to think through the force of facticity given through collectivities in the terms of the existential phenomenology outlined in *Being and Nothingness*.

For many commentators, there is a contested relationship between these two works in particular, the question being whether *Anti-Semite and Jew* "prefigured" certain themes in *The Second Sex*, or whether Beauvoir's influence in developing the account of relations with others in *Being and Nothingness* provided the basis for certain themes in *Anti-Semite and Jew*. Though it is not necessary to resolve this issue here, it is important to note the relationship between Beauvoir's and Sartre's efforts. *The Second Sex* is, after all, a full-length study, and, as such, its attempts at developing a genuine historical argument are more compelling than Sartre's in *Anti-Semite and Jew*. It tackles the question of collective otherness head-on, framing it specifically in the terms of a person's facticity and the meaning of that facticity:

> To decline to accept such notions as the eternal feminine, the black soul, the Jewish character, is not to deny that Jews, Negroes, women exist today—this denial does not represent a liberation for those concerned, but rather an inauthentic flight.[39]

Moreover, it was Beauvoir, earlier than Sartre, who tried to incorporate the work of Claude Lévi-Strauss into her analysis, thus giving it a richer and more sustained orientation toward anthropological method.[40] Although *Les Temps Modernes* published a number of articles by Lévi-Strauss, Sartre's first real written engagement with his work came in the *Critique*.

According to Sonia Kruks, Beauvoir must be credited with criticizing Sartre's notion of the absolute freedom of consciousness and his eventual turn toward a concern with collectivities. Karen Green sums up Kruks's argument nicely:

> Following de Beauvoir's own report that she had, in 1940, maintained against Sartre that from the point of view of freedom not every situation is equal, Kruks argues that with regard to the connected concepts of freedom and oppression, de Beauvoir led where Sartre followed. De Beauvoir never accepted that "the slave in chains is as free as his master." … She emphasized that the freedom of the individual depends on the freedom of others, and, most important, she challenged Sartre's assumption that "relations of otherness are conflictual relations between two *equal* freedoms."[41]

---

39   Simone de Beauvoir, *The Second Sex*, trans. H.M. Parshley (New York: Everyman's Library, 1993), xlii (translation modified).

40   Beauvoir reported in her biography that she read the manuscript for *The Elementary Structures of Kinship* before it was published, sitting for hours each day in Lévi-Strauss's house. Simone de Beauvoir, *Force of Circumstance, Vol. I: After the War*, trans. Richard Howard (New York: Paragon, 1992), 168.

41   Karen Green, "Sartre and de Beauvoir on Freedom and Oppression," in Green, ed., *Feminist Interpretations of Jean-Paul Sartre*, 176–7.

Kruks makes the point that, although Sartre appears to have been talking about relations of otherness in *Anti-Semite and Jew*, he tended to avoid the use of the words "Other" and "others" to describe the relationship of the anti-Semite and the Jew. It is Beauvoir in *The Second Sex* who first seriously collectivizes the Other—in this case, into feminine alterity. This has important political implications, as the freedom of a particular feminine other, in this view, is dependent on the freedom of all feminine others. Thus the freedom-oppression dyad appears in an entirely new light, as does politics in general.

This interpretation seems right, and it makes an important point. Sartre was not arguing—technically speaking—that the anti-Semite constitutes Jews as a collective (i.e., cultural or racial) Other. Instead, he argued that the anti-Semite hates Jews because he has chosen a particular relationship with "the Other" (i.e., the abstract interpersonal Other) that results from the inner conflicts that every human being must confront: "It has become evident that no external factor can induce anti-Semitism in the anti-Semite. Anti-Semitism is a free and total choice of oneself, a comprehensive attitude that one adopts not only toward Jews but toward men in general."[42] This points up a serious contradiction in *Anti-Semite and Jew*, then—one between the argument that an anti-Semite is a person who has chosen a particular attitude toward humanity (hatred) and that this attitude is not (and cannot be) influenced by any aspect of the world; and the argument that the anti-Semite is a specific historical creation, a product of a "traditional" relationship to property, for example.[43] He wanted to say, then, that consciousness is both free and constituted, but he never explains how this is possible.

The gulf between *Anti-Semite and Jew* and *The Second Sex* is thus quite vast. Consider, for example, Beauvoir's assertion in the introduction to her book that "he [man] is the Subject, he is the Absolute; she [woman] is the Other."[44] Beauvoir effectively reoriented the language of alterity given by Sartre in *Being and Nothingness* to collectivities of gender, averring that relationships of alterity between two groups will in some way constitute the relationship of alterity between two people from each group. Though she held that each woman is, of course, a free consciousness just like every man, and that

---

42   Jean-Paul Sartre, *Anti-Semite and Jew*, trans. George J. Becker (New York: Schocken Books, 1948), 17.

43   Which is why, Sartre argued (perhaps implausibly), anti-Semitism is a middle-class phenomenon rarely found among workers. Ibid., 36.

44   Beauvoir, *The Second Sex*, xlv. In a footnote to this sentence, Beauvoir cited a passage from Emmanuel Levinas's *Temps et l'autre* in which he wrote, "Otherness reaches its full flowering in the feminine."

all people constitute their subjectivity (which is never stable) out of the flux of experience, she also argued that collectivities and the human drive toward collectivity play a role in the construction of that subjectivity. The key difference here between Sartre and Beauvoir appears to lie in her reading of works of ethnography and sociology—she cited in particular Georges Dumézil and Lévi-Strauss—and her reading of Merleau-Ponty.[45] In her attempt to incorporate their works into Sartrean existentialism she effected a shift in the meaning of the term "the Other" in *The Second Sex*. From the start, it is related to collectivities:

> The category of the *Other* is just as primordial as consciousness itself. In the most primitive societies, in the most ancient mythologies, one finds the expression of a duality—that of the Self and the Other. This duality was not originally attached to the division of the sexes, it was not dependent upon any empirical facts ...
>
> Thus it is that no group ever sets itself up as the One without at once setting up the Other over against itself.[46]

Sartre did not typically use the term "Other" in this way. On the occasions in *Anti-Semite and Jew* when he did use the term, it was to refer to the interpersonal Other already described in *Being and Nothingness*.

But if Sartre was largely avoiding the language of Otherness so thoughtfully set up in his descriptions of the possible attitudes toward the Other in *Being and Nothingness* (and rightly so, since there is no bridge offered that would justify applying the concept of the Other to a group of people), then how did he explain the attitude of the anti-Semite: his passionate hatred? It is, of course, a manifestation of bad faith. But Sartre also relied here on a mode of analysis that is barely remarked upon in the vast literature on his work: the primitive-civilized dyad and, in particular, its elaboration by the influential early-twentieth-century philosopher and social anthropologist Lucien Lévy-Bruhl.[47] Indeed, Lévy-Bruhl's description of a "primitive mentality," whose structures are characterized by a lack of recognition of an analytical law of non-contradiction, plays varying roles in *Anti-Semite and Jew*, "Black Orpheus," and the

---

45   For a summary of the evolution of the relationship between Sartre's philosophy and that of Merleau-Ponty, see David Archard, *Marxism and Existentialism: The Political Philosophy of Sartre and Merleau-Ponty* (Hampshire, UK: Gregg Revivals, 1992).

46   Beauvoir, *The Second Sex*, xlv.

47   There are a few commentators who note this debt. See, for example, Stuart Zane Charmé, *Vulgarity and Authenticity: Dimensions of Otherness in the World of Jean-Paul Sartre* (Amherst: University of Massachusetts Press, 1991); and Howard Davies, *Sartre and "Les Temps Modernes"* (New York: Cambridge University Press, 1987).

Notebooks for an Ethics, all of which appeared in the late 1940s. It is somewhat puzzling that this intellectual debt has gone unrecognized, particularly since it poses certain problems for Sartre's understanding of consciousness as freedom, and also since it fits rather uneasily with his description of the fundamental structures of consciousness in *Being and Nothingness*, which do not admit of a general distinction between "primitive" and "civilized" mentalities. Perhaps the primary reason this debt to Lévy-Bruhl has been passed over by critics is that Lévi-Strauss, arguing directly against him in *The Savage Mind*, did so much to discredit Lévy-Bruhl's paradigm.[48] Indeed, although that book is well known for its attack on Sartre's own distinction between the analytical and the dialectical, it also took Lévy-Bruhl as a primary target—as the title's ironic play on Lévy-Bruhl's 1922 work, *Primitive Mentality*, indicates.

In that book, Lévy-Bruhl argued for a strict distinction between two organizations of mind: the first, primitive mental structure accepts the notion of "participationism," the idea that two or more objects or substances might coexist, thus defying the law of non-contradiction.[49] As an example, he pointed to animism, in which spiritual totems are understood to participate magically in the objective existence of a person or thing. This coexistence, or "possession," has important repercussions for the primitive's total view of the world, since he does not see it in terms of relations of cause and effect. For the primitive, inhabiting substances are the causes of observed phenomena, meaning, for example, that if someone is crushed by a fallen rock, this is not a result of chance or of the laws of gravity, but rather of the fact that the rock was inhabited by a spirit that willed it to fall and kill someone. Primitive mentality thus understands the world synthetically—that is, in terms of fatalism and participationism. Civilized mentality, on the other hand, observes both the law of non-contradiction and relationships of cause and effect. It does not impute to phenomena a hidden essence, invisible hand, or animating force. Its analytical structure is the foundation of scientific knowledge. For Lévy-Bruhl, the passage from a primitive mentality to a civilized one was a matter of historical progress. These are not two structures that coexist side by side as one mind— this is closer to Lévi-Strauss's argument in *The Savage Mind*—but, rather, each represents a stage of development of a particular society.

Sartre made enormous use of Lévy-Bruhl's distinction between the synthetic primitive and the analytical civilized in his essay on anti-Semitism,

---

48   See Claude Lévi-Strauss, *The Savage Mind*, trans. John Weightman and Doreen Weightman (Chicago: Chicago University Press, 1966).

49   See Lucien Lévy-Bruhl, *Primitive Mentality*, trans. Lilian A. Clare (New York: Macmillan, 1923).

arguing that the anti-Semite's structure of consciousness is synthetic and, in a word, "primitive"—thereby practically assimilating the concept of primitive-ness to his notion of bad faith. In his discussion of why anti-Semites like Action Française leader Charles Maurras believe that a Jew is incapable of under-standing Racine, Sartre argued that their view of property emphasizes land rather than abstract instruments such as money or stocks, because it affords a kind of mystical communion with French culture: "The anti-Semite can conceive only of a type of appropriation that is primitive and land-based, based on a veritable magical bond of possession and in which the possessed object and its possessor are united by a bond of mystical participation."[50]

To live in bad faith is not to recognize one's own freedom to choose oneself, even though with that freedom comes anguish. It is to be "attracted by the permanence of stone," to use his constant metaphor; that is, to deny one's human nature as for-itself and live instead as an inert substance. In *Anti-Semite and Jew*, Sartre consistently associated the bad faith of the anti-Semite with faith in the religious sense ("hate is a faith"); traditionalism (for the anti-Semite, the true Frenchman is "rooted in his province, in his country, borne along by a tradition twenty centuries old"); communalism ("the anti-Semite would under no circumstances dare to act or think on his own"); synthetic thought ("the anti-Semite has chosen to fall back on the spirit of synthesis in order to understand the world"); pseudo-science and irrationality (anti-Semites "behave toward social facts like primitives who endow the wind and the sun with little souls"); and "prelogical" thought.[51]

A look at Sartre's *Notebooks for an Ethics* just a few years later also shows the significance of the primitive-civilized dyad to his understanding of racism in the late 1940s. In the only part of the *Notebooks* to be published in Sartre's lifetime, an article entitled "Le Noir et le Blanc aux Etats-Unis" that appeared in *Combat* in 1949, Sartre once again associated the oppressor with a kind of primitive mentality.[52] In explaining, for example, the white supremacist view that Africans are incapable of invention, Sartre argued that a hierarchy of values always creeps into the racist's understanding of facts and that this is evidence of a primitive "participationism" of facts and values. Thus he wrote,

50   Sartre, *Anti-Semite and Jew*, 23–4 (translation modified).
51   Ibid., 19, 23, 32, 34, 37, 67.
52   Jean-Paul Sartre, "Le Noir et le Blanc aux Etats-Unis," *Combat*, June 16, 1949, reprinted in Sartre, *Notebooks for an Ethics*, trans. David Pellauer (Chicago: University of Chicago Press, 1992), 561–74. Francis Jeanson also comments on these pages, which he apparently saw in manuscript before they were published in *Combat*, in his essay "Sartre et le monde noir," *Présence Africaine* 7 (1949), 189–214.

If Blacks have invented less than Whites, it is that they are less inventive; and if invention is a good, we have the proof that they are less good. In this way concepts and values are a fixed and hierarchical series, and objects, just like men, participate in these concepts and these values, just as Aristotelian matter participates in the substantial forms. It is evident that conservative thought, when it is not realistic … has to be conceptual, participatory, and finalistic.

And to see clearly in an unjustifiable situation, it is not sufficient that the oppressor look at it openly and honestly, he must also change the structure of his eyes.[53]

One can imagine Sartre arguing here that the racist must pass from a primitive to a civilized mentality in order for this structural change to occur.

This is, of course, an odd argument, one that certainly does not require a theory of primitive "participationism" in order to make the point that perceptual schema often implicitly valorize the objects perceived. The point is simply that this vocabulary, and this primitive-civilized dyad, is still at work here, however dubiously. (And I would stress here that these represent unrevised notes.) In fact, it is quite difficult to understand why Lévy-Bruhl's work plays any role at all in Sartre's explanations. There is no attempt to relate the concepts of primitive and civilized structures of mind to the basic structures outlined in *Being and Nothingness*, which do not appear to admit of such differences.

I surmise that the reason Sartre relied on Lévy-Bruhl was because he was the dominant figure in French social anthropology in the 1920s and 1930s— that is, in the period when Sartre received his formal education. Lacking any explanation of his own for the origins of differences of power and recognition among groups, Sartre fell back upon the discourse that was available to him and that was considered legitimate at the time. After Sartre immersed himself in the work of Marx (and, later, Lévi-Strauss, whom Sartre seems to consider one of his few worthy interlocutors in the 1950s), the influence of Lévy-Bruhl's dyad drops precipitously.

Anti-Semite and Jew represented, then, something of a dead end for Sartre, even as it established what would become a life-long engagement with Jews and Jewishness and also develop into one of his most famous and commented-upon texts. The contradictory argumentation and the integration of a social theory that seems incompatible with existentialism reveal certain tensions both in Sartre's thinking and in the discourse available to describe collective phenomena (and, in particular, the relationships Europeans have with non-

---

53   Sartre, *Notebooks*, 571.

Europeans). In the first instance, Sartre had yet to admit that human freedom is circumscribed, even as he suggested that it is. In the second, the modernist vision of a developmental narrative of history had yet to be criticized. These tensions started to crack as the agitation for political independence from colonial rule heated up. Sartre's engagement with new political movements afforded him new relationships and situations from which to start thinking about the foundations of the relationship between collectivities and alterity, starting with racism and oppression. Indeed, as early as *Anti-Semite and Jew* Sartre demonstrated that he was taking not just anti-Semitism seriously, but racism in general as well. After all, he adapted Richard Wright's famous maxim that there was no "Black problem" in the United States, only a "White problem," to the situation of Jews in France: "In the same way, we must say that anti-Semitism is not a Jewish problem; it is *our* problem."[54]

---

54   Sartre, *Anti-Semite and Jew*, 152.

CHAPTER TWO

African Presence: Sartre on US and Colonial Racism in the late 1940s

In November 1947, the first issue of the influential postwar journal *Présence Africaine* appeared. This extraordinary publication, which eventually became the basis for a publishing house, was founded by Alioune Diop, one of the creators of the negritude movement. Members of the "Patrons' Committee" included André Gide, Paul Rivet, Emmanuel Mounier, Léopold Sédar Senghor, Richard Wright, Michel Leiris, Albert Camus, Aimé Césaire, and Jean-Paul Sartre. Members of the "Editorial Committee" included Bernard Dadié, Georges Balandier, Mamadou Dia, and Abdoulaye Sadji. The title, which signified the journal's intention to fill the "lack" both of knowledge about Africa and of African producers of that knowledge, had been suggested to Diop by Sartre, according to the anthropologist Balandier.[1]

The presence of Richard Wright on the masthead indicated that *Présence Africaine* aspired to be more than a journal of Africans and descendents of the African diaspora in the French colonies and metropole—indeed, the interwar cultural ties formed with African Americans continued into the postwar era.[2] This was significant for the development of Sartre's views on race and collectivities more generally. Sartre visited the United States for the first time in 1945, having been chosen by Camus to represent *Combat* on an official four-month press junket sponsored by the US government. While there, Beauvoir reported, Sartre became acutely interested in the condition of black Americans.[3] Thereafter, US race relations became one of his most frequently cited instances of oppression in the late 1940s; Francis Jeanson noted in a 1949 article in *Présence Africaine*, "Among these diverse 'black situations,' it is to disclosing those of Southern Negroes, in the United States, that Sartre seems to have especially

---

1   According to Balandier: "Diop and some friends envisaged the creation of a journal that would give a voice to the civilizations of Africa; it appeared in Paris soon after with a title, suggested by Sartre, that demanded the affirmation of an African *presence*." Georges Balandier, "1946, Rencontres Dakaroises: Diop, Senghor, Monod," in *Civilisés, dit-on* (Paris: Presses Universitaires de France, 2003), 75.
2   For more on these links, see Tyler Stovall, *Paris Noir: African Americans in the City of Light* (Boston: Houghton Mifflin, 1996).
3   Beauvoir, *Force of Circumstance*, Vol. I, 33.

attached himself."[4] Sartre's interest in Wright's work was strong enough that Wright appeared in the inaugural edition of *Les Temps Modernes* in October 1945.[5] Moreover, the themes of Sartre's 1946 play, *The Respectful Prostitute*, resonate strongly with Wright's observations of black-white interactions in *Native Son* (1940) and *Black Boy* (1945)—the latter was serialized alongside "What is Literature?" in *Les Temps Modernes* in 1947.[6] *The Respectful Prostitute*, whose plot was loosely based on the events of the 1931 Scottsboro Trial, dealt with Sartre's theme of the complicity of the oppressed in their own oppression; in this case, both the young black man accused of raping a poor white woman and the woman herself (who is a prostitute) bow to the will of the powerful whites who seem to control their destinies.[7] In this play, Sartre reduced the problem of racial discrimination in the United States to a strict and rather unproblematic function of class struggle. Wright gave Sartre some interesting comments on the play, making suggestions to reorganize the dramatic structure of the script and pointing out places where Sartre's lack of knowledge of the US resulted in flaws ("It is highly unlikely that Lizzie would sit or be allowed to sit, in a voyage from New York to, say, Atlanta, in a half-empty coach with Negroes, and surely not alone!").[8] Wright also wrote an introductory note to it for the US periodical *Twice A Year*, which published a translation of the play (and he also seems to have attempted to translate the introduction to *Being and Nothingness*).[9] Interestingly, Frantz Fanon also noticed the similarities between Sartre's play and *Native Son*, in particular the parallel characters of "The Negro" and Wright's Bigger Thomas.[10]

---

4   Francis Jeanson, "Sartre et le monde noir," 199.

5   Richard Wright, "Le feu dans la nuée," trans. Marcel Duhamel, *Les Temps Modernes* 1 (October 1945), 22–47.

6   See Sartre's comments on Wright's engagement in *What Is Literature?* 71–4.

7   Sartre changed the original ending, in which the black man is condemned by the false testimony of the prostitute, to a more optimistic version in which the black man goes free, both for the 1952 movie version and for its production in the USSR. Echoing the socialist realism aesthetic, Sartre gave the following justification for the change: "I've known too many young workers who had seen the play and had been discouraged to see it end sadly. And I realized that those who are really pushed to the limit, those who hang on to life the best they can, these people need to have hope." Michel Contat and Michel Rybalka, *The Writings of Jean-Paul Sartre, Vol. I: A Bibliographical Life*, trans. Richard C. McCleary (Evanstan, Ill.: Northwestern University Press, 1974), 140.

8   Yale University Archives, Richard Wright papers, "Reactions to the script of 'La Putain Respectueuse,' " n.d., Box 88, Folder 1081, p. 2.

9   See *Twice A Year*, special issue "Art and Action" (New York: Twice a Year Press, 1948); and Yale University Archives, Richard Wright papers, "Sartre, Jean-Paul, *L'être et le néant* [Introduction]," n.d., Box 88, Folder 1076.

10   See Fanon, *Black Skin, White Masks*, 138–40.

According to Wright's biographer, Hazel Rowley, Sartre and Wright first met in March 1946.[11] Wright, who lived as an expatriate in Paris in the late 1940s and the 1950s, gained fame in France with the publication of *Black Boy* by Gallimard, and both his literary sensibilities and politics made his personality a good fit for Sartre's. Of Wright's work, Beauvoir commented in an article in the *New York Times*: "The struggle of man against the resistances of the world is depicted. And it is just this which today in France appears to us to be the true mission of the writer."[12] Although the two shared a short-lived postwar optimism about the possibility of Europe as a "third force" between the United States and the USSR, Wright ultimately broke with Sartre in the early 1950s as a result of Sartre's relationship with the Communist Party.[13]

This interest in African Americans and intellectual affinity with Wright fostered a concern for racism that Sartre developed clearly in his *Notebooks for an Ethics*—the notes written in the mid-to-late 1940s that were meant to be the basis for a sequel to *Being and Nothingness*, but that went unpublished during his lifetime. Among these notes, which include copious references to US-style racism, is the text on slavery and its legacy in the United States that appeared in *Combat*. Seemingly intended as a full-length article, but never finished, it attempts not only a phenomenological analysis of black-white relations, but also ventures a (fairly undeveloped) justification for revolutionary violence—something that Sartre would take on later in the *Critique* and in his preface to *The Wretched of the Earth*.

This concern with racism is significant because Sartre eventually integrated it into his theory of European colonialism of the nineteenth and twentieth centuries. That is, he ultimately posited a relationship between racism and this form of colonialism. Indeed, I will argue that Sartre's theory of European colonialism relies on a marriage of two elements: an analysis of the material (i.e., economic) forces at work in the development and sedimentation of structures of exploitation and an analysis of the phenomenological conditions of oppression that set individuals in asymmetrical relations of recognition, thereby limiting their freedom. In the case of colonialism, the former consists of, for example, the appropriation of land, an occupying army, and a lack of equal juridical status for the native population; the latter consists

---

11   Hazel Rowley, *Richard Wright: The Life and Times* (New York: Henry Holt, 2001), 326.

12   Simone de Beauvoir, "An American Renaissance in France," *New York Times Book Review*, June 22, 1947, 29 (cited in Rowley, *Richard Wright*, 335).

13   See Addison Gayle, *Richard Wright: Ordeal of a Native Son* (Garden City, NY: Anchor Press/Doubleday, 1980), 234, 253.

of racism. Both of these, he will argue, are indeed forms of materiality—but distinct forms, each with its own characteristics.

Thus, racism played a key role in Sartre's thinking on colonialism, and it was present in his work from the beginning of his interest in anticolonial struggle. And this consideration of racism is not a simple rejection of it as wrong or evil, but a serious engagement with it as a powerful force to be reckoned with—as something that is not simply a "notion" that might be dismissed, but rather a set of beliefs and practices deeply embedded in a person's daily activities and an unthought system of values.

RACISM IN THE *NOTEBOOKS FOR AN ETHICS*

One of the central concerns of the *Notebooks* is oppression. This is remarkable since oppression figures little in *Being and Nothingness*, even though traces of a concern with it are present. For example, in a rare discussion of class consciousness, and after laying out the basic attitudes a person may have toward another, Sartre claimed,

> The primary fact is that the member of the oppressed collectivity, who as a simple person is engaged in fundamental conflicts with other members of this collectivity (love, hate, rivalry of interests, etc.), apprehends his condition and that of other members of this collectivity as looked-at and thought about by consciousnesses which escape him.[14]

This proposition captures the essence of what Sartre had to say about oppression in the *Notebooks*—though it supplies none of the details.

One of Sartre's goals in his projected work was, apparently, to supply a theory of the ontological conditions of oppression and, in so doing, to offer a critique of both Hegel's conception of the master-slave dialectic and Alexandre Kojève's application of it to the bourgeois-proletarian dyad—even as he acknowledged a deep debt to both. The master-slave dialectic became a mainstay of Sartre's understanding both of individual consciousness and of individual relations with others; where he differed with both Hegel and Kojève was in viewing it as irresolvable. As Shadia Drury notes of Sartre's philosophy,

> The master-slave dialectic is a permanent feature of human existence, both individually and globally. Every human encounter is an attempt by one party to reduce the other to an object or thing and the one who is so reduced must struggle to be *other* than what he is defined to be.[15]

---

14   Sartre, *Being and Nothingness*, 544.
15   Shadia B. Drury, *Alexandre Kojève: The Roots of Postmodern Politics* (London: Macmillan, 1994), 76.

Sartre seems to have had more in mind, however, than this particular criticism of the master-slave dialectic; in the *Notebooks*, he made it clear that not only is the dialectic irresolvable, it is also capable of taking different forms than those envisaged by Hegel and Kojève.

Evidence of this critique is perhaps most pronounced in the text on race-based slavery in the antebellum South. Sartre took Hegel (and, by implication, Kojève) to task for assigning only the task of work to the slave in the master-slave dialectic. This, however, misses a crucial feature of the dialectic as it was actually lived in the South, which is the pleasure that the domestic slave brought to the master:

> In reality, Hegel saw just one side of the slave: his labor. And his whole theory is wrong, or rather it applies to the proletarian, not to the slave. The proletarian does not have to please, he has relations only with things. The slave (at least the domestic and urban slave) has relations with things and with masters.[16]

Sartre thus posited a crucial—though at this point undeveloped—distinction between diverse forms of oppression (in this case, slavery and capitalist exploitation), not on the basis of material conditions alone, but on the basis of particular ontological relations among beings.

What are the ontological conditions of oppression? Sartre spelled them out at length in the middle of the *Notebooks*. He made the primary points that oppression without freedom—and, more precisely, a multiplicity of freedoms—is nonsensical. (A rock, he explains, can destroy a person, but it cannot oppress her.[17]) Sartre claimed that oppression "implies that neither the slave nor the tyrant fundamentally recognizes their own freedom. One oppresses only if one oppresses oneself." This is true, according to Sartre, because, conversely, "if I fully recognize my freedom, I also recognize that of others." Finally, and most controversially, Sartre averred, "There is a complicity of the oppressor and the oppressed."[18]

It is important to note here, as Alain Renaut does, that Sartre is concerned with two distinct forms of alienation in the *Notebooks*—the first concerns a consciousness's alienation from itself; the second concerns its alienation from others. This is clear in Sartre's evocation of a duality in every instance of oppression: an oppressor is both oppressed by himself, in the fact of not recognizing his own freedom, and oppressed by others. Or, in other words, "Oppression is both bad faith and mystification. The foundation of all mystification in the

---

16   Sartre, *Notebooks*, 566–7.
17   Ibid., 326.
18   Ibid., 325.

sense that Marx took it is the plan to make a man believe that he is not free or that I am not free."[19] (It is unclear to what extent one might say any particular instance of oppression may be a consequence of the structure of consciousness itself, or rather of the particular situation of that consciousness—or to what extent and precisely how these two forms of alienation might be related.) Though Renaut is right to emphasize that Sartre's notion of alienation in the *Notebooks* is not an orthodox Marxist one, and repeatedly to underscore Sartre's statement in the *Notebooks* that "alienation precedes oppression," he goes too far, claiming that Sartre was thus little concerned with others and with intersubjective relations.[20]

The *Notebooks* represent a serious engagement on Sartre's part with the notion of history, and hence with the problem of how individuals collectively create it. For such an engagement, a consideration of others—and of an alterity that is not simply the alterity of consciousness to itself—is obviously indispensable. Sartre gives an indication of what he means by "The Other in History": "woman, the preceding or succeeding generation, the other nation, the other class."[21] Also, as he says later on:

> The Orient (China, India, Japan). How can one dare to do a dialectic of history that does not take into account these 400 million human beings who, like us, have fifty centuries of history? The dialectic (whether Hegelian or Marxist) only considers *part* of humanity.[22]

These albeit infrequent musings demonstrate that Sartre was at the very least aware of the ethnocentric bias of the Hegelian dialectic, and they also show him using the word "Other" in a collective sense—although ultimately he developed neither of these points in the *Notebooks*.

One particularly pertinent example of how the ideas elaborated here gained full flesh in the late 1950s and early 1960s concerns revolutionary violence: its conditions and its justification. In the *Notebooks*, Sartre broached this issue through the example of US race relations:

> The hypocrisy of modern oppression can be seen, for example, in the case of Blacks in North America who have the right to vote but who, given the heavy poll taxes, do not vote ... Freedom being abstract, the concrete violence [of the oppressor who grants the right] is not defined in the right. One is free in

---

19   Ibid., 339.
20   See the section "Les *Cahiers*: morale de *L'Etre et le Néant*," in Renaut, *Sartre, le dernier philosophe*, 205–16.
21   Sartre, *Notebooks*, 47.
22   Ibid., 60.

terms of the status quo … But, on the contrary, to change this situation, the oppressed should use violence, to deny the right of property, therefore to refuse the right.[23]

Throughout the *Notebooks*, Sartre maintained a strict (if not particularly original) relationship between violence and right. "*There has never been any violence on earth*," he writes, "*that did not correspond to the affirmation of some right.*"[24] The fact that he used the example of African Americans—instead of the more traditional trope of the working class—is significant in that it shows already that he was aware of multiple layers of conflict, in any society, that cut across different types of groups, even if ultimately all of these conflicts may be related in diverse ways to regimes of property ownership. This is an issue to which he returned in the *Critique*, particularly in the section on colonialism.

Thus two of the main themes of his thinking that later draw heavy criticism from various quarters—History and revolutionary violence—were elaborated in broad strokes in these notes. Sartre did not broach the issue of colonialism here—not yet. Indeed, it barely seems to have been on his mind in the *Notebooks*, though a few mentions of it are made. Instead, the theory of oppression he developed here, as well as the praxis of rebellion he outlined, will eventually be applied to colonialism. And although he appears to have been working toward the idea of a universal History that takes into account collective "Others" both within Europe and outside of it, even this idea takes European man as its center (for example, certain nations in Asia count as legitimate actors since they, "like us," have fifty centuries of history). In this sense, Sartre simply reflected the dominant political strategy of anticolonialist rhetoric of his day, which aimed to legitimate (in the eyes of the colonial powers) subjugated peoples as nations with histories—thus effecting a distance from direct control of the colonial powers through political independence while simultaneously enfolding them into the structures of the nation-state and market economies already established by the colonial powers. Writing the history of an emerging political unit that defined itself as a nation was one of the main legitimating strategies of the Third Worldist movement in general—and a successful one, if political independence is used as the measure of success.[25] Critics of what later came to be known as neocolonialism would see in this strategy, however, a problem: a new form of domination had, on this view, been substituted for an

---

23 Ibid., 142 (translation modified).
24 Ibid., 177.
25 See Robert Malley, *The Call from Algeria: Third Worldism, Revolution, and the Turn to Islam* (Berkeley: University of California Press, 1996).

old one. To put it in dialectical terms, this attempt to "insert" a nation into history was a negative moment, one that necessarily relied on a mimicry of the positive (European colonial) moment.[26]

Though Sartre did not appear to have recognized this problem in the *Notebooks*, he clearly did recognize it in his 1948 essay "Black Orpheus," in which he squarely addressed the negritude movement as a reaction to white European cultural dominance that negates that dominance even as it relies upon it for its own existence.[27] "Black Orpheus" represents a clear shift in Sartre's politics in this period: in it, he synthesized ideas on freedom, collective Otherness, and the concrete situation that had been brewing since *Being and Nothingness*. He tied the writers involved in the negritude movement to his theory of intellectual engagement, first announced in *What Is Literature?* And he began to address one of the key political questions of his day: decolonization.

It is worth noting, however, that Sartre's commentators typically do not consider "Black Orpheus" to be a major text—a symptom of a general lack of interest in Sartre's anticolonialism before the Algerian War. Two major commentators on Sartre, Annie Cohen-Solal and Lévy, either pass over quickly or omit completely any mention of Sartre's early anticolonialism. Cohen-Solal, for example, devotes only one page of her book to a discussion of "Black Orpheus," and she does this only to demonstrate Fanon's early interest in Sartre's work.[28] She does not mention at all Sartre's affiliation with *Présence Africaine*. Like Cohen-Solal, Lévy focuses most of the (little) attention he gives to anticolonialism on Sartre's relationship with Fanon. Also like Cohen-Solal, he devotes only one page to "Black Orpheus," which he misreads as an appeal to find a black "essence" or "soul."[29] Both Cohen-Solal and Lévy are more interested in Sartre's relationship with communism—without doubt a central thematic of Sartre's work—so this is no surprise. But even in a non-narrative work such as Michel Contat and Michel Rybalka's *The Writings of Jean-Paul*

---

26   For a reading of the function of mimicry in colonialism, see Homi K. Bhabha, "Of Mimicry and Man: The Ambivalence of Colonial Discourse," in *The Location of Culture* (New York: Routledge, 1994), 85–92.

27   There is a large body of literature on the cultural politics of negritude. See, for example, Lilyan Kesteloot, *Les Ecrivains noirs de langue française: naissance d'une littérature* (Brussels: Institut de Sociologie, 1965); Irving Leonard Markovitz, *Léopold Sédar Senghor and the Politics of Negritude* (New York: Atheneum, 1969); and René Depestre, *Bonjour et adieu à la Négritude* (Paris: Laffont, 1980).

28   See Annie Cohen-Solal, *Sartre: A Life*, trans. Anna Cancogni (New York: Pantheon, 1987), 431–2. Cohen-Solal offers no analysis of the lengthy essay itself, only a quote from its opening paragraph.

29   Lévy, *Sartre*, 408.

Sartre, which is an exhaustive bibliography with commentary of Sartre's works, the early anticolonialism gets short shrift. To "Black Orpheus" the authors devote a commentary of only a few sentences. They note its significance only in terms of what they consider to be Sartre's masterful analysis of poetry ("This superb, inspired piece," they laud, "ought to be reread by those who claim that Sartre has no understanding of poetry"),[30] even though, by 1974—the year in which their bibliography was published—the political significance of negritude to the anticolonialist struggle was well known.

This is simply to say that an acknowledgement of Sartre's Algerian phase does not exhaust his thinking on colonialism and cannot adequately describe the relationship between his anticolonialism and his philosophical concerns. Long before the famed call to arms in *The Wretched of the Earth*—which, perhaps unfortunately, is the basis for most of the commentary on his anti-colonialism—Sartre started to forge the links between a thinking of collective Otherness and relations of oppression engendered by colonialism in his 1948 essay, "Black Orpheus."

BLACK MASKS, WHITE MASKS

Upon Sartre's death in 1980, Guadeloupan poet Daniel Maximin argued that the reason people in the Third World still held Sartre, among all French intellectuals, in such great esteem—in contrast to much opinion in France—was because he was the one who had actually listened to them. Maximin's essay, "Sartre Listens to the Savages," contrasted this position of acknowledging the subjectivity of people from the Third World positively with the positions of both Malraux and Camus, and he awarded a special place in Sartre's "listening" for the essay "Black Orpheus":

> With "Black Orpheus," a key study for the generation of independence, Sartre lent his ear to the cultural claims of negritude, understanding the necessity for the oppressed first to reclaim what the oppressor had denied him ... a veritable dialectical trap that pushed the rebel to stand before the master always as the better Christian, the better Marxist, the better academic, the better writer, the better activist, and the better revolutionary—not, above all, for his people and for himself, but through a secret wish for recognition by the Same, by polishing his image in the mirror of Europe's eyes.[31]

---

30 Contat and Rybalka, *The Writings of Jean-Paul Sartre*, 197.
31 Daniel Maximin, "Sartre à l'écoute des sauvages," *Le Nouvel Observateur*, May 5, 1980, 63.

Unlike in *Being and Nothingness*, in "Black Orpheus" the case of dueling looks is no longer a matter of an abstract, interpersonal for-itself trying to dominate another for-itself, but rather a racially marked for-itself engaging in a struggle with another racially marked for-itself. This represents a real shift in Sartre's language, one that closes the aforementioned gap between his own work and Beauvoir's in *The Second Sex* by emphasizing, rather than downplaying, the significance of a person's facticity for his relations with others. Even though he does not use the term "Other" here (again, as in *Anti-Semite and Jew*, the language of the Other is missing), this is a clear application of his description of the struggle between the for-itself and the Other from *Being and Nothingness*. But the question remains: Did Sartre try to justify this move from an interpersonal other toward a concrete other defined by his membership in a collectivity? And if so, how?

It must be noted that "Black Orpheus" was written for a certain occasion: the publication of a collection of poetry written by Francophone African and diasporic African writers. This occasion afforded Sartre an opportunity to join together a number of elements that had hitherto been addressed only in separate texts: the construction of racial differences, an analysis of culture, a critique of colonialism (however vague), and a justification of his new theory of literary engagement. It was and is a controversial text—a defense of the negritude movement, written by a white French writer who, as sociologist Anna-Maria Boschetti has shown, was at this time consolidating his dominance of the intellectual field in France.[32] At the time of its publication, "Black Orpheus" elicited a negative reaction among some black writers because, even though it evinced an admiration for the negritude poets, it was primarily an announcement that their poetry—their negritude—would soon be passé. As Fanon would famously remark:

> When I read that page, I felt that I had been robbed of my last chance. I said to my friends, "The generation of the younger black poets has just suffered a blow that can never be forgiven." Help had been sought from a friend of the colored peoples, and that friend had found no better response than to point out the relativity of what they were doing.[33]

In retrospect, negritude has been condemned by many as a movement of elites that was not genuinely revolutionary. "Its success," Irving Markovitz would later note, "had little to do with any forceful revolutionary appeal. Rather,

---

32   Boschetti, *Intellectual Enterprise*.
33   Fanon, *Black Skin, White Masks*, 133.

negritude served as a type of 'passive resistance.' It 'worked' because it contained a moral appeal to the French intelligentsia couched in terms of their own culture and tradition."[34]

Negritude was certainly a movement of black elites who had been educated in the metropole and who had assimilated the legitimate French culture of their era. That many of them became masters of the Surrealist style testifies to this fact. Indeed, Sartre's argument in "Black Orpheus" is based on the idea that negritude is a moment of negation that relies for its content upon white culture's attempt to posit a black essence—even as he showed that both of these terms are corrupt, that neither ultimately has a fixed meaning.[35] Whether negritude actually was revolutionary or not, it certainly was viewed that way by many contemporary commentators, perhaps largely because of Sartre's provocative introduction to it. "Black Orpheus" recognizes and celebrates the political moment of negritude and its historical significance for European culture—marking negritude as the only truly revolutionary poetry of the immediate postwar era. Thus, he wrote,

> The originality of Césaire is to have cast his direct and powerful concern for the Negro, for the oppressed and for the militant into the world of the most destructive, the freest and the most metaphysical poetry at a time when Eluard and Aragon were failing to give political content to their verse.[36]

René Depestre noted Sartre's prescience in conjoining his ideas on the poetry of negritude to anticolonialism: "From a reading of sixteen poets judiciously chosen by Senghor, Sartre deduced that negritude would be called sooner or later to make common cause with the movement for liberation of colonial peoples."[37] Perhaps the poetry of negritude represented a kind of "passive resistance," but it gave its adherents the terms and the arguments for something more. And although Sartre did not know it at the time, the political import of negritude would eventually outstrip the contents of the poetry: many of the poets were already, or were to become, prominent politicians—Senghor (Senegal), Césaire (Martinique/France), and Rabemananjara (Madagascar) included. Many of those who were influenced by negritude, such as Fanon, played a role in the disintegration of the French empire.

---

34   Markovitz, *Léopold Sédar Senghor and the Politics of Negritude*, 42.

35   For another view on the construction of a "black essence" and of Afrocentric knowledge as moments of historical negation, see Achille Mbembe, *On the Postcolony* (Berkeley: University of California Press, 2001), esp. 11–14.

36   Sartre, *Black Orpheus*, 39.

37   Depestre, *Bonjour et adieu à la négritude*, 155.

The language of negation and of self-affirmation served as a powerful political tool during the era of decolonization and beyond—allowing for reason-giving and the building of justifications of alternate paths toward modernization, whatever their outcomes may have been, and to whatever audiences they were directed, European or non-European. What is at issue in "Black Orpheus" is the negation of white supremacy, forged through colonial exploitation, particularly in terms of values. Sartre noted that the negritude poets were building a set of values that reverses the polarity of the demeaning terms given to them by whites—terms that had objectified them in a particularly humiliating way, as a mode of justifying their integration into the capitalist system as particularly exploited workers. According to Depestre, in addition to analyzing correctly many of the fundamental premises of negritude,

> Sartre was also the first European intellectual to understand the importance that a concern for the rehabilitation of black skin, of the physical beauty of blacks, would have for intelligentsias "of color" through the rationalization of the socio-economic concept of *race*.[38]

For Sartre, negritude was not, however, a negation of the *system* of racial differentiation, but rather a negation of a specific differentiation. "Black Orpheus," then, is an evocation of the hope that such distinctions would disappear in the future, once the economic conditions upon which exploitation was based also disappeared. Later on, in the *Critique*, Sartre would return to the subject of values and race, but there he argued that racism is a *system* of values—and that the system itself must be overturned for people to recapture that part of their humanity that racism allows others to make into an object.

In addition to noting negritude's move to place a positive valuation on terms of humiliation assigned to blacks, Sartre argued that this dialectic of racial difference-making bore a certain relationship to the anticolonial struggle. Depestre took Sartre to task for what he saw as a delimitation of race and colonialism that is too strict; for Depestre, Sartre had followed the poets of negritude too far in positing a black "soul" or "nature" as the foundation of race consciousness among blacks. This, however, represents a clear misreading on Depestre's part—one that is made often enough to warrant comment here.[39] In "Black Orpheus," Sartre took care to distinguish racial oppression

---

38   Ibid., 155–6.
39   For a contemporary instance of this misreading, see Albert Franklin, "Réflexions sur 'Orphée noir,' " *Présence Africaine* 14 (November 1952), 287–303.

from colonial oppression, even as he tried to show the ways in which they reinforce one another. At the same time, Sartre clearly saw negritude as a
movement whose goal was to posit an essence—even though, on his view, none
actually exists. Sartre played, perhaps dangerously given this misreading, with
the stereotypes of blacks that the negritude movement tried to rehabilitate and
make its own. This play should be read as an attempt to align himself with the
poet of negritude he admired most, Aimé Césaire.

In "Black Orpheus," Sartre introduced the split between an analysis of the
subjective and objective conditions of oppression that would be transformed
to fit a theory of European colonialism in the *Critique*:

> Class consciousness of the European worker depends on the nature of profit
> and surplus-value, on the current conditions of the ownership of the means of
> production, in short, on the objective characteristics of the proletarian's *situa-
> tion*. But since the contempt that whites have for blacks—and which has no
> equivalent in the attitude of the bourgeoisie vis-à-vis the working class—tries
> to touch them at their core, blacks must oppose this with a more just view of
> black *subjectivity*.[40]

Sartre explicitly argued *against* the picture given by many of the negritude
poets of a black essence. Insofar as he employed the rhetoric of a black "soul" or
essence, it was only to show how the poets of negritude were recuperating
such a notion in direct response to its assertion by whites who had used it as a
(illegitimate) justification for their oppression. They thus participated in the
mystification entailed by any form of racism, but since theirs was a moment in
a progression, Sartre found it justified. As Depestre himself acknowledged,
Sartre foresaw a dialectical movement that would eliminate ascriptions of race
that are determining and essentialized, that would eliminate the dichotomous
content of the reified terms "white" and "black" with which he so forcefully
played throughout the text. Still, he argued that it is impossible to ignore these
ascriptions in the present if one is to pursue a revolutionary politics.

It is clear that, far from simply commenting on and analyzing the poetry
of negritude, Sartre had learned a great deal from it. Though he still held to
the central claims and the language of *Being and Nothingness*, the writers of
negritude appear to have given Sartre pause concerning the significance of
one's objectivity for others, causing him more forthrightly to acknowledge the
fact and the weight of differences of situation—something Beauvoir had been
urging since 1940, as we have seen. The situation of a black man in the Ivory
Coast in 1948 was not the situation of a white man in the French metropole, and

---

40   Sartre, *Black Orpheus*, 16 (translation modified).

Sartre acknowledged that this difference did bear upon the choice of his original project—hitherto free from any outside influence—and how that project might be pursued. Thus, for example, Sartre wrote,

> The situation of the black, his original "laceration," the alienation which a foreign intellectual imposes upon him under the name of assimilation, place him under the obligation to regain his existentialist integrity as a Negro, or, if one prefers, the original purity of his existence, by a progressive ascent, beyond the world of discourse. Negritude, as liberty, is the basic concept and the point of departure; the task is to cause it to pass from the immediate to the mediate, to develop its theme … It is not a question for him to *know*, nor to tear away from himself in ecstasy, but to discover and at the same time to become that which he is.[41]

Moreover, Sartre added a modifier to the word "consciousness" in this essay—"black" consciousness—a move that would have been unthinkable in *Being and Nothingness*, in which Sartre argued that no aspect of facticity might modify the for-itself. In a certain sense, the notion of a black consciousness (or a white consciousness) is confusing: how, on Sartre's terms, might a consciousness "be" one or the other, when as pure negation a consciousness cannot "be" anything? Sartre argued, however, that black consciousness is a certain kind of practical activity that arises under certain specific conditions (the oppression of blacks in a system of colonial rule, as one example). Negritude is

> a tension of the soul, a choice of oneself and of the Other, a way of transcending the brute facts of experience; in brief, a *project*, completely similar to a voluntary act. Negritude, to employ the language of Heidegger, is the *being-in-the-world* of the Negro.[42]

And this kind of practical activity—which takes the form of an anti-racist racism—will disappear when those conditions disappear. After that occurs, Sartre seems to have believed that all that will remain is a naked, colorless consciousness, a truly free consciousness that no longer has need of any modifiers like "black," "white," "proletarian," and so on.

---

41   Ibid., 30–1 (translation modified). It is interesting to note that Sartre's original rendering of the first sentence—crossed out in the manuscript—did not mention "the alienation that foreign thinking imposes through assimilation." He had initially written of "the ambiguity of the concepts that he [the black person] uses." Read broadly, this passage from the "ambiguity" of a person's situation to the "alienation" brought about by it could well characterize a turn toward Marxism. See Jean-Paul Sartre, Manuscript for *Orphée noir*, Bibliothèque Nationale, site Richelieu, Microfilm 3461, p. 30.

42   Ibid., 41.

It is unclear why he asserts this outcome. After accepting the notion—as Sartre certainly appears to have done in "Black Orpheus"—that consciousness can be modified by facticity or situation (instead of just "bounded" by it, which is the weaker term he used in *Being and Nothingness*), there is no reason to believe that it can ever be immune from it, and Sartre did not present an argument for this claim. Several times in the essay, Sartre pointed to "experience" as the foundation of a black consciousness—specifically, a common experience (or memory of the experience) of suffering in the form of slavery.[43] Sartre went to great lengths to detail the specificity of the situation of black writers of the French language at this point in history, only to say that, in the future, situation, history, and experience will no longer matter—as though the need for intellectual engagement that is the hallmark of Sartrean politics would vanish through a rather vague historical process. That process, which was only dimly visible in "Black Orpheus," is decolonization, and the anti-racist racism of the negritude poets represents a moment in the dialectic that was bringing it about, according to Sartre. Their posing of a black "essence" to counter an imposed universality—which was in fact nothing more than a positing of a white "essence" by colonizing Europeans—was a strategic move on the road to *both* political and existential liberation. Here Sartre seems to be firmly within the optimistic horizon of his 1946 defense of humanism, *Existentialism Is a Humanism*, and his 1946 essay "Materialism and Revolution," in which he claimed that "the philosophy of revolution" represents "the philosophy of *man* in the general sense."[44] Negritude, in this case, represented a moment on the path toward a realizable humanism. The dialectic Sartre described in "Black Orpheus" is not a negative one in which differences might always be maintained; nor is it the nonteleological dialectic of successive totalizations and detotalizations that he would outline later in the *Critique*.

For the moment, however, Sartre advanced a number of claims about the relationship between racism and colonialism. Since he was specifically addressing cultural products—the poetry of negritude—he gave great weight to the function of the French language as a medium of expression imposed by the fact of colonization. Sartre saw French as an alienating, yet unavoidable,

---

43 Ibid., 52. The evocation of "experience" as the bridge between the for-itself and the world would suggest the influence of Merleau-Ponty. See Archard, *Marxism and Existentialism*, 23. On a related issue, Sartre argued that although other groups, such as the "white proletariat," experience suffering, they do not use poetic language as do the black writers of French expression, because they are not in a position of negating white culture to affirm themselves. See *Black Orpheus*, 11–12.

44 Jean-Paul Sartre, "Materialism and Revolution," in *Literary and Philosophical Essays* [*Situations I* and *II*], trans. Annette Michelson (New York: Criterion Books, 1955), 237.

force for blacks who use it, even though it cannot be considered a "foreign" language for those who have grown up with it:

> Blacks rediscover themselves only on the terrain full of the traps which white men have set for them. The colonist rises between the colonials to be the eternal mediator; he is there, always there, even though absent, in the most secret counsels.[45]

It is language, then, that for the negritude poet is the locus of the "original laceration" that Sartre averred is the fate of colonized blacks. And it is Césaire who best represents what Sartre saw as the power of negritude's engagement with the French language and colonialism:

> This dense mass of words, hurled into the air like rocks by a volcano is the negritude that arrays itself against Europe and colonialism. What Césaire destroys is not all culture, it is the white culture; that which he conjures forth is not the desire of all, it is the revolutionary aspirations of the oppressed Negro; what he touches in the depths of his being is not the soul, it is a certain form of humanity concrete and well determined.[46]

Such grandiose claims for the power of poetry must be set in the context of Sartre's recently elaborated theory of literature as engagement—into whose horizon he attempted to enfold, rightly or wrongly, the negritude movement.

One of the major difficulties of dealing with "Black Orpheus" is that, even though Sartre admitted that there is a relationship between the "concrete and determined humanity" of a situation and consciousness (that is, not just anyone can be a black writer of the French language: this is not simply a matter of one's free choice of oneself), he did not tell us what this relationship is or how it is constituted. It is not one of simple cause and effect, as though the poets of negritude were mere effects of their situations; indeed, Sartre reserved a strong role for a constituting subject, which is why Césaire emerged as the real hero of negritude for Sartre. He, above the other poets, represents both a synthesis of the then-current situation of blacks and also a transcendence of that situation. His poetry is many things at once: a negation of white culture even as it is the product of it; the epitome of Surrealism even as it destroys it; an attempt to plumb the depths of a "black soul" even as it historicizes it. Césaire seems to be the kind of "new man" that the dialectic of negritude was bound to bring forth; still, we do not get a sense of why Césaire among all the other

---

45 Sartre, *Black Orpheus*, 22–3.
46 Ibid., 36–7.

negritude poets is, on Sartre's view, able to live his negritude in this particular way. Hence, the problem of the relationship between freedom and facticity persisted.

Another controversial aspect of "Black Orpheus" is Sartre's reliance, once again, on the primitive-civilized dyad. Part of Sartre's argument concerning the content of negritude is that it is a negation of the technocratic, lifeless, asexual rationality of European culture, and hence a celebration of everything associated with nature. In his description of the poetry of negritude, Sartre assimilated the category of the primitive to "black" culture, and the category of the civilized to "white" culture. As a result, contemporaries such as *Présence Africaine* editor Albert Franklin accused Sartre of participating in the perpetuation of racist stereotypes:

> One might think that Sartre only calls this racism 'anti-racist' because he himself judges it to be dangerous. But it is nothing of the sort. Sartre wants to contribute to this anti-racist racism. He believes it works, it is the only thing that works![47]

Sartre was indeed on dangerous ground—ground that he must have actively sought considering the audacity of the label "anti-racist racism." Like many of the prefaces yet to come, "Black Orpheus" seemed designed to provoke controversy, and thereby attract attention both to Sartre and to the book itself—a powerful strategy given Sartre's intellectual dominance, and one that certainly was effective.[48] In this instance, however, his usage of the primitive-civilized dyad was different than it had been in *Anti-Semite and Jew*. There, he had used it as an explanatory schema. In "Black Orpheus," Sartre culled images of the primitive from the texts of the negritude poets in order to describe what he viewed as their own project: to negate a certain "white" modernity.[49] While Sartre certainly was guilty of a certain primitivism—that is, of assigning a positive value to characteristics called "primitive"—it seems wrong to say that Sartre had fallen into a kind of trap here, however unintentionally. In comparison with *Anti-Semite and Jew*, Sartre had taken a step back from the notion that the primitive-civilized dyad was capable of explaining anything at all. He

---

47 Franklin, "Réflexions sur 'Orphée noir,' " 295.
48 For discussions of both the ritual function of Sartre's symbolic capital and its importance to his prefaces, see Lamouchi, *Jean-Paul Sartre et le tiers monde*, esp. 185–8; and Genevieve Idt, "Fonction rituelle du métalangage dans les préfaces hétérographes," *Littérature* 27 (October 1977), 65–74.
49 On the use of the "primitive" in constituting the notion of modernity among twentieth-century French intellectuals, see Marianna Torgovnick, *Gone Primitive: Savage Intellects, Modern Lives* (Chicago: University of Chicago Press, 1990).

suggested instead that it was an invention of a white culture that seeks justifications for its domination, and that it too would disappear through a dialectical progression. In fact, Sartre was trying to subvert what he saw as negritude's inevitable assimilation of stereotypical images of blacks, following the lead of some of the poets of negritude, notably Césaire.

It would be possible to make a case for the role of the imagination in Sartre's views on race in "Black Orpheus"—and, in particular, of the imaginary afforded by the primitive-civilized dyad. Sartre saw the poets of negritude as participants in an admirable and yet quixotic quest for an African essence that was, in fact, a mere phantom—it faints in the arms of the poetic hero as he brings her out of the shadows of hell. Here Sartre was no doubt influenced by Michel Leiris, whose book *L'Afrique fantôme* he cited in both the *Notebooks* and "Black Orpheus": "Phantom Africa vacillating like a flame, between being and nothingness, more true than the 'eternal boulevards and their legions of cops,' but yet absent, disintegrating Europe by its black invisible rays, beyond reach, Africa, imaginary continent."[50] But the fact that the common wish of the negritude poets is an imaginary one does not make the fact of "black" consciousness any less real. The image, as Sartre argued in his 1936 book, *L'imagination*, "*is a certain type of consciousness. The image is an act and not a thing. The image is consciousness of something.*"[51] Or, as Thomas Flynn puts it, "The imagination is … consciousness itself 'intending' the world in a specific way."[52] It stands to reason, then, that black writers of French expression might, in forging images of Africa, in fact be forging a common practice—one whose aim was "tearing off our white underclothing"[53]—a practice named "negritude," which Sartre defined as "a certain quality common to the thoughts and to the behavior of Negroes."[54] Understood in these terms, negritude was a kind of fiction with force: it decentered the white modernist imagination that valorized "Africa" and the "primitive" negatively (justifying white domination)—hence acting as a kind of counter-imaginary.

Thus, "Black Orpheus" represents in general something quite interesting —something very different from *Anti-Semite and Jew*, though only two years separate the texts. In it, we understand that Sartre was as much the object of the

---

50   Sartre, *Black Orpheus*, 19 (translation modified). In the *Notebooks* Sartre writes, "It is absolutely impossible to *reach* the primitive at his core because this core does not exist; as we see in Leiris's *L'Afrique fantôme*." Sartre, *Notebooks*, 374 (translation modified).

51   Jean-Paul Sartre, *L'Imagination* (Paris: Presses Universitaires de France, 1936), 162.

52   Flynn, *Sartre and Marxist Existentialism*, 4.

53   Sartre, *Black Orpheus*, 11.

54   Ibid., 17.

criticisms of negritude as are Europeans in general. That is, Sartre did not simply set himself in the role of the objective observer in this text (although that is one of his roles); he understood that he, too, was implicated, and therefore had to choose sides. For existentialism to be meaningful as a philosophy for all people, it had to address questions that appear meaningful to those who are not white European men. In "Black Orpheus," Sartre gave for the first time an indication that he thought that Europeans were in trouble, not because of the existential anguish that plagues everyone as a result of their freedom, but because of a kind of anguish that stems directly from the European's situation as "oppressor." In this sense, "Black Orpheus" can be understood as a justification for Sartre's anticolonialism, as well as a defense of the significance of existentialism for thinking through the lived situations of black men and women. It also represents an attempt at evading a reliance on purely pragmatic reasons for anticolonialism and developing instead a theory of colonialism and anticolonialism that relies on an analysis of the twin, related conditions of racism and economic exploitation—the foundations of his expansive analysis of colonialism in the *Critique of Dialectical Reason.*

CHAPTER THREE

From Gide to Sartre:
The Practice of Anticolonialism

Until "Black Orpheus," Sartre had paid frequent but unsustained attention to colonialism in his writing. When he did mention it, typically it was one significant entry in a list of abusive practices and institutions. This is not to say that colonialism was not on his political radar. Even a cursory examination of the contents of *Les Temps Modernes* from its founding shows that anticolonial struggle was a consistent concern of the editorial team. Indeed, the first article to denounce the war in Indochina appeared in only the fifth edition of the journal, in February 1946, written by Vietnamese Marxist philosopher and Merleau-Ponty student Tran Duc Thao.[1] By the end of that year, the journal had taken a public position on the war that had just begun in Indochina.

"It would be to forget one of the principal conditions of Sartre's success and its duration," notes Anna Boschetti, "if one did not take into account *Les Temps Modernes*, the journal that he started in October 1945, at the very moment that the vogue for existentialism exploded."[2] In her examination of the social conditions of Sartre's dominance of the intellectual field in the immediate postwar era, Boschetti argues that Sartre's choice of the journal format for publicizing his writing corresponds both to the break his postwar conception of intellectual engagement represented and to a continuity with prewar forms of intellectual expression—both of which were effects of his position in the intellectual field. Concerning the former, Boschetti contends that, at the moment of the Liberation, Sartre was perfectly placed to "live to its maximum intensity" the contradiction that the end of the war posed for intellectuals: the fact that the Communist Party was the most powerful political force in a country whose general mood was characterized by crisis, rupture, and expectation of revolution; and the fact that the values of the intellectual field, in particular those of academic philosophy, tended to exclude Marxist materialism, meaning it was not acknowledged as "legitimate culture."[3]

---

1 Tran Duc Thao, "Sur l'Indochine," *Les Temps Modernes* 5 (February 1946), 876–89. The author gives an account of how he was arrested (and then released) by the military for having written antiwar tracts addressed to French public opinion and the United Nations.

2 Boschetti, *Intellectual Enterprise*, 137 (translation modified).

3 Ibid., 106.

Concerning the adoption of the specific format of the journal, Boschetti makes the point that he reproduced—and modernized—the conjuncture between writer at the pinnacle of his profession and the journal format that Gide and the *Nouvelle Revue Française* had represented in the interwar era.[4]

LES TEMPS MODERNES AND INTELLECTUAL ANTICOLONIALISM

While Boschetti's analysis here is powerful, it tells us little about another dimension of *Les Temps Modernes*: the choice of its specific contents. In particular, it tells us nothing about what, by any account, is an early engagement with anticolonial struggle compared to its French competitors.[5] Indeed, Boschetti appears to fall into the same trap as so many other of Sartre's commentators by focusing exclusively on the Cold War and communism as the sole frames of reference for Sartre's activity. For Boschetti, the engagement with anticolonialism is practically nonexistent—so much so that, in order to tag along belatedly as an official anticolonialist, Sartre had to associate himself with the leader of the FLN support network known as the *porteurs de valise* (and former *Les Temps Modernes* editor), Francis Jeanson, in 1960:

> [Jeanson's] fighting at the sides of the FLN and his 1955 book, *L'Algérie hors la loi*, had made him one of the leaders of the intellectual movement against the war in Algeria. Thus, Sartre's intervention in the "Jeanson trial" of 1960, in favor of clandestine action, is in fact the result of an exchange: in associating himself with his disciple, the master rediscovers a role in avant-garde politics that was in the process of escaping him.[6]

There are two points that need to be made here. First, Boschetti's mode of argumentation is problematic. Jeanson is represented as someone who "sincerely" laid title to anticolonialism through his fighting, his book, and—as she notes elsewhere—his involvement in the resistance during World War II (that is, not through his position in the intellectual field), whereas Sartre "cynically" took advantage of a particular opportunity to bolster his flagging position in the

---

4   Ibid., 137. That the postwar intellectual field represents a historical passage from Gide to Sartre is a standard interpretation. See, for example, Régis Debray, *Le Pouvoir intellectuel en France* (Paris: Editions Ramsay, 1979); Michel Winock, *Le Siècle des intellectuels* (Paris: Editions du Seuil, 1997); and Lévy, *Sartre.*

5   And also to Sartre's intellectual competitors. See Marie-Christine Granjon, "Raymond Aron, Jean-Paul Sartre et le conflit algérien," *Les Cahiers de l'institut de l'histoire du temps present* 10, special issue "La Guerre d'Algérie et les intellectuels français" (November 1988), 79–94, esp. 81.

6   Boschetti, *Intellectual Enterprise*, 233–4 (translation modified).

intellectual field. There does not seem to be any basis for this distinction, however. Second, and more important, Boschetti's analysis relies on some incorrect facts. It is well known (reported by Beauvoir and Cohen-Solal, mentioned by Lévy) that Sartre, who was traveling in Brazil at the time, did not write the famed letter supporting Jeanson at his trial—the letter in which the phrase "porteurs de valise" was launched. In fact, he had evinced little interest in getting involved with the trial, even though he had supported the Jeanson network, having contributed an interview to their clandestine publication *Vérités pour...* in 1959. The letter signed by him and submitted to the court in favor of the accused was actually written by *Les Temps Modernes* editor Marcel Péju after his entreaties to Sartre fell on deaf ears. Instead, Sartre authorized Péju to write a letter for him and submit it—illegally—in his name. Thus, this famous letter was neither written nor the text even approved by him before entering the public domain—making it difficult to sustain Boschetti's argument that this was a cynical ploy on Sartre's part.[7]

The fact that Boschetti ignores this significant—and emerging—political position does not negate her claims as they relate to the social conditions of Sartre's dominance of the intellectual field in the immediate postwar era. It does, however, complicate the picture insofar as the anticolonialist stance did not fit easily with—and to a great extent outraged—the sensibilities of the grand public (including those on the Left and those who sympathized with anticolonialism) that Sartre so adeptly wooed on his way to becoming the "total intellectual," which is a crucial element of Boschetti's argument.[8]

What does looking at the contents reveal? It shows that the journal took a fairly radical position at the very beginning of the war in Indochina. In fact, it can be argued that the famous split between Sartre and Camus that took place in 1952 had its roots in debates that were taking place in these years, in which colonialism was a central point of contention. In late November 1946, Camus penned a series of articles criticizing the use of revolutionary violence in

---

7   For a full account of the story, see Jean Lacouture and Dominique Chagnollaud, "Les sommations des *Temps modernes* (entretien avec Marcel Péju)," in *Le Désempire: Figures et thèmes de l'anticolonialisme* (Paris: Editions Denoël, 1993), 230–2. For a first-hand account of the Jeanson-Sartre relationship, see John Gerassi's interview with Jeanson, Yale University Archives, John Gerassi Collection of Jean-Paul Sartre, GEN MSS 411, Box 3, Folder 44, "Interview with Francis Jeanson, November 13–14, 1973"; especially pp. 20–1 on the Jeanson-Sartre interview in *Vérités Pour...*; and pp. 30–2 on the Jeanson Network trial.

8   As Paul Clay Sorum asserts, "The weekly *Octobre* and the monthlies *Les Temps Modernes* and *Esprit* were almost alone in supporting the cause of the Vietminh." Sorum, *Intellectuals and Decolonization in France* (Chapel Hill: University of North Carolina Press, 1977), 72.

Combat, which he titled "Neither Executioners Nor Victims."[9] These articles were explicitly critical of communism and the often violent repression of freedom in the Soviet Union, and proposed alternative arrangements for establishing a socialist society that would reject war—internal or external—as one of its main devices.

Les Temps Modernes replied to Camus immediately, in December 1946, with its first collectively signed editorial, "Both Executioners and Victims," effectively criticizing his attempt to avoid "dirty hands."[10] The contents? A denunciation of the war in Indochina, and a comparison of French colonialism there with the Nazi occupation of France. Effectively, the journal took issue with the idea that nonviolence is an acceptable (or effective) response to violence, and they used the insurgency in Indochina as a means to express their critique. This editorial, penned by Jean Pouillon, was one of the earliest public statements against the war to appear in France, and it laid blame for *all* the violence taking place in Indochina at the feet of both the French army and the French people. The editors lambasted the press coverage of the war in Indochina, which evinced in their minds a "warlike fury." They cited pragmatic reasons for ending the war—in particular the fact that, after eighty years of French presence, the occupier had not found a way to make itself feel wanted by the Vietnamese people. "Let us suppose, moreover," the editors opined, "that the Vietnamese are the only ones to torture, to commit crimes, to commit traitorous ambushes, one would still have to ask: 'But who then left them no other escape? Who then, if not us, pushes them to these desperate acts?' " Perhaps taking aim at Camus, they wrote,

> It is unimaginable that after four years of occupation, the French do not recognize the face that is theirs today in Indochina, that they do not see that it is the face of the Germans in France ... For our part, we thought there was a deeper meaning in the Resistance, and it is precisely this meaning that we are attempting to recover in protesting against what is going on in Indochina.[11]

---

9   Camus's articles have been gathered in Albert Camus, *Neither Victims Nor Executioners*, trans. Dwight Macdonald (Chicago: World Without War Publications, 1972).

10   *Les Temps Modernes* [Jean Pouillon], "Et bourreaux, et victimes."

11   Ibid. This comparison between the resistance to German occupation and resistance to colonial rule would go on to have a long history in intellectual critiques of colonialism in France—particularly during the war in Algeria, when knowledge of the army's widespread use of torture became public. Its earliest instance may in fact be this 1946 article—and not, as Paul Clay Sorum has noted, a 1951 article in *L'Observateur* by Claude Bourdet entitled "Is There an Algerian Gestapo?" See Sorum, *Intellectuals and Decolonization in France*, 113.

While they avoid using the word "independence," the editors' call for an end to the war and for the withdrawal of the French army would seem to have supported that political claim.

Indeed, Sartre himself returned to Camus's essays in "What Is Literature?" half a year later, retorting that, as Ronald Aronson puts it, "violence is nonetheless 'the only means' for ending violence." Again making reference to the colonial war in Indochina, Sartre argued that Camus's articles, by then published in a book called *Neither Victims Nor Executioners*, were interesting but ultimately naïve: one cannot simply "refuse to participate indirectly in all violence ... Thus, we must meditate upon the modern problem of ends and means not only in theory but in each concrete case."[12]

Catholic intellectual François Mauriac, also a critic of colonialism—who was stunned at the comparison *Les Temps Modernes* wanted to make between Nazi occupation and colonialism, and also at what he saw as an undesirable solution to the problem of the war—wrote a stinging reply in February 1947. Although Jean Pouillon had drafted the editorial (later collectively signed by the team at *Les Temps Modernes*),[13] Mauriac presumed Sartre to be the author in his front-page retort in *Le Figaro*, "The Philosopher and Indochina."[14] Mauriac, who said the editorial had "provoked in me a veritable bewilderment," disagreed that there could be any moral equivalence between French and Indochinese resistance, arguing that Sartre had abandoned any pretense of attacking the problem in the concrete—relying instead on an "absolute morality." According to Mauriac, the colonialism practiced in the nineteenth century had been, to be sure, execrable. Nonetheless, he wrote, "it would be a betrayal of its [France's] own history to break a union so deeply inscribed in the real and in a place where so many French and native destinies find themselves engaged." What was crucial, in Mauriac's view, was to find a way for the two peoples to work together, something that he believed was quite possible: "It is up to us to discover, before it is too late, new foundations of understanding and cooperation with those to whom we have been linked by a half century of History." Finally, inaugurating what would later become a traditional critique of Third Worldism, Mauriac wondered at Sartre's pessimism toward his own country and, in particular, at the "masochistic fury" that had taken over the "apostle" of *Les Temps Modernes*.[15]

---

12 Quoted in Aronson, *Camus and Sartre*, 96, 97.

13 See Michel-Antoine Burnier, *L'adieu à Sartre, suivi du Testament de Sartre* (Paris: Plon, 2000), 94.

14 François Mauriac, "Le philosophe et l'Indochine," *Le Figaro*, February 4, 1947, 1.

15 For the most extreme (and popular) example of this genre of critique, see Pascal

Sartre and Merleau-Ponty were sufficiently moved by Mauriac's charges that they decided not only to publish a lengthy collective response (this time penned by Merleau-Ponty, who once claimed that the colonies were France's gulags), but also to include it in a set of articles about the war in Indochina in the next issue of the journal.[16] In "Indochina S.O.S.," penned by Merleau-Ponty but again signed "T.M.," the editors defended their call for a halt to hostilities, denied the accusation that their claims were based on an abstract morality, and reiterated the moral parallel between the situations in Indochina and occupied France. Although they recognized that Mauriac had, on other occasions, had clear-sighted things to say, here they strongly denounced his brand of anticolonialism, which held that France still had a positive mission to accomplish in its colonies, by mocking his idea that, although nineteenth-century colonialism was bad, the contemporary system had somehow changed. Mauriac's call for reformulating the foundations of French-Indochinese relations served, in their eyes, as a moralizing cover-up for a system that was, in fact, based on violence.[17]

More than just setting out the stakes of the debate, this exchange points up the extremity of Les Temps Modernes's position, particularly in the immediate postwar era. This position-taking, moreover, was consistent: in the years between 1945 and the end of 1951, for example, Les Temps Modernes published thirty-one articles whose explicit subject was colonialism, and a further seven whose content was indirectly related to that theme (excluding articles on the Korean conflict). Alain Ruscio, in his comparison of Les Temps Modernes to Esprit (noncommunist left), Démocratie nouvelle (PCF), Revue de Paris (moderate right), and Études (Jesuit), finds it to have published the most articles (seventeen) on the war in Indochina.[18] Though the main focus of attention was the war in Indochina, a deeper examination of Les Temps Modernes's contents shows articles on Madagascar, the Ivory Coast, Martinique, Guadeloupe, South Africa, and Algeria. Additionally, Les Temps Modernes reviewed works that were analyses of colonial relations, such as Italian-born

Bruckner, The Tears of the White Man: Compassion as Contempt, trans. William R. Beer (New York: Free Press, 1986).

16   The other two articles were written by Tran Duc Thao and Claude Lefort. See Les Temps Modernes 18 (March 1947).

17   T.M. [Maurice Merleau-Ponty], "Indochine S.O.S.," Les Temps Modernes 18 (March 1947).

18   Alain Ruscio, "Les intellectuels français et la guerre d'Indochine: une répétition générale?" Les Cahiers de l'Institut d'Histoire du temps present 34, special issue, Charles-Robert Ageron and Philippe Devillers, eds, "Les guerres d'Indochine de 1945 à 1975" (June 1996), 114.

psychologist (and Lacan student) Octave Mannoni's *Prospero and Caliban: The Psychology of Colonization*; fictional depictions of it, such as Marguerite Duras's *Un barrage contre le pacifique* and Jean Hougron's *Tu recolteras la tempête*; or, in one instance, a new journal devoted to anticolonial struggle, as was the case with Francis Jeanson's review of *Consciences Algériennes*, whose editorial team was led by the Catholic, leftist intellectual André Mandouze. Moreover, *Les Temps Modernes* published an article in 1950 that came to be known as the seminal thesis putting into question the anthropological discipline's relationship to the history of colonialism: Michel Leiris's "L'Ethnographe devant le colonialisme."[19]

Marcel Péju, who joined *Les Temps Modernes* in 1950 and became one of the lead writers on the issue of colonialism, insisted that, by the time of his arrival,

> The journal's anticolonialist determination was already complete and without concession ... Through the entire duration of the war, the principle of supporting Vietnam's struggle for independence was never in doubt. And the same determination was found when it was a question of the Maghreb.[20]

Péju's contention here is borne out by a reading of these early articles, in contrast with Nourredine Lamouchi's claim that Sartre's early anticolonialism (up to 1950) was "abstract and moralizing" since he did not explicitly advocate independence. This lack of use of the word "independence" should not, however, be taken necessarily as a sign of being "abstract and moralizing": in the mid-to-late 1940s, demands for total independence were formulated only rarely, as many indigenous political and labor movements sought real concessions concerning political equality and alleviation of working conditions within the colonial framework. Nonetheless, these stood beside claims for independence such as Ho Chi Minh's.[21]

Indeed, Lamouchi's periodization—which traces Sartre's passage after 1950 from a political anticolonialism to a strident Third Worldism—might be challenged. He faults *Les Temps Modernes* for having waited until 1950 to

---

19   Michel Leiris, "L'Ethnographe devant le colonialisme," *Les Temps Modernes* 58 (August 1950), 356–74. The spur for the article, Leiris relates in a prefatory note, was a lecture he gave and the ensuing discussion at the Association des Travailleurs Scientifiques in March 1950.

20   Lacouture and Chagnollaud, "Les sommations des *Temps Modernes*," 222.

21   On this point, see Yves Person, "French West Africa and Decolonization," in Prosser Gifford and William Roger Louis, eds, *The Transfer of Power in Africa: Decolonization, 1940–1960* (New Haven: Yale University Press, 1982).

condemn the violent repression of the March 1947 revolt in Madagascar and the subsequent trials of Malagasy political leaders on trumped-up charges.[22] In fact, *Les Temps Modernes* started covering the situation in Madagascar just after the Tananarive trial, which had taken place in 1948. It was on the occasion of the appearance of an abridged version of "Black Orpheus" in *Les Temps Modernes*[23] that the journal published a critical piece on the trial of alleged instigators of the violently repressed revolt in Madagascar in 1947. (It is possible that Lamouchi errs here owing to a too-faithful following of Contat and Rybalka's *The Writings of Sartre*, rather than looking at the contents of *Les Temps Modernes* in detail.) Among those on trial was the poet Jacques Rabemananjara, a leader of the Mouvement Démocratique de Rénovation Malgache, who figured prominently in the collection of poetry edited by Senghor, a selection of which appeared in the "Black Orpheus" edition of *Les Temps Modernes*. Accompanying the article was a transcript from debates in the National Assembly calling for an investigation of the trial.[24] Interestingly, issues are raised here that were reprised during the French-Algerian War, but that only became grounds for a general battle cry among the French Left in that later conflict. In the forefront was the issue of torture, the practice of which had been admitted by the government.[25]

Given the evidence, it seems implausible this anticolonialism was ever so impossibly abstract as Lamouchi (or Mauriac) claims in this early period, even if it is true that it was not a key concern for Sartre. The contents of *Les Temps Modernes* demonstrate, from the very beginning, both an engagement with colonialism and attempts at informed analyses of the institutions and practices of colonialism. It is fair to assume that, as director of the review and as party to the collectively signed editorials, Sartre guided these contents and sympathized with their methods. Though it is true that Sartre remained, at this time, within a certain horizon of an abstract humanism, he nonetheless tried to base his few

---

22   Lamouchi, *Jean-Paul Sartre et le tiers monde*, 78.

23   Jean-Paul Sartre, "Orphée Noir," *Les Temps Modernes* 37 (October 1948), 577–606. The editors note that the unabridged version is in press.

24   See Roger Stéphane, "Le Procès de Tananarive," *Les Temps Modernes* 37 (October 1948), 696–709; "Fixation de la date de discussion d'une interpellation sur le procès de Madagascar (Extraits du *Compte rendu analytique official* du septembre 1948)," *Les Temps Modernes* 37 (October 1948), 710–18; and a short, unsigned, follow-up article on government hypocrisy on the issue of torture in "Les cours des choses," *Les Temps Modernes* 48 (October 1949), 766.

25   Indeed, the revolt in Madagascar received renewed attention after long being overshadowed by the war in Algeria. One article in *Le Monde Diplomatique* argues that it marked "the beginning of the end." See Philippe Leymarie, "Madagascar 1947, le début de la fin..." *Le Monde diplomatique/Manière de voir* 58 (July/August 2001).

analyses of colonialism on discussions of the lived experiences of concrete human beings.

FROM GIDE TO SARTRE

On the occasion of Gide's death in 1951, Sartre wrote a brief essay for *Les Temps Modernes* about the famed novelist in which he made passing reference to Gide's daring in publishing *Travels in the Congo*, a book that denounced the practices of colonialist exploitation.[26] Yet, four years earlier, one can imagine that the anticolonialism of Gide's reformist and decidedly paternalistic stamp could have been one of the targets of Sartre's article in the inaugural issue of *Présence Africaine*. An examination of the differences between Gide and Sartre, both of whom contributed to this first edition as patrons of the journal, provides an excellent synopsis of the shift to a postwar anticolonialist French intellectual discourse.

As Gide's contribution to the journal makes clear, his critique of colonialism was not primarily political, but rather moral. Hence, the solutions to the problems besetting the colonial system were to be found in the hearts of men—not in their political institutions (or, only secondarily there). As Jean Lacouture and Dominique Chagnollaud aver, "All of the indignation that he built up, and that fed *Travels in the Congo* and *Return to Chad*, did not lead Gide openly to call into question colonialism and its principles."[27] Colonialism needed to be, in a word, humanized. Natives needed to be treated not just as colonial subjects, but also as *potential* interlocutors, after they raised themselves out of darkness (with European help): "We now understand that these men, formerly despised, might themselves have something to say; that it is not only a question of seeking to instruct them, but also to listen to them."[28] What Gide proposed, then, was a dialogue of sorts, but not a dialogue of equals; it was a tutelage. The native, in this discourse, is certainly capable of subjectivity, but does not bear it outright—or at least does not bear recognition of it outright.

Drawing on the discourse of the primitive-civilized dyad, Gide cited the work of Arthur de Gobineau at length as an authority underpinning his belief that, indeed, Africans are more artistic and sensual than Europeans, and that an infusion of African culture might enrich and "regenerate our declining forces." Although Gide mostly cited Gobineau approvingly, he was sensitive to the

---

26   Jean-Paul Sartre, "The Living Gide," in *Situations* [*Situations IV*], trans. Benita Eisler (New York: George Braziller, 1965), 64.

27   Lacouture and Chagnollaud, *Le Désempire*, 187.

28   André Gide, "Avant-propos," *Présence Africaine* 1 (October–November 1947), 3.

notion that Gobineau's views on race might be problematic—he objected, for example, to Gobineau's claim that Africans are incapable of appreciating art ("Goodness! Oh Gobineau, how you are *dated!*"). He described "three periods, three attitudes" in the cultural meeting of France and black people: "First, exploitation; then condescending pity; finally a certain understanding that leads us no longer to seek only to help them, to raise them up, and progressively educate them, but also to allow ourselves to be educated by them."[29] Averring that Africans and the French were then in this final phase, Gide was, on the whole, optimistic and nonconfrontational. In rather banal language, he remarked that "until now," Europeans have "maintained" blacks in a state of inferiority.[30] Gide thus manages to turn Gobineau on his head. In his *Essay on the Inequality of Human Races*, Gobineau had advanced the thesis that, although racial intermixture was necessary to the creation of any civilization (since each race had its own special "genius" that needed to be complemented by other "geniuses" for innovation to occur), it also, he thought, led necessarily to degeneration. Gide, on the other hand, seems to have believed here at least that a too-strict separation of peoples is in some way a cause of "decline."

Gide's tone is conciliatory and reassuring (especially, perhaps, to worried Europeans); in "Black Presence," Sartre's contribution to the journal, Sartre was fiery and disruptive—true to his polemical style. Like Gide, he affirmed the "African presence" that this journal aimed to represent, thinking, as Gide did, that the "old body" of Europe could be reinvigorated by new blood. But he excoriated the hypocrisy of well-intentioned whites in the metropole who, by embracing jazz and the friendship of the random exchange student from Senegal, believed that they were truly accepting of blacks. According to Sartre, this self-declared non-racism was the resulting fiction of the convenient split between metropole and colony that allowed blacks to be treated as equals in one place and as subhuman in another. Playing forcefully on the contradictions between "here" and "there," Sartre wrote,

> These few guests who have been permitted entry after forcing them to submit to all the rites of initiation—these are hostages and symbols. They attest, in our eyes, to our civilizing mission; in honoring them, we are conscious of honoring ourselves; each handshake made *here* to a black erases all the violence we have done *over there*. *Here*, blacks are beautiful, polite strangers who dance with our women; *over there*, they are "natives" who are not received by French families and who do not frequent the same public places. *Here*, we go to their meetings,

---

29   Ibid., 5, 4, 4 (italics in original).
30   Ibid., 6.

to their balls; *over there*, the presence of a black man in a French café would cause a scandal ... *Over there*: but we don't go over there to see; we resemble a puritan who really wants to eat meat, on the condition that he is allowed to imagine that it grows on trees, and who always refuses to go to the slaughter-house to see the true origin of the beef he is served.[31]

Sartre emphasized that French culture and the French language—far from being the blessings Gide believed them to be for Africans, who are to be patiently instructed in them to obtain the status of free subjects—are indeed a problem, precisely because they were not chosen by Africans but rather forced upon them. Nonetheless, according to Sartre, Africans are undoubtedly as capable of making the "instruments" of French culture and language their own as are any other people, even if "it is necessary that they retailor this piece of clothing completely."[32]

This heightened sense of a full, unconditional subjectivity—with all of its attendant rights and responsibilities—marks the key shift from an interwar to a postwar anticolonialist discourse, the shift from Gide to Sartre. It is also both a symptom and a spur of a shift in the contents of anticolonialist discourse. In the first instance, the Sartrean emphasis on the free subjectivity of all persons fit well with the emerging claims for autonomy or independence made by organized political movements in the colonies. In the second, Sartrean existentialism offered concepts and methods for thinking the human condition that were adopted by a generation of anticolonialists, especially as Sartre began to pay more attention to the material conditions of oppression and as he tried to integrate existentialism into Marxism.

It seems clear enough that this double movement was closely related to Sartre's affiliation with and promotion of writers and thinkers from outside the metropole, such as negritude poets Senghor and Césaire, and *Les Temps Modernes* collaborators Tran Duc Thao and Richard Wright. And there is no need to deny the significance of other forces—in particular, the experience of World War II, the beginning of the Cold War, and Sartre's occupation in the immediate postwar era of the dominant position in the French intellectual field—in order to make this claim. Indeed, all of these concerns fit together, making it difficult to try to rank them. Sartre's anticolonialism could be viewed, for example, as a logical outgrowth of a commitment to resisting oppression won during World War II, as a manifestation of Sartre's oft-

---

31 Jean-Paul Sartre, "Présence noire," *Présence africaine* 1 (October–November 1947), 28–9.

32 Ibid., 29.

expressed wish in this era for a "third force" between the United States and the Soviet Union (even if the term "Third World" did not yet exist), and also as part of his general avant-gardism on all political and social issues, which was one of the hallmarks of *Les Temps Modernes* and the source of its strength vis-à-vis its competitors.

There was thus a convergence between the claims of colonized peoples—which were really only taken seriously by political elites in the metropole after World War II—and Sartre's own political and philosophical concerns of these years. This convergence was best represented in the late 1940s in "Black Orpheus," but we have seen various elements of it in earlier works and interests—in particular in "The Childhood of a Leader," the section on freedom and facticity in *Being and Nothingness*, the analysis of anti-Semitism, the relationship with Richard Wright and interest in US racism, his manifesto on literary engagement, the collaboration with *Présence Africaine*, and, more generally, in the contents of *Les Temps Modernes*. Nonetheless, though Sartre had laid the foundations for a strident anticolonialism, he had yet to flesh it out in any rigorous way. The lack of a set of conceptual tools adequate to the problem meant that he sometimes had to rely on modes of analysis—such as Lévy-Bruhl's notion of a primitive mental structure and the idea of a historical passage from primitive to civilized mentalities—that fit uneasily with existentialism, and that would seem to disallow a critique of the supposed civilizing mission of colonialism.

This lack also meant that he was unable to describe in any clear way the relationship of consciousness to facticity, in spite of Beauvoir's encouragement that he think through the issue. Without this, the notions of collective otherness to which Sartre referred in "Black Orpheus"—in particular, those of racialized consciousness and of dueling looks exchanged between racialized bodies—do not make much sense. The political will for a critique of colonialism was there, and indeed "Black Orpheus" supplied a public space in the metropole for debate and for a real advancement of anticolonial claims; but it was only in treating more thoroughly the conditions of the creation of collective otherness that Sartre arrived at his rigorous treatment of colonialism in *Critique of Dialectical Reason*. In Part II, we will see how Sartre's more direct relationship with anticolonial struggle in the 1950s fed his thinking on colonialism and shaped a concern for theorizing relations of collective alterity in the *Critique*.

PART II

SARTRE AND THE ENDS OF

ANTICOLONIALISM, 1954–1962

CHAPTER FOUR

Toward a Theory of Colonialism: Sartre's Engagement with the "Subhuman"

This man coming towards us, you will know immediately whether you see him *first* as a German, a Chinese, a Jew, or first as a man. And you will decide what you are on deciding what he is. Consider this coolie as a Chinese grasshopper, and you immediately become a French frog. By getting your models to pose, you will give them time to become other: other than you; other than people; other than themselves. The "pose" produces the elite and the pariahs, the generals and the Papuans, the Breton-looking Bretons, the Chinese-looking Chinese, and the ladies bountiful: the ideal.[1]

The years 1949 and 1950 marked a period of a kind of colonial tourism for Jean-Paul Sartre. In 1949 he took a long journey around the Americas and the Caribbean islands; in 1950 he and Simone de Beauvoir spent ten weeks on a tour that took them from Algeria, across the Sahara, and into West Africa. Sartre had always traveled, but he usually confined himself to European countries or, after Camus's call to write for *Combat*, the United States. Even during the war he and Beauvoir bicycled around Free France, where they encountered André Gide and André Malraux, among others, in an attempt to drum up support for their intellectual resistance group, "Socialism and Liberty." But by the late 1940s, Sartre's political engagements, coupled with his growing international fame, led him to test new waters—though Italy always remained the place he loved to visit above all others. "The Anti-Ambassador," as Annie Cohen-Solal was to name this new, more well-rounded traveler, would eventually make numerous trips to the Soviet Union, visit Mao's China, and be present for the "honeymoon" of the Cuban Revolution. Indeed, during his trip to Havana in 1960, Sartre (with Beauvoir) had a dramatic midnight meeting

---

1 Jean-Paul Sartre, "From One China to Another," in *Colonialism and Neocolonialism*, trans. Azzedine Haddour, Steve Brewer, and Terry McWilliams (New York: Routledge, 2001), 20–1.

with Che Guevara—an avid admirer of Sartre's and a student of existentialism, according to his ex-wife, Hilda Gadea.[2]

"The support for the Chinese experiment [and] the Cuban experiment in effect lent itself to the fight Sartre led with his French friends for achieving an independent Algeria," writes Cohen-Solal.[3] But one need not look only to his travels in countries with communist revolutions in progress to understand Sartre's support for the Algerian cause. Sartre brought his critical framework for observing and diagnosing oppression and injustice to other situations as well—and, as I have argued in the case of the United States, learned much that would be of continuing theoretical value to him from those situations.[4]

A GROWING ENGAGEMENT

In the case of his 1949 tour, a series of interviews that appeared in *Franc-Tireur* in October 1949 are particularly illuminating: focusing solely on Haiti, Sartre spoke plainly about a link between the long-standing political freedom of Haiti's black population and the possibility for individual black people to claim a full and unconditional humanity—though he took care, of course, to note that one does not follow unproblematically and immediately from the other. In these interviews, he addressed issues of *métissage*, American imperialism, income inequality, the dominance of the French language, and cultural hybridity. He noted the special influence of two poets on Haitian culture and political life: Aimé Césaire and André Breton. And although we do not know whether Sartre had read C.L.R. James's *The Black Jacobins*—published in French translation by Gallimard that year and reviewed in *Les Temps Modernes* in February 1950—he evoked similar themes of the radicalism of Toussaint Louverture and his powerful legacy in this "black Republic."[5]

---

2   Young, "Preface," in Sartre, *Colonialism and Neocolonialism*, xv.

3   Annie Cohen-Solal, *Sartre: A Life*, trans. Anna Cancogni (New York: Pantheon Books, 1987), 399 (translation modified).

4   I do not mean to suggest that tourism is an unproblematic endeavor. As James Clifford, among many others, has shown, the touristic experience is always mediated both by preconceptions of the culture visited and by cultural mediators one meets when one arrives in it. See Valene Smith, ed., *Hosts and Guests: The Anthropology of Tourism* (Philadelphia: University of Pennsylvania Press, 1977); James Clifford, *Routes: Travel and Translation in the Late Twentieth Century* (Cambridge: Harvard University Press, 1997); and Barbara Kirshenblatt-Gimblett, *Destination Culture: Tourism, Museums, and Heritage* (Berkeley: University of California Press, 1998).

5   Georges Altman (interview with Sartre), " 'J'ai vu à Haïti un peuple noir fier de sa tradition de liberté," *Franc-Tireur*, October 21, 1949, 1–2; Altman (interview with Sartre), "Haïti se jette avec passion sur tout ce qui évoque la culture française," *Franc-Tireur*, October

Pascal Bruckner, one of France's most forceful critics of Third Worldism, took specific aim at Sartre in his 1983 book, *The Tears of the White Man*. According to Bruckner, Sartre's political engagements in favor of Third World liberation movements represented a "strange mixture of masochism and indifference." Bruckner averred that Sartre demonstrated "incompetence vis-à-vis the countries and the cases he treated (let us reread here the disturbing analyses of colonialism and neocolonialism in *Situations V*); his quasi-total ignorance of foreign cultures."[6] Bruckner cited Sartre's *lack* of travel as one of the reasons for his complete failure to comprehend anything at all about anything non-French, comparing him unfavorably in this regard with the well-traveled and better-informed Malraux.

Bruckner's book was a polemic, and should be considered part of the wave of literature, beginning in the mid-to-late 1970s, that is often called France's antitotalitarian moment (in this case, the totalitarianism in question is that of Third World dictatorships). Still, one might have expected Bruckner to give corroborating evidence or more informed textual analysis to support his claims. Indeed, it is true that Sartre often toured communist countries like the USSR, China, and Cuba under the status of an "official guest"—and his corresponding analyses of the openness of these societies thus suffered dramatically and, in retrospect, often embarrassingly.[7] It is also true, however, that even though Sartre was never, as Malraux had been, a statesman, he visited the four corners of the globe and, as his trips in 1949 and 1950 demonstrate (as do his trips to the United States in this era), he often did so in a spirit of fact-finding and with apparently genuine curiosity.[8] Concerning his later trips to Cuba and Brazil, Beauvoir noted, perhaps naïvely, that even though their age had slowed down both their capacity and appetite for travel, they decided to go because "Cuba's experiment did concern us," and "a visit to Brazil would enlighten us about the problems of underdeveloped countries."[9]

22–23, 1949, 1, 3; Altman (interview with Sartre), "Haïti, vu par J.-P. Sartre," *Franc-Tireur*, October 24, 1949, 2. In addition to the review of C.L.R. James's now-classic book, *Les Temps Modernes* published a special section in the February 1950 edition on the Antilles called "Martinique, Guadeloupe, Haïti." Michel Leiris wrote the lead essay.

6   Pascal Bruckner, *The Tears of the White Man: Compassion as Contempt*, trans. William R. Beer (New York: Free Press, 1986), 184–5 (translation modified).

7   For a treatment of Sartre's 1954 visit to the Soviet Union, a country in which Sartre infamously claimed "The freedom to criticize is total in the USSR," see Bernard-Henri Lévy, *Sartre*, 328–30.

8   Cohen-Solal describes Sartre's effort to make his trip to Brazil during the French-Algerian War a campaign of counter-propaganda waged against Malraux's visit there (at the time, Malraux was minister of cultural affairs). Cohen-Solal, *Sartre*, 400.

9   Simone de Beauvoir, *Force of Circumstance, Vol. I: After the War*, trans. Richard

In the case of Sartre and Beauvoir's voyage to Africa, it was Sartre's colleague at *Les Temps Modernes*, Michel Leiris, who gave him the idea. "Leiris, an ethnographer whose specialty is Black Africa, suggested to Sartre that we go and see what was happening there for ourselves," Beauvoir recounts. "The Europeans had tried, in vain, to repeal the Houphouët law voted by the Constituent Assembly in 1947 which suppressed forced labor."[10] One of Sartre's projects on this trip was to make contact with the leaders of the Rassemblement Démocratique Africaine, a political party that spanned French West Africa and that was allied at that time with the PCF. In the end, Beauvoir notes, the trip was a failure. Though *Paris-Match* reported that "one of the main goals of his voyage was a deep social investigation of the black problem,"[11] Sartre did not meet any underground political leaders, as he had hoped to do, nor did he and Beauvoir find enough ways to have meaningful encounters with the "proletarianized natives."[12]

From the failure of his postwar political party, the Rassemblement Démocratique Révolutionnaire in the late 1940s, to 1952, the year he made his rapprochement with the PCF, Sartre's political activity diminished.[13] Beauvoir described the situation in 1951, when Sartre was reorienting the politics of *Les Temps Modernes* with new editors Claude Lanzmann and Marcel Péju, in a way that set her and Sartre's particular concerns in sharp relief:

> The Left was divided and unable either to stop the war in Indochina or make any dents in the current colonialist policy, despite the trouble brewing throughout Black Africa; except for a few *graffiti*—US go home—they had no way of fighting the ichneumon-like invasion Sartre had predicted a year

Howard (New York: Paragon, 1992), 487. She remarked a bit later on: "To understand the world outside the Cold War, we had to get to know an underdeveloped, semi-colonized country where the revolutionary forces had not yet been unleashed, and perhaps would not for some time. The Brazilians we met persuaded Sartre that by combating Malraux's propaganda in their country he would be rendering a useful service to Algeria and the French Left; their insistence finally convinced us that we should make the trip." Ibid., 509.

10   Ibid., 204. In fact, the "loi Houphouët-Boigny," named for the deputy from the Ivory Coast, was passed in 1946. For a more exact description of the practice of forced labor and its abolition, see Frederick Cooper, *Decolonization and African Society: The Labor Question in French and British Africa* (New York: Cambridge University Press, 1996), esp. 110–66, 176–224.

11   Yves Salgues, "Sartre de retour d'Afrique," *Paris-Match*, May 20, 1950, 26. For more on the RDA, see Roger E. Kanet, "The Soviet Union, the French Communist Party, and Africa, 1945–1950," *Survey* 22 (Winter 1976), 74–92; and the chapter "Communism and Decolonization," in Irwin Wall, *French Communism in the Era of Stalin: The Quest for Unity and Integration, 1945–1962* (Westport, Conn.: Greenwood Press, 1983), esp. 186–7.

12   Beauvoir, *Force of Circumstance, Vol. I*, 222–3 (translation modified).

13   Cohen-Solal, *Sartre*, 311.

before. In the States, Macarthur [*sic*] had gone so far as to attack General Marshall during June, and then Dean Acheson as well; investigations were instituted into the lives of American officials working for the United Nations. These persecutions were presented undisguised as the preliminaries of a preventive war Eisenhower himself announced in an interview he gave to *Paris-Match* in October: the armies of the West were to prepare for imminent battle in the suburbs of Leningrad.[14]

As usual, critique here centered on the incapacity of the Left in France to serve as an effective counterweight both to the perception of an aggressive US imperialism and to reactionary colonial policies that denied negotiations with indigenous political movements. Bernard-Henri Lévy, though he deplores Sartre's turn toward communism as a kind of self-betrayal, recognizes the conditions in which such a turn might have been possible by asking his reader to imagine a republic in which the head of government was an "inefficiently recycled Pétainist" and the president had voted "yes" to Vichy in July 1940—that is, they had supported the collaborationist French government during World War II; in which the public seemed genuinely to fear a Soviet invasion and was already organizing maquis to fight it; and in which a young sailor named Henri Martin was sentenced to five years in prison simply for denouncing the war in Indochina.[15]

It is interesting to note, as do both Lévy and Cohen-Solal, as well as Sartre himself, that Sartre's first real engagement with the PCF came when he agreed to use his intellectual weight to help free Henri Martin in early 1952.[16] Martin, a Communist, had enlisted in the French navy in order to fight the Japanese in the Pacific theater during World War II. After the end of the war, he was appalled to find himself sent to fight what he saw as a war of oppression in Indochina. In protest, he handed out antiwar leaflets to his fellow sailors and

---

14   Beauvoir, *Force of Circumstance, Vol. I*, 252–3. Beauvoir likely meant Senator Eugene "McCarthy," not General Douglas "Macarthur," since it was McCarthy who attacked Secretary of Defense George Marshall in the Senate on June 14, 1951, as part of his campaign against communist infiltration of the US government and those who were soft on communism. In the original French, she wrote the name "Macarthy," which perhaps caused the translation error.

15   Lévy, *Sartre*, 358.

16   See Cohen-Solal, *Sartre*, 325–7; Beauvoir, *Force of Circumstance, Vol. I*, 260. Sartre himself also claims this was the turning point (Yale University Archives, John Gerassi Collection of Jean-Paul Sartre, GEN MSS 411, Box 1, Folder 14, "Interview with Jean-Paul Sartre, October 29, 1971," 585). Others, however, do not note the fact that an anticolonialist protest served as the first real meeting point between Sartre and the PCF; a notable case is Jean-François Sirinelli, *Sartre et Aron, deux intellectuels dans le siècle* (Paris: Hachette, 1982).

was subsequently arrested and convicted of demoralization of the military.[17] As part of his efforts on behalf of Martin, Sartre wrote a long commentary for a set of essays collected in *L'Affaire Henri Martin* (1953), whose other contributors included Leiris, Vercors, Francis Jeanson, and Jean-Marie Domenach.[18] This intervention—in the end unnecessary, as Martin was freed just before the book's publication—bears direct comparison with the Dreyfus case, as it centers on the unjust imprisonment of a single individual (also, in this case, a member of the military). Sartre's commentary focused thus on the legal aspects of the case, rather than on a denunciation of colonialism itself. Though he condemned the government's continuance of the war and rejection of any negotiations, in this case he defended justice in the universal sense of the Dreyfusards: "Right now we must choose. Either we publicly denounce the arbitrary or we make ourselves complicitous in it. Because it is in our name that Martin is kept in prison and that this guilty Justice claims to be our Justice."[19] The fact that Sartre used this particular tactic—criticizing the legal system from within—is somewhat surprising, given his analysis of the law as a tool of repression targeted against specific groups (such as workers, and blacks in the US) in his *Notebooks for an Ethics*. He later noted of this piece of writing that "it was a bourgeois critique of the bourgeois government: I reproached it for having violated bourgeois legality."[20] But there is a way in which Sartre's participation in *l'affaire* Henri Martin made a great deal of sense: throughout his life, he was inclined to take up the cause of individuals wrongly accused or unjustly treated.

Though his political engagement may have ebbed during this time, Sartre's commitment to writing did not. In 1952 he published a massive quasi-biography, sections of which had already appeared in *Les Temps Modernes*, entitled *Saint Genet: Actor and Martyr*; originally intended as a preface, it had ballooned to a full-length study of the delinquent-turned-writer, Jean Genet. In the context of his move toward thinking through the relevance of facticity for consciousness, *Saint Genet* marked an important moment, providing an examination of how the circumstances of Genet's youth—and, in particular, certain key situations—influenced his choices in becoming both a criminal and a homosexual. Sartre homed in here on the concept of a person's objectivity for

---

17   For details of the Martin case, see Jean-Paul Sartre, *L'Affaire Henri Martin* (Paris: Gallimard, 1953).

18   Albert Camus was asked to contribute, but declined because of the involvement of Sartre, with whom he had had a falling out the year before. See Aronson, *Camus and Sartre*, 161.

19   Ibid., 201.

20   Philippe Gavi, Jean-Paul Sartre, Pierre Victor, *On a raison de se révolter* (Paris: Gallimard, 1974), 31.

others; in Genet's case, Sartre claimed that Genet was symbolically raped from behind by the look of another who had caught him in the act of stealing, calling him "thief." Genet then made it his project to realize the objectivity that the other had imputed to him.[21]

While it would be an interesting digression to consider how *Saint Genet's* discussion of the creation of the marginal figure—in this case a gay French man—might fit with Sartre's treatment of marginality defined by race or colonial status, this would take me perhaps too far afield. Nonetheless, it is evidence of Sartre's continuing attempt to come to terms with the weight and force of what he defined as a person's objectivity for others. In this and the following two chapters, I will explore further the notion of an otherness that is defined in terms of characteristics shared by collectivities—first, by exploring Sartre's views in the 1950s and early 1960s on how both economic exploitation and racism created the relationship between colonizer and colonized; second, by setting these views in the context of similar discussions on collective otherness. I will also revisit Lévi-Strauss's criticism of the *Critique*—but taking, I hope, a new perspective. Rather than addressing the relationship between analytical and dialectical reason, I will describe Lévi-Strauss's own views on race, as he discussed them in his 1952 pamphlet for UNESCO, *Race and History*. As both François Dosse and Kristin Ross have argued, structuralism in general, and Lévi-Strauss in particular, had an orientation toward "untouched" societies that made his work unappealing and, in the eyes of many, irrelevant to an understanding of the dynamic processes at work in many non-Western societies that had, indeed, been "touched" by colonialism.[22] "Structuralism's avoidance of the question of decolonization took the form of political lethargy on the part of its proponents as well," Ross points out. "One looks in vain for the names of prominent or soon-to-be-prominent structuralists such as Barthes, Lacan, Lévi-Strauss, or others, as signatories of [the Manifesto of the

---

21   Jean-Paul Sartre, *Saint Genet: Actor and Martyr*, trans. Bernard Frechtman (New York: George Braziller, 1963). Mark Poster argues that this work represents a turn in Sartre's work toward an analysis of "the Other," though Poster does not make a distinction between the abstract interpersonal Other of *Being and Nothingness* and a concrete, limited "Other" defined by marginality. See Mark Poster, *Existential Marxism in Postwar France: From Sartre to Althusser* (Princeton: Princeton University Press, 1975), 195–201.

22   See François Dosse, "Africa: The Continental Divide of Structuralism," in *History of Structuralism, Vol. I: The Rising Sign, 1945–1966*, trans. Deborah Glassman (Minneapolis: University of Minnesota Press, 1997); and Kristin Ross, *Fast Cars, Clean Bodies: Decolonization and the Reordering of French Culture* (Cambridge: MIT Press, 1995), 162. For a sociological account (on the Bourdieusian model) of the rise of structuralism, see Niilo Kauppi, *French Intellectual Nobility: Institutional and Symbolic Transformations in the Post-Sartrian Era* (Albany: State University of New York Press, 1996).

121]."[23] In a related critique, Sartre himself postulated a certain association between the growth of postwar technocratic culture (and the social sciences that supported it) and the turn toward structuralism.[24] Re-examining the stakes of the intellectual conflict between Sartre and Lévi-Strauss through this lens should provide some insight into the uses and legacies of phenomenology and structuralism for understanding both the definitions and politics of the cultural other in the 1960s and beyond.

THE HUMAN AND THE SUBHUMAN

The two key terms under dispute between Sartre's existential Marxism and structuralism were History and the status of the human.[25] As Sartre himself put it in 1967 to Israeli philosopher Menahem Brinker, who had asked him about the project in the *Critique*: "Now I believe that only a historical approach can explain man"[26]—a methodology and a goal that would have been flatly rejected by a structuralist.

For, as much as Lévi-Strauss's structuralism had been devoted to dissolving man as the only path to a scientific anthropology, Sartre's anti-colonial interventions in the 1950s delivered a consistent argument: the category of the "human" and its vexed properties of agency and responsibility were indispensable if one wished to understand the dynamic world of colonial relations and the process of decolonization (as well as other kinds of relations and processes). Moreover, not only was the human a key concept, but so also was the *subhuman*—those against whom people who dominate in a system of oppression make determinations concerning their own properties and rights.

Sartre's 1947 contribution to *Présence Africaine* had already demonstrated an early interest in what would become an enduring—and, indeed, signature—theme. Evoking tropes created centuries before, during the encounter between Europeans and the "new world," Sartre viewed racism as the consequence of a world divided between humans and subhumans.[27] The latter, denied the status

---

23   Ross, *Fast Cars, Clean Bodies*, 162.

24   Jean-Paul Sartre, "Jean-Paul Sartre répond," *L'Arc* 30, no. 4 (1966), 94.

25   See Poster, *Existential Marxism in Postwar France*; and Kate Soper, *Humanism and Anti-Humanism* (London: Hutchinson, 1986).

26   Quoted in Cohen-Solal, *Sartre*, 412. In a similar vein, he wrote in the *Critique* that "both sociology and economism must be dissolved *in History*." Sartre, *Critique*, Vol. I, 716.

27   See Michèle Duchet, *Anthropologie et histoire au siècle des lumières: Buffon, Voltaire, Rousseau, Helvetius, Diderot* (Paris: Maspéro, 1971); Tzvetan Todorov, *On Human Diversity: Nationalism, Racism, and Exoticism in French Thought*, trans. Catherine Porter (Cambridge: Harvard University Press, 1993); Ivan Hannaford, *Race: The History of an Idea in the West* (Washington, D.C.: Woodrow Wilson Center Press, 1996); Anthony Pagden, *The*

of human, could on that basis alone also be denied the basic set of rights and the recognition that humans (in this case, Europeans) reserved for themselves. Thus, as Sartre said in a 1953 interview for the newspaper *La République algérienne*, evoking the lack of human rights for the colonized,

> neither the "right of peoples to decide their own fate" nor the "rights of man" formulated in 1789 have been recognized for the colonized by the colonizers. Nowhere is the exploitation of man by man more apparent; the colonizers can only justify themselves—even in their own eyes—by a racism that will finish by infecting the "metropole" itself.[28]

Throughout the 1950s, Sartre's anticolonialist articles made reference to the function of the category of the subhuman in the system of colonialism and, more specifically, in the thinking and practice of racism. Yet his first serious consideration of this imposed division between the human and the subhuman came in the *Notebooks for an Ethics*. Already in the late 1940s, Sartre had argued that the distinction was one of the pillars of the system of oppression in place in the US South. His consideration of slavery and its legacy—US-style racism— once again supplied a key critique that he later adapted to his analysis of colonialism.

One of Sartre's most notorious lines, written for the preface to Albert Memmi's *The Colonizer and the Colonized*, evoked the paradox that to treat a human being as a subhuman being already implied a certain recognition of the person's humanity: "Nobody can treat a man 'like a dog' unless he first considers him as a man."[29] The meaning of this claim was not immediately evident, and Sartre made little effort in this particular text to spell out his intent. His essay on the condition of black Americans in the US South— published in the *Notebooks for an Ethics*, as we have seen, but which also appeared in *Combat* in 1949—provided a more concrete explanation. Here, Sartre described at some length the bad faith behind white supremacist beliefs in the antebellum South. He pointed out that before the eighteenth century,

---

Fall of Natural Man: The American Indian and the Origins of Comparative Ethnology (New York: Cambridge University Press, 1982); "Ethno-graphy: Speech, or the Space of the Other: Jean de Léry," in Michel de Certeau, *The Writing of History*, trans. Tom Conley (New York: Columbia University Press, 1988).

28   Interview with Jean-Paul Sartre, "Jean-Paul Sartre: 'Le problème colonial et celui de la démocratie sociale en France sont indissolublement liées," *La République algérienne*, January 16, 1953, 1.

29   Jean-Paul Sartre, "Albert Memmi's *The Colonizer and the Colonized*," in *Colonialism and Neocolonialism* 52. This essay in fact opens with an evocation of racism in the US South.

certain slave owners had prohibited the instruction of their slaves in Christian teachings. Sartre's interpretation was that, had the slave owners permitted it, they would have had to recognize the fact that they were dealing with creatures who possessed souls, and who would thereby have a claim not to be enslaved. In fact, Sartre wrote, when the slave owners "prevented [the slaves] from becoming Christians, they knew quite well that the Christian faith lay within their possibilities."[30] The prohibition was itself recognition of the status of being human.[31]

Sartre also made specific use of the term "subhuman" in this text, this time in the context of the prohibition against educating slaves because of their presumed incapacity for learning. "Not only are they from an extremely primitive civilization," Sartre wrote from the point of view of the racist,

> but even more they have lost their adaptation to this civilization, as to the original situation wherein they found themselves, an adaptation that concrete men in a situation rightly make. Plunged into a world they were unaware of, they originally count *less* than they did even in Africa. They are subhumans.[32]

Along the same lines as the previous example, Sartre pointed out the bad faith inherent in such an argument: it relied on an unjustified equivalence between the propositions "they don't know how to read" and "these are creatures whose nature is not to be able to read." So powerful, however, is the racist's capacity for self-deception, that even when she is confronted with a black man who knows how to read, she devises a method of comprehending this fact while still

---

30   Sartre, *Notebooks*, 581.

31   Sartre rehearses the same argument more than a decade later in the *Critique*: "As for oppression," he writes, "it consists, rather, in treating the Other as an *animal*. The Southerners, in the name of their respect for animality, condemned the Northern industrialists who treated the workers as material; but in fact it is animals, not 'material,' which are forced to work by breaking-in, blows and threats. However, the slave acquires his animality, through the master, only *after* his humanity has been recognized. Thus American plantation owners in the seventeenth century refused to raise black children in the Christian faith, so as to keep the right to treat them as sub-human, which was an implicit recognition that they were *already* men: they evidently differed from their masters only in lacking a religious faith, and the care their masters took to keep it from them was a recognition of their capacity to acquire it … This is the contradiction of racism, colonialism and all forms of tyranny: in order to *treat a man like a dog*, one must first recognize him as a man. The concealed discomfort of the master is that he always has to consider the *human reality* of his slaves (whether through his reliance on their skill and their synthetic understanding of situations, or through his precautions against the permanent possibility of revolt or escape), while at the same time refusing them the economic and political status which, *in this period*, defines human beings." Sartre, *Critique*, 110–11.

32   Sartre, *Notebooks*, 581 (translation modified).

maintaining the other person in a position of subhumanity. Appealing to the language of magical participation of substances, or "primitive mentality," Sartre argued that the racist tells herself that the black reader has a "stolen power" whose use could only be put to evil ends. In the end, Sartre argues, the prohibition on teaching a slave to read stems from the wish to deny that black human beings are projects, or for-itselves—if this were recognized, again, these people would then have claims to political freedom stemming directly from their existential freedom.

Spelling out the relationship between existential freedom and political freedom was one of the central tasks of the *Notebooks*, according to Thomas C. Anderson. Key to this relationship is a reciprocal recognition of the Other's freedom, even as each person remains an object for the Other. Here Sartre tried to come to terms with the idea that, no matter what humans do, part of their being will always be constituted from without. But, Anderson writes, "my objectivity need not be a cause of alienation and conflict." Indeed, it is only through renouncing the impossible, God-like project of being totally self-constituting that humans can live authentically. He quotes Sartre: "It only becomes so if the Other refuses to see a freedom in me too. But if, on the contrary, he makes me exist as an existing freedom, as well as a *Being/object* ... he enriches the world and me."[33] In the place of alienation as the constitutive relationship among humans (and the dominant focus of *Being and Nothingness*), in the *Notebooks* Sartre begins to theorize the possibility of relationships founded on reciprocity—a project that would continue until his dialogues with former Maoist Benny Lévy, and until his death in 1980.

Refusing to see a freedom in the Other: this was the basis for the distinction between the human and the subhuman that informed so much of Sartre's writing on colonialism and, more generally, systems of discrimination and oppression. According to Sartre, the only way a colonist can in effect believe himself to have a clear conscience—in bad faith, to be sure—is to treat natives as subhuman, and hence not entitled to any human rights. Though it may seem odd that Sartre appealed to rights in any form as a foundation of justice, given his criticism of law and right in the *Notebooks*, it is true that he returned again and again to human rights as a touchstone for judging issues of basic fairness, not just in the 1950s, but after as well. When he criticized human rights, or what is presently often called "human rights discourse," it was typically on the grounds of hypocrisy. On the one hand, as we have seen, colonial Europeans

33   Thomas C. Anderson, *Sartre's Two Ethics: From Authenticity to Integral Humanity* (Chicago: Open Court, 1993), 66. The quotation from Sartre is from *Notebooks*, 500.

proclaimed human rights as core values on their own soil, even as they denied them to their colonial subjects. This hypocrisy might be overcome rather simply through political means, however, by just extending those basic rights to more and more people until everyone possessed them. On the other hand, Sartre sometimes argued that the hypocrisy stemmed from the fact that, even when rights were recognized, the conditions necessary for exercising them were absent[34]—as was the case with voting rights for blacks in the US South, which were often nullified by other barriers. These obstacles of capability were much more difficult to overcome than obstacles of political recognition, since surmounting them would in his view involve a significant reorganization of society and a redistribution of resources.

Although Sartre's anticolonialist articles in the 1950s made consistent appeals to the principle of human rights and the moral necessity of upholding them for everyone (that is, to the first criticism of human rights), this may have been more a function of playing to an audience, as the articles for *Les Temps Modernes* and *L'Express* were destined for a grand public. These appeals often situated him more in proximity to leftist critics of the war in Algeria such as Pierre Vidal-Naquet than to more extreme positions, such as those of Frantz Fanon and Francis Jeanson.[35] Like Sartre, Vidal-Naquet, a leading antiwar activist and author of the anti-torture tract *L'Affaire Audin* (1958), also criticized the judicial system from within, going so far as to assert: "That a judge or a president of a military tribunal should make himself the accomplice of torturers, this is just as grave as the president of the Republic himself brandishing the *magnéto* [a well-known torture device]."[36] But it is clear in the

---

34   In this sense, his project might share something with Amartya Sen's. See for example Amartya Sen, *Development as Freedom* (New York: Oxford, 1999).

35   Pierre-Henri Simon noted with approval this aspect of Sartre's rhetoric, as well as Sartre's patriotism, although he disapproved of Sartre's apology for violence, in his review of *Situations V*. Pierre-Henri Simon, "Histoire Contemporaine: *Situations V* de Jean-Paul Sartre," *Le Monde*, October 21, 1964, pp. 12, 13.

36   Pierre Vidal-Naquet, *Face à la raison d'État: Un historien dans la guerre d'Algérie* (Paris: Éditions de la Découverte, 1989), 158. Vidal-Naquet also set forth a useful analytical division between three types of intellectual response to the French-Algerian War: Dreyfusard, Bolshevik, and Third Worldist. Although by 1960 Sartre could be identified most closely with the Third Worldist camp, given the radicalization represented in the preface to *The Wretched of the Earth* and his support for the Cuban Revolution, until then his position in such a typology would have been rather ambiguous. Even after 1960—in particular during the Vietnam War and his participation in the Russell Tribunal in 1967—the defense of human rights and an appeal to international legal instruments such as the 1948 Geneva Convention on the Prevention and Punishment of Genocide were important parts of his criticism. See Jean-Paul Sartre, *On Genocide* (Boston: Beacon Press, 1968).

Critique that Sartre's problems with the Western human rights regime lay more in the social than in the political realm—which is, of course, not surprising given his turn toward Marxism. What is interesting is that this focus on the second, rather than the first, criticism of human rights is yet another indication of Sartre's continuing emphasis on freedom in a broad sense—both existential and social—and on the ensuing relationship between freedom and anti-colonialism.

Sartre argued that, even though colonialism induced this split between the human and the subhuman, granting the status of human to the colonizer, it also, simultaneously, *dehumanized* him. To understand why Sartre thinks this is so, it is sufficient to return to one of the key arguments in *Anti-Semite and Jew*: the anti-Semite is a person who does not wish to think for himself, to recognize his own freedom; instead, he wishes to have others think for him, to become inert, with the "impermeability of stone." This metaphor of person-as-stone, a person who rejects his own freedom in favor of the status of thingliness, is reprised in Sartre's anticolonial texts. He used it in partly the same way it was used in *Anti-Semite and Jew*, which was to criticize the inherent bad faith of the settler or the racist who, rather than making himself or a freely formed community the basis of his values, instead just adopts the preformed values given by others in a system of exploitation. Thus, the settler or the racist stays close to the inert given, the "stone," which is the world of the inhuman; in identifying himself with things, he no longer recognizes himself as human.

Sartre also adapted the stone metaphor to a new use in addressing colonialism, one that is presaged in the *Notebooks*'s discussion of oppression: it describes the attitude of the oppressor in a situation that, according to Sartre, is characterized by a negative reciprocity. In the preface to Albert Memmi's *The Colonizer and the Colonized*, Sartre described a colonial system in which the violence of the colonizer begets the "counter-violence" of the subhuman. Through acts of counter-violence, Sartre believed it would be possible for the subhuman to reassert his own humanity. Thus, the process of decolonization is the result of a "pitiless reciprocity":

> It is the oppressors themselves who, by their slightest gesture, resuscitate the humanity they wish to destroy; and, as they deny it to others, they find it every-where like an enemy force. To escape from this, they must harden, give themselves the opaque consistency and impermeability of stone; in short, they must dehumanize themselves.[37]

---

37   Sartre, "Albert Memmi's *The Colonizer and the Colonized*," in *Colonialism and Neocolonialism*, 52–3.

Though the writing and terminology here is classically Sartrean, the idea of the reciprocity of the colonizer-colonized dyad was in fact popularized by Memmi himself. His central claim in *The Colonizer and the Colonized* was that the colonial situation is a social fact: it gives objective existence to both of these figures and specifies "an obvious logic in the reciprocal behavior of the two colonial partners."[38]

In a certain way, this theme of the subhuman was a kind of rereading and critique of the primitive-civilized dyad that was so important to the justification of colonialism's civilizing mission. Moreover, without acknowledging it, Sartre had tapped into another, related debate handed down from the Enlightenment: the question of whether or not different races constitute different species.[39] Extending Sartre's analysis of colonialism through this lens, one could argue that the logic of the human-subhuman divide upon which colonialism rested necessitated certain forms of discrimination—social norms against intermarriage, for example, or political restrictions against "naturalization" of citizenship—in order to prevent the harmful consequences of mixing species (or on the grounds that mixing species as a natural fact is impossible). We might be able to discern a certain critique of the genealogical (in its broad, social sense) basis of oppression at work here, in addition to the simple critique of the claim that subhumans are not entitled to human rights because they are not members of the human species.

THE SUBHUMAN AS A SHIFT IN SARTRE'S WORK

Like his criticism of the primitive-civilized dyad in his late-1940s text, "Black Orpheus," Sartre's focus on the human-subhuman dyad was an attempt to break a dichotomy created by what he characterized as a regime of the most extreme oppression. The force of the dichotomy, which was engendered by the force of the system of oppression itself, was so strong that in Sartre's view only violence would ultimately undo it. On this issue, the gap between "Black Orpheus" and his preface to *The Wretched of the Earth* is enormous. Although there is much that unites these texts thematically—for example, the reliance on a dialectical structure of negation and an appeal to a new form of humanism—the differences in tone and, more important, in the prophecy offered are undeniable.

---

38   "1965 Preface" in Albert Memmi, *The Colonizer and the Colonized*, trans. Howard Greenfeld (Boston: Beacon Press, 1991), ix.

39   For an illuminating treatment of these discussions, see Todorov, *On Human Diversity*, Ch. 2.

Sartre's preface to *The Wretched of the Earth* expressed his most extreme views on the violence of the colonial system, as well as the most uncompromising prescriptions for its destruction. When taken in the context of his other essays on colonialism, collected in *Colonialism and Neocolonialism*, it actually put into sharp relief his more habitual mode of anticolonial rhetoric. This mode, while it made no concessions to colonialism or reformism under any guise, often took the form of defending the democratic institutions and traditions of France—which include the tradition of human rights—as well as France's moral integrity.[40] The arguments from hypocrisy that I described above played a central role, as did the human-subhuman split. For Sartre in these essays, Algerian independence was inextricably linked to the maintenance of democracy in France, as well as to the moral integrity of each individual French citizen. He pointed to the real source of the Algerian problem, which was the very existence of colonizers (i.e., the settlers), themselves French citizens. Their claims by definition could not be reconciled with the basic tenets of the republic, since on Sartre's view they required the maintenance of native Algerians—who outnumbered the settlers nine to one—in a state of permanent "subhumanity." The settlers viewed any act of resistance as an existential threat. Thus, he wrote,

> This rebellion was not restricted to contesting the power of the colonists; they felt that their very existence was in question. For most of the Europeans of Algeria, there are two complementary and inseparable truths: the colonists are human beings by divine right, and the natives are subhumans.[41]

And it was thus that torture, for example, could be justified. This anticolonialism, which professed a deep humanism and commitment to democracy and to freedom of the individual, might be overlooked in a too-rigid focus on the preface to *The Wretched of the Earth*. It is true that Sartre seemed to be disgusted with France, with what he saw as the impotence of the citizenry to exercise, or even properly recognize, what he viewed as its responsibilities;[42] hence the criticism of de Gaulle beginning in 1958, and a heightened tone of despair:

---

40   This is one reason why de Gaulle was one of Sartre's favorite targets; his assumption of power in May 1958 was, for Sartre, a military coup. De Gaulle was chosen on the strength of his person, Sartre argued, not on the strength of his political program (which, though he may have had one, was unknown). See especially the essays "The Pretender" and "The Frogs Who Demand a King," in Sartre, *Colonialism and Neocolonialism*.

41   "A Victory," in Sartre, *Colonialism and Neocolonialism*, 75.

42   There is also some degree to which Sartre's numerous references to collective guilt echoed the postwar debates in Germany (prompted by Karl Jaspers, whose reflections on the

An exhausted, humiliated country, undermined by dissent, which, disgraced
and sulking, sinks deeper into hopeless wars and degrades itself a little more
each day by selling its sovereignty and then laying the sheaf of its freedoms at
the jackbooted feet of the military.[43]

But during the 1950s, Sartre's militancy had not yet called for the shooting
down of Frenchmen, in spite of his disgust for their silence.[44]

Nonetheless, the paradigmatic function that the preface to Fanon assumed
in discussions of Sartre's anticolonialism almost immediately upon its publication almost necessitates a comparison with "Black Orpheus." In the former, he
evinced an extreme pessimism, though not complete hopelessness. In the
latter, he was cautiously optimistic; in his solidarity with the poet Césaire,
Sartre believed that a reconciliation of warring terms would be achieved.
Bloodshed and violence were not mentioned. Of course, one key to understanding these differences lies in the dates: "Black Orpheus" appeared in 1948,
during what was still an era of a careful postwar confidence, in spite of the
recent repression in Madagascar; Sartre wrote the preface to *The Wretched of
the Earth* in 1961, one of the darker years of French history in the twentieth
century.

Indeed, William McBride notes the significance of context to a valid interpretation of Sartre's claims in his preface to Fanon's book:

Those who now criticize Sartre's acceptance in this essay of violence as (in the
Engelsian phrase that he recalls) "the midwife of history" ought to reread the
chronicles of the Algerian War as it was carried out both in Algeria (widespread practices of torture by the French Army) and in Metropolitan France

---

Schuldfrage were translated into French in 1948) on collective guilt for the crimes of the Nazi
regime. In this context, a consideration of his 1959 play *The Condemned of Altona* is indispensable, as the play directly addresses the issues of torture and responsibility—and yet is set
in postwar Germany instead of France, and takes a former member of the SS as its perpetrator instead of a *para*. See Michel Contat, *Explication des* Séquestrés d'Altona *de Jean-Paul
Sartre* (Paris: Archives des lettres modernes, 1968). Moreover, two of his essays in *Colonialism
and Neocolonialism*—"You Are Wonderful" (1957) and "We Are All Murderers" (1958)—
deal explicitly with the theme of complicity with state-sponsored injustice, though he did not
exhaust the subject there. Clearly he did not think individual French people in the metropole
were responsible for crimes under any legal definition; instead, he argued for a more general
ethico-political duty to speak out against injustice and to try to change the offending political
regime.

43   "The Frogs Who Demand a King," in Sartre, *Colonialism and Neocolonialism*, 106.

44   For an account of Sartre's political positions on Algerian independence, see
Noureddine Lamouchi, *Jean-Paul Sartre et le tiers monde: Rhétorique d'un discours anti-
colonialiste* (Paris: L'Harmattan, 1996), Ch. 5. Unfortunately, Lamouchi did not include the
Critique of Dialectical Reason in his analysis, but otherwise it is quite exhaustive.

(the open campaign of terror, of which Sartre was one victim, carried on by the "Organisation Armée Sécrète" against those relatively few who publicly opposed the French government's position) in order to see whether such criticism makes any sense in light of the context.[45]

I note this because McBride's point is a good one (and much needed, considering how a simple reference to this scandalous text on Fanon is enough, in the eyes of many, to de-legitimize all of Sartre's views on colonialism); but as I turn in the next two chapters to Sartre's discussion of colonialism in the *Critique of Dialectical Reason* and the preface to *The Wretched of the Earth*, as well as the reception to these works, my aim will be a bit different. I am not primarily interested in making empirical and moral judgments about whether Sartre was "right" or "wrong" on the issues of, first, his analysis of colonialism, and, second, his justification of the practice of violent resistance. In the former case, given the state of knowledge about the economic consequences of colonialism for African and other colonies in the 1950s—which, as economic historian David Fieldhouse has pointed out, was not particularly advanced—it would be pointless to hold Sartre's analyses to any standard of accuracy.[46] On the other hand, an evaluation of his defense of violent resistance, though interesting, would veer into the territory of moral philosophy, not history.

Instead I aim to show how Sartre's interest in Third World independence movements was deeply related to other intellectual and philosophical engagements. Already in his 1956 essay "Colonialism Is a System," which was based on a speech he gave at a meeting of the Comité d'Action des Intellectuels contre la

---

45   William L. McBride, *Sartre's Political Theory* (Bloomington: Indiana University Press, 1991), 175.

46   Fieldhouse also notes that "the absence of a comprehensive rationale of decolonization until the later 1950s or early 1960s meant that Marxist historians of Africa had to make do with a limited range of not very relevant general dogmas and to interpret African history along lines more suited to Europe. Their main tools were monopoly capitalism, extraction of surplus value, the use of force to exploit indigenous commodity resources, unequal development, and the pauperization of the indigenous artisan and peasant classes, to which some added the principle of the adverse terms of trade between more and less developed economies." David Fieldhouse, "Decolonization, Development, and Dependence," in Prosser Gifford and William Roger Louis, eds, *The Transfer of Power in Africa: Decolonization, 1940–1960* (New Haven: Yale University Press, 1982), 500. One of Sartre's central goals in the *Critique* was to argue against the idea that colonialism simply *is* this set of exterior determinations that Fieldhouse has described (he takes on, in particular, "pauperization" as an inevitable outcome of contact between French and Algerian societies), arguing instead for a recognition of individual agency to be reinserted into this process. Nonetheless, Sartre's descriptions could only be based on the literature available to him at the time. And since there is still debate concerning the consequences of state policy for economic development, it would seem futile to try to address the question of the accuracy of Sartre's analyses.

Poursuite de la Guerre en Algérie,[47] Sartre sketched the main themes and key elements of his theory of colonialism as the most extreme form of exploitation—as well as what he saw as its consequences for individuals caught in the system, and his vision of the future of that system. In it, he began to unite multiple strands of thinking concerning oppression, racism, and the existential and social conditions of freedom. Colonialism was a system, he claimed—one created by individual agents, and in which they were caught. It was not inevitable that the system in Algeria, for example, should have become what it was, but because it had, its destruction through violence was inevitable. For Sartre, just as individuals had built it, the collective action of individuals, be they subhumans or primitives, would bring it down.

---

47   See Cohen-Solal, *Sartre*, 368–70.

CHAPTER FIVE

Colonialism and the
Critique of Dialectical Reason

The human-subhuman dyad did a lot of critical work in Sartre's occasional journalistic articles, but he had yet to justify it in the realm of theory. How, as a practical matter, are such groups created? And how are their divisions enforced both through institutions and through schemas of perception? These questions go straight to the heart of any definition of collective alterity—if any such definition can be maintained—and they also introduce the *inhuman* into a consideration of how the human is defined.

Though it was never Sartre's intent to address collective Otherness as such, it was through the invention of a new set of concepts in the *Critique* to describe concrete human relations that Sartre came closest to defending earlier claims about collective identity and alienation—for example, the coalescence of blacks through a memory of past suffering that he described in "Black Orpheus"; or the inertia of the anti-Semite who hates all of humanity. In these cases, individual human beings live their Otherness as members of a collective (and Otherness does not necessarily refer only to marginal Otherness). Experiencing otherness in this way has special consequences, in particular for political action. That this kind of Otherness is different than the kind Sartre often dwelled on in *Being and Nothingness* can be grasped by taking one of his favored examples: his own ugliness.[1] An objectivity such as "ugliness" is not lived through the awareness of a membership in a collective of ugly people, who might together activate themselves as a unit. We might imagine that an ugly person may indeed be socially marginalized and inhumanely treated, but it is difficult to see what the political prescription for remedying such a situation would be—or even whether we could call the discrimination such a person faces "oppression." On the other hand, a native of Algeria would have, in Sartre's view, experienced his Otherness, his status of "subhumanity," as a member of an oppressed collectivity.[2]

---

1   On Sartre and ugliness, see Alain Buisine, *Laideurs de Sartre* (Lille: Presses universitaires de Lille, 1986).

2   In keeping with Sartre's understanding of the subject, this awareness or experience of oppression would typically be prereflexive.

THE IMPORTANCE OF MEDIATION

The key terms that Sartre introduced in the *Critique* to indicate the mediation of all human relations and all forms of materiality are the "practico-inert" and the "mediating third." Put simply, the practico-inert is worked matter that functions as an inhuman mediation of external relations between people. Human beings, who are the source of all praxis (Sartre always uses the Greek term), create the practico-inert through their intentional actions in the world.[3] The problem is that, in so doing, they create arrangements of matter that limit their own possibilities: "Alienation," he explained, "substitutes the practico-inert field for the free practical field of the individual."[4] For Sartre, thought was as much a kind of materiality as is a table or a bureaucratic institution; thus, alienation operates in limiting and arranging the objective possibilities of thought as it does for other things. Nonetheless, as he had in *Being and Nothingness*, Sartre held fast to a conception of freedom in which human beings create future-oriented projects that transcend what is given in the present; here his intent was to show the often severe ways that freedom is constrained.

The concept of the mediating third does the work of accounting for what Sartre called "relations of interiority" between people. The mediating third is always some other person who is necessarily in the position of "totalizing" the relationship between any other two people. Here he gave the example of sitting at his window while on vacation, watching a gardener and a construction worker laboring outside, each of them unaware of the other because they were separated by a wall. Sartre noted,

> It would be a mistake to suppose that my perception reveals me to myself as *a man* confronted by two other *men*: the concept of man is an abstraction which never occurs in concrete intuition. It is in fact as a "holiday-maker," confronting a gardener and a road-mender, that I come to conceive myself; and in making myself what I am I discover them as they make themselves, that is, as their work produces them.[5]

---

3   Many commentators have noted that the terms "praxis" and "practico-inert" in the *Critique* do much of the same work that the "for-itself" and the "in-itself" did in *Being and Nothingness*—one of the key points of contention in the debate over the relationship between the "early" and the "late" Sartre. Dominick LaCapra, for example, believes there has been a simple substitution of terms. See Dominick LaCapra, *A Preface to Sartre* (Ithaca: Cornell University Press, 1978), 121.

4   Sartre, *Critique*, 668.

5   Ibid., 101.

Sartre's assumption, made clear in this instance, is that labor is the foundation of relations between people because it is the basic human activity in the world (one works in order to satisfy a need, to fill a lack), thus becoming the source of relations of recognition among people as well. This in turn affects one's own perceptions and experiences. The role of the "Other" as the perpetual mediating third, the person who is outside the binary relation but who gives the relation its meaning, is crucial:

> The organisation of the practical field in the world determines a real relation for everyone, but one which can only be defined by the experience of all the individuals who figure in the field ... Each centre stands in relation to the Other as a point of flight, as an *other* unification.[6]

At the same time, Sartre acknowledged that the relation of the mediating third is not a simple one—nor is it necessarily easy for any given observer to grasp:

> It will no doubt have been noticed that this Trinity seems like an embryonic hierarchy: the third party as mediator is a synthetic power and the bond between him and the dyad is unreciprocal ... It is already fairly obvious, in fact, that the problem will become infinitely complex since social reality comprises an indefinite multiplicity of third parties.[7]

Although this analytical division between relations of exteriority and relations of interiority would seem to imply yet another Sartrean dualism between facticity and consciousness, the persistent thesis of the *Critique* is that, in practice, these relations are constantly mediated and mediating.[8] Thus, understanding must grasp these mediations if it is to be truthful. After all, this was a defense of dialectical reason, even if Sartre often employed analytical reason in it. Moreover, commentators such as Bernard-Henri Lévy have argued that it would be wrong to suppose that Sartre's notion of the subject was ever as Cartesian as his many detractors have claimed, in spite of his often dualistic terminology. For Lévy, Sartre's subject represented a clear rejection of the Husserlian transcendental Ego that, "although caught up in things, still managed to hang over

---

6   Ibid., 105–6.

7   Ibid., 119.

8   One of the clearest explications of Sartre's rejection of subject-object dualism in the *Critique* appears among André Gorz's hard criticisms of Pietro Chiodi's book, *Sartre e il marxismo*. Gorz rails against "the doctrinal, political, and methodological objections that Chiodi addresses to Sartre, as well as the often erroneous interpretations that he gives of Sartrean philosophy, [which also] are widely dispersed in Western Europe and in North America." André Gorz, "Sartre et le marxisme," in *Le socialisme difficile* (Paris: Editions du Seuil, 1967), 215.

them."[9] Instead, Lévy sees the Sartrean subject as action, movement, strongly weighted toward exteriority; Lévy contends, "[Sartre] indeed says: there is no consciousness which is not directed at 'something' which is different from it and will confer its being ... This subject, firstly, no longer has any interiority." Lévy's goal, incidentally, is to set Sartre up as an antihumanist *avant la lettre*— the precursor to Foucault and Althusser. Thus he claims that the anti-Sartrean "rage" of the antihumanists was based on a certain resentment, since Sartre's critique of "Man" "anticipated their most productive moves: twenty or twenty-five years in advance!"[10] Yet Sartre's subject, as we know, is not identical to the contents or things it takes as its objects, so it cannot be "pure" exteriority. In the *Critique*, it still holds true for Sartre that consciousness cannot "be" anything at all, since its essence, for lack of a better term, is negation. In the *Critique*, Sartre tried to show how this negating power creates the practico-inert, which in turn presents obstacles to that same negating power.

"COLONIALISM IS A SYSTEM"

It is unsurprising, given the time of the *Critique*'s composition in the late 1950s, that Sartre turned to colonialism to illustrate in concrete terms how these mediations actually work on the level of practice. It is true that colonialism is not the central concern of the work, and that examples taken from class struggle generally and the French Revolution in particular play a more important role. Indeed, one influential commentator, Robert J.C. Young, may have overemphasized the place of colonialism in the *Critique*, perhaps owing to the fact that in the English edition the editors imposed a set of chapter titles and subheadings that do not appear in the French original.[11] Nonetheless, for a synthesis of his ideas on violence, it is on colonialism—this most extreme

---

9   Lévy, *Sartre*, 190.

10   Ibid., 187, 191. For an attempt to establish Sartre's influence on postmodernism, see William L. McBride, "Sartre and His Successors: Existential Marxism and Postmodernism at Our *Fin de Siècle*," *Praxis International* 11 (April 1991), 78–92; and Nik Farrell Fox, *The New Sartre: Explorations in Postmodernism* (New York: Continuum, 2003). For a similar defense of the Sartrean subject, see Jean Khalfa's intriguing examination of the points of contact between Sartre and Gilles Deleuze. Khalfa claims that both thinkers viewed individuation as expressive of the world in its entirety. Comparing this to Leibniz's monad, Khalfa argues, "the unconscious is nothing other than the presence of the world 'in' me," meaning that "if the monad is without doors or windows, it is not that it is enclosed in its psychological being, it is that it is exteriority through and through." Jean Khalfa, "Deleuze et Sartre: Idée d'une conscience impersonelle," *Les Temps Modernes* 608 (March–May 2000), 212–13.

11   For example, a chapter section cited by Young, "Racism and Colonialism as Praxis and Process," does not appear in the French version, and nothing marks it off from the text that surrounds it. Moreover, in the English version, this section comes at the end of a chapter

example of alienation, "where exploitation is super-exploitation,"[12] where racism and economic oppression combine to form a system of brutality both psychological and physical—that Sartre's ideas converge. Much of what is expressed about colonialism in the *Critique* had, however, clearly been brewing for some time. The outline for Sartre's understanding of colonialism in Algeria was already on display in his 1956 essay, "Colonialism Is a System." Sartre added to this analysis and fleshed out its philosophical foundations, but he did not amend it. With the continuance of the war—viewed by Sartre, as it was by many, as an illegitimate war of repression—he seemed to become more and more convinced of the systematic nature of violence and counter-violence that he saw in colonial relations. This perhaps motivated his conclusion in the *Critique* that

> we have thus shown, in the simple example of colonisation, that the relation-ship between oppressors and oppressed was, from beginning to end, a *struggle*, and that it was this struggle, as a double reciprocal *praxis*, which ensured—at least until the insurrectional phase—the rigid development of the *process* of exploitation.[13]

Sartre's analysis of colonialism revolves around two axes: the practico-inert structures created by colonizer and colonized alike that serve to regulate the exploitative relationship between them, often (or even typically) reinforcing it; and the praxes that create bonds of alterity and/or reciprocity, depending on the situation, among the colonizers (the settlers) and among the colonized (the natives). In the first instance, Sartre examined the historical conditions of the colonization of Algeria as his prime example. In the second instance, he exam-ined a number of things: the division of settlers and natives into perceptual groups of humans and subhumans (as I have already discussed); the settlers' racism; the participation of the natives in their own oppression; feelings of infe-riority among the native population; and also the capacity for genuine group action ("counter-violence") on the part of the natives.

Starting with the practico-inert, and following his nonteleological view of history, Sartre noted that nothing was inevitable about the events that became known as the colonization of Algeria:

---

crated in that translation, "The Place of History," giving it the appearance of "summing up" Sartre's views on the subject of History. This is not the case in the French version. The rele-vant pages are: *Critique of Dialectical Reason*, 716–34, and *Critique de la raison dialectique, Vol. I: Théorie des ensembles pratiques* (Paris: Gallimard, 1985[1960]), 797–814.

12   Sartre, *Critique*, 733.
13   Ibid.

If some contemporary work of sociology says that "pauperisation," as the destruction of the social structures of the Muslim community, was a necessary result of contact between two particular societies, one backward (or underdeveloped), agricultural and feudal, the other industrialised, then intelligibility and necessity are both absent from this type of determination. The two can be connected only in so far as the real, conscious activity of each colonialist (especially on the economic plane) is seen as realising, by itself, in particular cases, for limited objectives, but in the light of a common objective, the "pauperisation" which the contact between two societies ... could not produce apart from individual contacts between the individuals who compose them.[14]

In contrast to the "dogmatism" of this kind of explanation, Sartre began by familiarly situating the contacts between France and Algeria in a narrative of the expansion of French capitalism and the growing importance of the French bourgeoisie, focusing on the claim that the "key-condition of the colonial undertaking" was a search for "low wages." Sartre argued that it was in fact the innumerable individual acts of violence, particularly in the nineteenth century, that structured the practico-inert in such a way as to invent the "couple" consisting of the colonizer and the colonized, and to make the counter-violent resistance to French violence the only way out of colonialism by the 1950s. The need to enforce low wages—the condition of the system—meant that

> the victory of arms was not enough; it had to be renewed every day. It would be even more effective and economical to *maintain* it by institutionalising it, that is to say, by endowing it, for the natives, with the character of a practico-inert statute.[15]

Sartre defined violence broadly—it can refer both to individual acts and to long-term processes. In his angrier moments, he used the terms "extermination" and "plunder,"[16] but he did have a set of specific ideas in mind, and he

---

14   Ibid., 716–17. The word he uses in the French is *clochardisation*, meaning the creation of vagabonds or homeless people, and not *pauperisation*, which has roughly the same meaning as its English cognate.

15   Ibid., 723. I say "familiarly" because this narrative, frequently employed, treats Algeria as an "outside" ready to be integrated into a European story. Much of the work of the postcolonialist school of Subaltern Studies has taken a critique of this narrative as one of its foundations. See Gyan Prakash, "Subaltern Studies as Postcolonial Criticism," *American Historical Review* 99 (December 1994), 1,475–90. Moreover, though Sartre rails against sociological "determinism," his own account, at least on the surface, appears to be much the same. It is his methodological emphasis on the primacy of the individual, and apparently not so much a dispute about particular facts, that accounts for his strong words in this case.

16   Sartre, *Critique*, 723.

emphasized that, no matter the occasion, in the end this dialectic of violence, like any dialectic, is produced "as a practical relation between free, situated organisms."[17] He put in this category: the military violence of conquest; the "petrified violence" that the maintenance of a military presence represents; the "inertia" internalized by natives as a result of their existence in a system of exploitation, and which results in their "impotence" to effect changes in their favor; demographic factors such as high birth rates and endemic disease that are, Sartre claimed, "a controlled process"; and, of course, economic "super-exploitation." This last instance of violence is the most important for Sartre, and it also forms the basis for his analysis in "Colonialism Is a System." His view was that colonialism as it developed in Algeria (it is left unclear how generalizable to other colonial situations this particular description of super-exploitation might be) rested on the growth of the native population and, following the expropriation of the best arable land, their subsequent starvation. In this bleak picture Sartre saw the "key-condition" of low wages being satisfied and reinforced: by having wages kept low, the native population could only sustain itself on the edge of starvation—just enough to feed and multiply, but not enough to improve its standard of living.[18] Any proposal of paying fair wages would of necessity be resisted in such a system, as would any proposal of granting Muslims civil rights, and thus political leverage. Each of these alternatives would lead to a mitigation of the subhuman condition of the natives upon which the system depended—in effect, it would spell the end of colonialism as it was then known, and the eventual disappearance of the "colonizers" and "colonized" who were historical inventions of that system. Joseph Catalano, in his commentary on Sartre's *Critique*, gives the following summary:

---

17   Ibid., 697.

18   For a critique of Sartre's empirical claims about colonialism in Algeria, see Tony Smith, "Idealism and People's War: Sartre on Algeria," *Political Theory* 1, no. 4 (November 1973), 426–49. Smith argues, against Sartre, that impoverishment was a result of the *weakness* of the French economy of Algeria, which did not have the strength to integrate enough Muslims, rather than of its dominance. He also notes that no one has been able to show that the vehemence with which France sought to keep its colonies after World War II was caused by the need for cheap labor or foreign markets. He concludes: "What hope is there that Sartre's categories of explanation could comprehend the amazing phenomenon of Mollet's Socialist government launching the Suez invasion, calculating thereby to end the Algerian uprising?" (432). For Smith, "Sartre's analysis is more powerful on ground which he himself has pioneered, especially in his work of the group minds locked in conflict in Algeria" (433). It should be noted, however, that Sartre never wrote about "group minds".

Although a handful of Muslims may be educated, the aim of colonialism is generally to keep those colonized from entering into the society of the occupying country. The goal is cheap labor, and this goal requires the daily practice of keeping the Muslim on a subhuman level.[19]

There was little sense that a mass of Muslims, even were they to be granted political rights, would also then possess the cultural identity of French men and women, in spite of France's civilizing mission—itself a contemporary fiction that Sartre's analysis aimed to expose.

THE "SOCIAL BEING" OF COLONIZERS AND COLONIZED

Caught in a circular set of violent contradictions, this "practico-inert hell," Sartre argued, creates the violence of the native. In a certain way, it provides a "destiny" for the native, leading him to choose particular projects (joining the FLN, for example), and not others, to organize his praxis. Here, a person's membership in a collectivity is of paramount importance in determining the projects available to him. Though Sartre did not write about the phenomenon of "social being" in the section on colonialism in the *Critique*, his earlier analysis of it clearly applies—and it offers an explanation for how collective differences become congealed both in the practico-inert and also in the projects that each individual organism chooses for himself.[20]

The idea of a social *being* is not one that Sartre would obviously adopt, given his argument in *Being and Nothingness* that the for-itself is precisely nothing—it has no essence.[21] In "Black Orpheus," however, Sartre ascribed certain modifiers to consciousness that linked it to its facticity. In that essay, consciousness could be "black" or "white," for example, depending on its historical situation. Nonetheless, Sartre held firmly that this was not a return to

---

19   Joseph S. Catalano, *A Commentary on Jean-Paul Sartre's* Critique of Dialectical Reason, Volume 1: Theory of Practical Ensembles (Chicago: University of Chicago Press, 1986), 242.

20   Sartre did, however, relate the social being of the colonized to a destiny of violence in his 1965 interview with *Playboy*. "Take a child who was born in Algeria in 1930 or 1935. He was doomed to an explosion into death and the tortures that were his destiny." Interviewer: "Is there no hope, 'no exit' from this destiny?" Sartre: "Certainly there is. You can take action against what people have made of you and transform yourself. That Algerian child, though predestined to torture or to death, is living out his revolt today; it's he who makes that revolution." Madeline Gobeil, "Jean-Paul Sartre," *Playboy*, May 1965, 71.

21   For a philosophical treatment of the concept of social being and its trajectory in Sartre's work, see Juliette Simont, " 'Ni synthèse, ni collection' ou de l'intersubjectivité et de l'être social," in *Jean-Paul Sartre: Un demi-siècle de liberté* (Brussels: De Boeck Université, 1998).

essences—that it was, indeed, the opposite. Similarly, in the *Critique* Sartre questioned himself as to the suitability of a notion of social being for his philosophy:

> Existentialism denied the *a priori* existence of essences; must we not now admit that they do exist and that they are the *a priori* characteristics of our passive being? And if they exist, how is praxis possible? I used to say that one never *is* a coward or a thief. Accordingly, should I now say that one *makes oneself* a bourgeois or a proletarian?[22]

In a way, the argument for social being—collective memberships that are "passive syntheses of materiality,"[23] differential structures that exist objectively in the social field and that are expressed by individual organisms acting in the social milieu—can be directly related to "Black Orpheus" through this comparison. Looking ahead to the 1960s and 1970s, social being will be central to Sartre's massive, unfinished work on Gustave Flaubert.

To answer his own question, Sartre replied, "There can be no doubt that one *makes oneself* a bourgeois. In this case, every moment of activity is embourgeoisement. But in order to make oneself bourgeois, one must be bourgeois." The practico-inert is an objective reality and the condition of praxis. It is "the *crystallised practice* of previous generations: individuals find an existence already sketched out for them at birth; they 'have their position in life and their personal development assigned to them by their class.' "[24] Moreover, this movement of the bourgeois always toward adapting herself to the *other* bourgeois, toward others' tastes, desires, and projects, results in the setting of exclusions that in effect create the social being of the worker:

> An exploiting class, by tightening its bonds against an enemy and by becoming aware of itself as a unity of individuals *in solidarity*, shows the exploited classes their material being as a collective and as a point of departure for a constant effort to establish lived bonds of solidarity between its members.[25]

Sartre's general agreement with Marx concerning a theory of the social *reproduction* of identities—rather than, as one might have expected from the author of *Being and Nothingness*, more attention being focused on the possibility that individual praxis might disrupt any process of reproduction—is a

22 Sartre, *Critique*, 231.
23 Ibid., 232.
24 Ibid., 231, 232. Sartre notes that he is quoting Karl Marx's *The German Ideology*.
25 Ibid., 346.

sure mark of his general pessimism about the human condition in general in the year 1960, and presumably about the wherewithal of individual French people to stand up against systems of oppression. In the case of colonialism, the cards seem to have been doubly stacked against all the actors—colonizers, colonized, and the inhabitants of the metropole. The constitution of the social being of individuals in each of these collectives was such that breaking the bonds of alterity conditioning their relations was all but impossible.

THE BOND OF ALTERITY

The reason for this difficulty is the fact that the particular nature of collectives is that they are "serial" in structure. For Sartre, the condition of all alienating human praxis is scarcity; in his vision of the world, history is set in motion by a primary struggle of individuals to overcome a situation of lack that threatens their existence (hunger, for example).[26] Seriality is a particular social structure that arises when there is competition for scarce resources, which is only the case in societies that have, so to speak, "entered" History. In a sort of rewriting of both the primitive-civilized dyad and Lévi-Strauss's distinction between "hot" and "cold" societies, Sartre argues that there is a difference between primitive (ahistorical) and advanced (historical) societies, based on the social regulation of scarcity. In primitive societies, so this argument goes, an equilibrium is established among social elements that prevents competitive antagonism from occurring; as a result, primitive societies do not know History, since they exist in a state of timeless repetition. It is only when a disruption of the equilibrium occurs that the logic of competition sets in, leading to the creation of socially differentiated groups that eventually become classes.

Given the condition of living in "History," whenever individuals have the aim of obtaining the same object, they are necessarily, and objectively, ordered. The example he gives is of people waiting in line to board a bus: because there may not be enough places for every person who wants to get on, Sartre argued that the line itself forms an objective unity (in this case, of like-minded intentions) in which people are hierarchized in relation to each other in terms of their intentions to board. That is, they are ordered and modified by scarcity in the world outside of themselves. It would be difficult to rival the complexity of Sartre's interpretation of so simple a thing as a line of people:

---

26 Raymond Aron gives a helpful explanation of the relationship between scarcity and history in the section "L'histoire n'est pas nécessaire" in his article, "Sartre et le marxisme," *Le Figaro littéraire*, October 29, 1964.

The bus designates the present commuters, it constitutes them in their *inter-changeability* ... In other words, their being-outside (that is to say, their interest as regular users of the bus service) is unified ... it is a simple identity ... At this moment of the investigation, the unit-being [*être-unique*] of the group lies outside itself, in a future object, and everyone, in so far as he is determined by the common interest, differentiates himself from everyone else only by the simple materiality of the organism.[27]

This kind of serial ordering happens in our everyday lives in a myriad of simple ways, such as a bus line; but it also regulates more complex structures, Sartre says, such as the French army, economic classes, colonizers, Jews, and so on.

Seriality is a particularly important explanatory tool for Sartre not only for its pervasiveness in people's daily lives, but also because it is constitutive of a particular relationship among people: the bond of alterity. Indeed, his explanation for the praxis that created, and that maintains, the system of colonialism (and its violence) relied on the related concepts of seriality and alterity. Essentially, alterity is a relation of separation among individuals—it is a bond, to be sure, but a negative one. Sartre opposed it to reciprocity, which is a much rarer phenomenon. To sharpen the significance of seriality, Sartre turned to a familiar example:

> *The* Jew (as the internal, serial unity of Jewish multiplicities), or *the* colonialist, or *the* professional soldier, etc., are not ideas, any more than *the* militant or, as we shall see, *the* petty bourgeois, or *the* manual worker. The theoretical error (it is not a practical one, because praxis really does constitute them in alterity) was to conceive of these beings as concepts, whereas—as the fundamental basis of extremely complex relations—they are *primarily* serial unities. In fact, the being-Jewish of every Jew in a hostile society which persecutes and insults them, and opens itself to them only to reject them again, cannot be the only relation between the individual Jew and the anti-Semitic, racist society which surrounds him; it is this relation in so far as it is lived by every Jew in his direct or indirect relations with all the other Jews, and in so far as it constitutes him, through them all, as Other and threatens him in and through the Others ... *The* Jew, far from being *the type* common to each separate instance, represents *on the contrary* the perpetual *being-outside-themselves-in-the-other* of the members of this practico-inert grouping.[28]

Like Sartre's analysis of the bus line, this example emphasizes a significant point about seriality: it constitutes each member of the series as an "Other" vis-à-vis all others (and hence, identical and interchangeable). This Otherness is

---

27 Sartre, *Critique*, 260.
28 Sartre, *Critique*, 267–8.

always constituted from the outside, because one is "designated" in the series by the very *object* that unites the series: whether it is getting a place on the bus or "being" Jewish, or a colonialist, and so on. For Sartre, this was evidence that serial collectivities (of which most of the ensembles to which human beings belong are composed) induce an identification of free beings with inhuman matter through the mediation of the unifying object. Thus, the bond among these united individuals—alterity—is a negative one.

It is important to note here that, for Sartre, alterity in this case does not refer to a "cultural Other" or collective Otherness. It refers instead to a situation in which each self identifies itself with a not-myself, in which each self becomes the Other *in his own collectivity*. "*The Other*," Sartre writes, "as formula of the series and as a factor in every particular case of alterity, therefore becomes, beyond its structure of identity and its structure of alterity, a being common to all (as negated and preserved interchangeability)."[29] The Other is always an "exigency"—that is, an exigency to act a certain way (the same way as the Other). In some cases, Sartre goes so far as to say that the Other can act as an imperative. In the case of colonialism, the seriality of the *colons'* behavior arises from the fact that people in the colonial system who are *colons* reaffirm their own status as *colon* through their everyday practices, chosen in preference to practices that acknowledge both their own freedom and the freedom of others. One of the *colons'* most sinister everyday practices is racism.

RACISM: THE IDEA AS IMPERATIVE

Like the system of colonialism, for Sartre the practice of racism is perhaps the most extreme example of the bond of alterity at work in serial collectivities. There is an intimate link in his theory between super-exploitation and racism —the latter is not simply a "psychological defense" of colonialists, but rather their necessary practice. Confirming his earlier arguments in *Being and Nothingness*, *Anti-Semite and Jew*, "Black Orpheus," and the *Notebooks for an Ethics*, racism in the *Critique* is inessential and historical. Though it relies in many cases on identifiable physical differences between populations, those differences cannot be the foundation of racism. Nor is racism a matter of psychology, as Octave Mannoni had argued in *Prospero and Caliban*.

Sartre focused on the relationship between the practico-inert and thought in his attempt to explain the phenomenon of racism in the *Critique*, taking colonialism in Algeria as its clearest primary example. Sartre argued that

---

29   Sartre, *Critique*, 266.

racism is a practice that was created in Algeria by the necessities of super-exploitation and all of its attending practices and institutions, such as conquest, military presence, expropriation, and so on. The multiplication of these human practices in the inhuman practico-inert hardened over time. As the settlers became more and more instruments of this system—that is, themselves more and more inhuman—the bond of alterity uniting them as a collective strengthened as well. The result was a certain type of thought:

> It is in fact *Other-Thought* [*Pensée-Autre*] produced objectively by the colonial system and by super-exploitation: man is defined by the wage and by the nature of labour, and therefore it is true that wages, as they tend towards zero, and labour, as an alternation between unemployment and 'forced labour', reduce a colonised person to the sub-human which he is for the colonialist. Racist thinking is simply an activity which realises in alterity a practical truth inscribed in worked matter.[30]

On this level, Sartre was in no way interested in racism as a psychological phenomenon.

This genre of explanation, which seems to give all the weight to the practico-inert and none to free praxis, is perhaps not really so far from the Sartre of "Black Orpheus," in which black consciousness and white consciousness are in conflict on the basis of their divergent experiences and collective memories—though the example in the *Critique* is much more complex. But here Sartre introduced a certain nuance by reserving a special description and explanation of the *idea* of racism. Thinking is a kind of practice, and ideas form part of the practico-inert structure of the human world—so the fact that there is a separate discussion of them seems significant. It is also interesting that Sartre chose racism to exemplify his views on thinking and ideas, and their role in the dialectical relationship between human praxis and the inhuman practico-inert. In effect, it was here that he laid out some preliminary views on values and value systems.

There are two places in the *Critique* where Sartre discussed the idea of racism. The first comes in his section on the social being of individuals, in an extremely rich, epic-length footnote (the longest of the book) that spans four pages of small type in the French edition. The second is in a later section in which he addressed colonialism at length. He argued in both instances that an *idea* can be the object that unifies a serial collectivity: "In reality, racism is the colonial interest lived as a link of all the colonialists of the colony through

---

30 Ibid., 714.

the serial flight of alterity."[31] Once again invoking the metaphor of petrifica-
tion, thus demonstrating a continuity with *Anti-Semite and Jew*, Sartre argued
that racism is "an Idea of stone"—that it is, in fact, inert through and through,
but without any content. It is the meaningless repetition of contentless phrases
("the native is lazy, dishonest, and dirty"), defining the essence of alienated,
serial practice:[32]

> These phrases were never the translation of a real, concrete thought; they were
> not even *the object* of thought. Furthermore, they have not by themselves any
> meaning, at least in so far as they claim to express knowledge about the colo-
> nised. They arose with the establishment of the colonial system and have never
> been anything more than this system itself producing itself as a determination
> of the language of the colonists in the milieu of alterity. And, from this point of
> view, they must be seen as material exigencies of language … addressed to
> colonialists as members of a series and *signifying* them as colonialists both in
> their own eyes and in those of others.[33]

In a certain way, this begs the question of what constitutes "real, concrete
thought," but since Sartre saw racism as the best example of alienated thinking
—so alienated, in fact, that it is no longer movement, but rather stone—
presumably "real, concrete thought" must be generated from freedom and
relations of reciprocity, rather than from serial alterity.

Unfortunately, the conditions of colonialism as a system make such a
generative process nearly impossible, on Sartre's view. The extremity of the
situation means that racism is not just an opinion or a set of claims—each of
which might be refuted through reason—but rather a "system of other values,
entirely governed by alterity."[34] For the racist colonialist in Algeria, freedom is
completely absent; the Other dominates through the force of imperatives given
by this system of values.

---

31   Sartre, *Critique*, 300fn.
32   Ibid., 300fn, 301fn.
33   Ibid., 301fn. There is some unintended affinity here between Sartre's thoughts on
racism and Hannah Arendt's discussion of anti-Semitism in *Eichmann in Jerusalem: A Report
on the Banality of Evil* (New York: Viking Press, 1963)—for example, the "banality" of these
phrases and the fact of their contentlessness and their repetition. Sartre continues: "It is
pointless to say that they [the racist phrases] circulate, that people repeat them to one
another in some form; the truth is that they *cannot* circulate because they cannot be objects of
exchange. They have *a priori* the structure of a collective and when two colonialists, in
conversation, appear to be *exchanging* these ideas, they actually merely reactualise them one
after the other in so far as they represent a certain aspect of serial reason."
34   Sartre, *Critique*, 720.

A SOLUTION OF SORTS: THE GROUP

In his *Notebooks for an Ethics*, Sartre argued that, for an oppressor to see a situation of oppression clearly, he would literally have to "change the structure of his eyes." In the *Critique*, Sartre similarly noted that the colonialist's racism actually "signifies" him as a colonialist in both his eyes and in the eyes of others. Given the stone-like quality of this kind of thinking, it is perhaps unsurprising to find that Sartre saw no way out of colonialism except through violence. The picture he painted was grim, but he did also want to argue that there might be a basis—however unstable—for the creation of new values, this time based on reciprocity rather than on alterity.

In the rich, difficult language Sartre devised for the *Critique*, "reciprocity" acts as the flip-side of alterity. It, too, is a bond uniting people, but it represents individual praxes acting in coordination as a "common person" and for a "common goal," rather than individual praxes acting in competition for an object each would like to steal from the other. In this language, alterity is the bond unifying a serial "collectivity," and reciprocity is the bond that unifies a "group." Though Sartre keeps a rigid analytical separation of the two kinds of human ensembles in his descriptions, the complexity of the world means that, in practice, there is no rigid separation: serial collectivities can turn into groups that can then turn back into serial collectivities; in fact, this is exactly what "History" means to Sartre.

The best example of group formation, for Sartre, is found in any revolutionary undertaking. His own example is the taking of the Bastille during the French Revolution—an act in which he believes there was a coherent unity of nonantagonistic intention on the part of all of the actors. Clearly, however, another example would be organized colonial resistance, such as that undertaken by the FLN (or, to take another controversial example from this period, the Castroist revolution in Cuba). Later, Sartre's theory of group formation and, specifically, the "group-in-fusion" would inspire analyses of the May 1968 *groupuscules*.

Sartre's theory of the group-in-fusion was intended as an answer to the question of how the revolutionary activity of the Bolshevik Revolution could degenerate into the repressive, bureaucratic institutions of Joseph Stalin—that is, how actions aiming toward freedom could become their opposite. While it is not important to describe his detailed argument here, it is important to note that Sartre believed the unity of revolutionary action that the group-in-fusion represents to be highly unstable, and thus always of short duration. The group-in-fusion is a utopian moment, a moment of authentic human freedom—but it is only a moment, and is always doomed to institutionalize itself. It is also important to note that groups seem to be fairly rare phenomena. For Sartre, classes are not groups; the proletariat and the bourgeoisie are serial collectivities. Thus, like a number of Western Marxists at this point in time, Sartre did not believe there was anything inherently revolutionary in the proletariat—as Deleuze and Guattari later noted of him in their influential work, *Anti-Oedipus: Capitalism and Schizophrenia*.[35]

Although Sartre did not broach the issues of group formation and anticolonial action directly in the *Critique*, the link between the two is clear—and it is solidified in his preface to Fanon's *The Wretched of the Earth*. In the *Critique*, he focused on the violence of the native as counter-violence: "The only possible way out was to confront total negation with total negation, violence with equal violence; to negate dispersal and atomization by an initially negative unity whose content would be defined in struggle: the Algerian nation."[36] In the dialectic Sartre described here, there is one serial collectivity whose bond is an extreme form of alterity confronting another serial collectivity whose bond of alterity is equally as extreme. This is a universe in which extreme alienation reigns, so Sartre did not yet pass to an analysis of the utopian moment of group formation emerging from anticolonial struggle.

What is crucial to understand is that this grisly picture, far from extolling any virtue in violence, instead tries to demonstrate that violence is the outcome of only the most inhuman conditions. Not quite the "apologist" or "advocate" of violence commentators on his preface to Fanon's book have accused him of being, here he painted himself as its angry, highly pessimistic observer. The war continues, he seems to have been saying, and its violence is a fact.

It is only in the preface to *The Wretched of the Earth*, which ought to be read in the full context of the *Critique*, that Sartre set forth some analysis of the revolutionary, anticolonialist group. And here his analysis is frankly puzzling. Sartre agreed with Fanon that it is in the revolution that a new culture, a new humanism, and hence a new set of values will be born: the fraternal bond of the revolutionary group provides the heat in which the new culture may be forged.

---

35 According to Deleuze and Guattari, "Sartre's analysis in *Critique de la raison dialectique* appears to us profoundly correct where he concludes that there does not exist any class spontaneity, but only a 'group' spontaneity: whence the necessity for distinguishing 'groups-in-fusion' from the class, which remains 'serial,' represented by the party or the State." Gilles Deleuze and Félix Guattari, *Anti-Oedipus: Capitalism and Schizophrenia*, trans. Robert Hurley, Mark Seem, and Helen R. Lane (Minneapolis: University of Minnesota Press, 1983), 256–7.

36 Sartre, *Critique*, 733.

Sartre seems fairly confident that what will emerge from the FLN's struggle will count, generally, as progress. Yet, in the *Critique*, he seemed much more ambivalent concerning how to evaluate the outcomes of revolutionary action. The unstable group-in-fusion, as I pointed out above, is not dependable. The group eventually lapses back into a serial collectivity; though it hopes to create structures that enable bonds of reciprocity, these structures may, as it turns out, simply impose new bonds of alterity on humans. This is what happened in the cases of both the French and Russian Revolutions, the latter leading to the central example of Stalinism.

Moreover, not only is the fraternal bond illusory in the *Critique*—it also acts as the basis for terror. Here, Sartre was not so much concerned with terror directed at those outside the communal bond, but at those *within* it; he was theorizing the basis of party discipline. In the situation Sartre imagined, each member of the group acts as a regulating third of all other members by taking a pledge of loyalty. The point of the pledge is to try to bind each person to common action and common belief—to stave off the inevitability of institutionalization by freezing the members' dispositions. The effect of the pledge is to give each member sovereignty over the life of every other member. If a member strays—becomes "Other"—then violence is used against her. So the violence of the pledged group moves in two directions, outward toward reshaping the practico-inert, and inward toward disciplining the group:

> [The revolutionary] realises sovereign freedom in himself as unity and ubiquity; at the same time, however, he commits violence on the enemy (in fact this is simply counter-violence) and he uses perpetual violence *in order to reorganise himself*, even going so far as to kill some of his fellow members.[37]

This understanding of revolutionary action has clear applications to the infighting among Algerian groups during the war; it was well known at the time that political murders were taking place, both in Algeria and in France. Oddly, in his preface to *Wretched*, Sartre completely ignored this fact, painting a fairly rosy picture of the FLN's political prospects. He focused only on the unity of the group and its capacity for reshaping the world, making no mention of his argument that this unity is based on a fear of internal treachery that may lead to fraternal bloodshed.

Taking these rather fundamental differences between the two texts into consideration, we might conclude either that Sartre's preface is not actually as utopian as it seems when read in the context of the *Critique*, or that Sartre was

---

37   Sartre, *Critique*, 406.

so swept away both by events and by Fanon's persuasiveness that he under-played or forgot his own arguments on these points.[38] I would stand somewhere between these conclusions. Clearly, Sartre's preface to *The Wretched of the Earth* must be read alongside the *Critique of Dialectical Reason*. In fact, I would argue that it is better to read it with the *Critique* than it is to read it with *The Wretched of the Earth*, because the ambivalence of the *Critique* tempers the excesses of the preface.[39] For example, although Sartre's preface is often taken as a sign of radical Western masochism, this interpretation misses many moments in the text in which Sartre made it clear that his project was to "save" France from itself, to weed the bad out from the good. Typically, the dividing line runs between the same two poles as it did in his essays in the 1950s: between, on one hand, the "fascist" politics represented by de Gaulle's coup and his plebiscitarianism, as well as the "putschism" of certain military leaders, and, on the other, French republican values. Hence, he wrote,

> When one wants to protect, with the full rigour of the law, the morale of the Nation and the Army, it is not a good thing for the latter to systematically demoralize the former. Nor is it a good thing that a country with a republican tradition should entrust its young people in their hundreds of thousands to putschist officers.[40]

After all, his text was addressed to French people, so logically he must have thought there was some hope for the political change he desired. "Will we recover?" Sartre asked himself on the final page, and the answer he gave was "yes."[41]

---

38   For Sartre's retrospective views on this text, parts of which he said he later disagreed with, see Jean-Paul Sartre and Benny Lévy, *Hope Now: The 1980s Interviews*, trans. Adrian van den Hoven (Chicago: University of Chicago Press, 1996), 91–5.

39   An English-language contemporary of Sartre noted, in a similar vein, that "*Situations V* now enables us to see how the ideas and prejudices of *La Critique de la raison dialectique* are related to actual political problems"—"Review of *La Critique de la raison dialectique*," *The Times*, Nov. 5, 1964. *Situations V* (*Colonialism and Neocolonialism* in English) included Sartre's preface to *The Wretched of the Earth*. For other views on *Situations V*, see Simon, "Histoire Contemporaine: *Situations V*"; "Review of *Situations V*," *Présence Africaine* (third trimester, 1964); Christian Dedet, "Review of *Situations V*," *Revue de Paris* (October 1964); Maurice-Pierre Boye, "Review of *Situations V*," *Fiches bibliographiques* (1964); "Review of *Situations V*," *Afrique Contemporaine* (January/February 1965); L. de Biéville, "Le Colonialisme vu par J.-P. Sartre," *Le Christianisme au XXe siècle*, April 8, 1965; François Bondy, "Jean-Paul Sartre et la révolution," *Preuves* (December 1967), 57–69; Claude Roy, "Sartre et la politique," *Libération*, September 22, 1964; and Maurice Catel, "Review of *Situations IV et V*," *Livres de France* (October 1964).

40   Sartre, "Preface to *The Wretched of the Earth*," in *Colonialism and Neocolonialism*, 154.

41   Ibid., 155.

CHAPTER SIX

The Aftermath of the *Critique*: Struggles over the Meanings of Colonialism

The first volume of the *Critique of Dialectical Reason* appeared in January 1960. This "verbose, heavy, and shapeless book" was not the cultural phenomenon that *Being and Nothingness* had been—in fact, quite the opposite.[1] Yet its exploration of social being drew attention from some significant interlocutors. During the academic year 1960–61, Claude Lévi-Strauss and his students studied the *Critique* in several special seminars organized by Jean Pouillon, an editor of *Les Temps Modernes* and also one of Lévi-Strauss's close collaborators on his journal, *L'Homme*. It was in these seminars that Lévi-Strauss developed his sharp criticisms of Sartre's anthropological method, which he wrote about in *The Savage Mind*.[2] Moreover, according to James Miller, Michel Foucault had planned to include criticism of the *Critique* in *The Order of Things*, but had it removed before publication.[3]

The *Critique* was not a watershed in French intellectual life, as my analysis will show. It nonetheless had appeal and a certain influence on those interested in the politics of colonialism and anticolonialism—in marked contrast to Lévi-Strauss's disaffected stance. Specifically, Georges Balandier, a leading "Third Worldist" anthropologist and intellectual counterweight to Lévi-Strauss, recognized the sympathies between Sartre's approach to colonialism and his

---

1   Luc Guérin, "Review of *La Critique de la raison dialectique*," *Contrat Social* (July 1960).

2   In *The Savage Mind*, Lévi-Strauss wrote, "If I have felt obliged to give expression to my disagreement with Sartre regarding the points which bear on the philosophical fundaments of anthropology, I have only determined to do so after several readings of the work in question [*Critique of Dialectical Reason, Vol. I*] which occupied my pupils at the Ecole des Hautes Etudes and myself during many sessions of the year 1960–1. Over and above our inevitable divergences I hope that Sartre will recognize above all that a discussion to which so much care has been given constitutes on behalf of all of us a homage of admiration and respect." Lévi-Strauss, *The Savage Mind*, xii. On Pouillon's role, see Contat and Rybalka, *The Writings of Jean-Paul Sartre, Vol. I*, 372. For Lévi-Strauss's reflections on Pouillon and his role both at *Les Temps Modernes* and at *L'Homme*, see Claude Lévi-Strauss, "Jean Pouillon," *Les Temps Modernes* 620–1 (August/November 2002), 8–11.

3   James Miller, *The Passion of Michel Foucault* (Cambridge: Harvard University Press, 1993), 44.

own approach to political anthropology. This implicit polarization of the anthropological field in the 1960s represented a larger cleavage in French intellectual life that would have important consequences for intellectuals' political activity in the 1960s and beyond.

THE RECEPTION OF THE *CRITIQUE*

Perhaps the most remarked-upon aspect of the *Critique* was the book's length. Critics often opened their reviews with cutting remarks about it: "I have just finished the 755 pages of the *Critique of Dialectical Reason*. I don't know how, but I finally did it."[4] If Sartre was the original mediatized intellectual, then the *Critique* was perhaps his work least suited to mediatization. It is difficult, boring, repetitive, and poorly written. It has paragraphs that go on for pages and chapters that have no clearly demarcated sections. It relies on a set of conceptual vocabulary newly invented by Sartre, meaning that there are few passages in the book that are written in plain language. Serge Doubrovski commented in the *Nouvelle Revue Française* that the book is characterized by "abstraction that becomes jargon, jargon that turns into deliriousness"[5]—an apt description, given that Sartre was taking large doses of the amphetamine corydrane while writing it. In spite of this opacity, the *Critique* was widely reviewed in many different kinds of publications—newspapers, literary journals, philosophy journals—and even announced in wire stories from *Agence France-Presse*.[6]

Perhaps because of the length and density of the text, most of the early reviews focused on the more concise and clearly argued introduction, called "Questions of Method," already published in *Les Temps Modernes* in 1957, in which Sartre attacked the Hegelian notion of history as dialectic, from the perspective of Kierkegaardian singularity. Critics were generally either neutral or favorable toward the "Questions of Method," calling it a "demystified Marxism"[7] that was sure to challenge the communists.

---

4   Jacques Clodu, "Notre agent à la Havane: Jacques Clodu écrit à Jean-Paul," *Démocratie*, August 25, 1960.

5   Serge Doubrovski, "J.-P. Sartre et le mythe de la raison dialectique," *Nouvelle Revue Française* (September 1961), 492. Doubrovski's review is fairly respectful, though he doubted Sartre would be able to prove what he wanted to prove: that dialectical reason can be its own foundation. See also Serge Doubrovski, "Jean-Paul Sartre et le mythe de la raison dialectique (fin)," *Nouvelle Revue Française* (November 1961), 879–88.

6   See Claire Hugon, "Jean-Paul Sartre revient à la philosophie," *Agence France-Presse*, n.d., 1960; and André Weber, "Jean-Paul Sartre face au marxisme," *Agence France-Presse*, n.d., 1960.

7   Josane Duranteau, "Review of *La Critique de la raison dialectique*," *Le Combat*, July 21, 1960. For another favorable review, see André Maurois, *Lettres Françaises*, July 14, 1960.

And it did. In July 1960, PCF intellectual Roger Garaudy published strong criticisms of the *Critique* in *Lettres Françaises*. Garaudy's review itself became a news story, with both *L'Express* and *Le Monde* running short articles announcing the attack on Sartre.[8] Ignoring most of what was new in the book, Garaudy wasted no time in going straight to the heart of the old differend between Sartre and the communists:

> Instead of concrete human relations, which are not—Marx demonstrated this—relations between individuals, but relations between classes, Sartre substitutes a game of mirrors: relations of the Other to the Other. This so-called dialectic ignores real history ... Separated from their economic and social foundations, alienation and reification resemble more the theologians' "original sin" than Marx's "commodity fetish."[9]

As this citation suggests, the main thrust of the review was an attack on existentialism and, in particular, on the possibility of a "philosophy of consciousness" being the foundation of knowledge about social phenomena. Many of Garaudy's criticisms would therefore already have been familiar to those who had read Georg Lukács's 1947 essay "Existentialism or Marxism?" or Merleau-Ponty's *Adventures of the Dialectic*.[10]

Of course, precisely this emphasis on the relationship of "the Other to the Other"—and Sartre's refusal to let go of it, even as he had moved toward the communists—was what had made existentialism such an attractive tool for critics of colonialism such as Fanon and Memmi. And it is perhaps unsurprising that, in spite of the facts that the *Critique* appeared in the middle of a

----

8   "Roger Garaudy condamne le dernier livre de J.-P. Sartre," *Le Monde*, July 14, 1960; and "Sartre vu par les communistes et les anti-communistes," *L'Express*, August 4, 1960.

9   Roger Garaudy, "Critique de la Raison Dialectique," *Lettres Françaises*, July 14, 1960, 8.

10   See, for example, Merleau-Ponty's comment, "For Sartre, the social remains the relationship of 'two individual consciousnesses' which look at each other." Maurice Merleau-Ponty, *Adventures of the Dialectic*, trans. Joseph Bien (Evanston, Ill.: Northwestern University Press, 1973), 152—quoted in Thomas R. Flynn, "Merleau-Ponty and the *Critique of Dialectical Reason*," in Jon Stewart, ed., *The Debate between Sartre and Merleau-Ponty* (Evanston, Ill.: Northwestern University Press, 1998), 272. Flynn makes the argument that, without abandoning the existentialist commitments to freedom and responsibility, the *Critique* was at least partly a response to Merleau's criticisms: "Many of the basic flaws which Merleau-Ponty noted in Sartre's existentialism are remedied by his taking a dialectical turn in the *Critique*, even to the point of adopting Merleau-Ponty's use of the 'interworld' as the proper locus for social phenomena. Given the immense respect Sartre continued to maintain for Merleau-Ponty, even after *Adventures*, it is reasonable to suppose that the latter's strictures were in Sartre's mind as he explicitly addressed the very issues for which he had been taken to task in that work." Ibid., 277.

colonial war and that many of the *Critique*'s analyses are directly or indirectly related to colonialism, Garaudy made no mention of colonialism or Algeria in his review. Garaudy was by no means alone among reviewers in this oversight, but it was perhaps particularly symptomatic of the concerns of the PCF at this time. Of the Sartre-Garaudy contretemps, one observer wrote,

> What separates Sartre from the communists more than anything is, quite paradoxically, the war in Algeria. In effect, the Stalinists' attitude toward the war is more than dubious. Already in 1945, at the time of the first attempt at insurrection, the communists were for a brutal repression, treating Messali Hadj as a "fascist bandit" … The communists feel themselves to be overtaken on the left, something which, all in all, is not very difficult.[11]

Raymond Aron also ignored the colonial context of the book. Writing in *Le Figaro littéraire*, Aron focused on Sartre's contention that he would, ultimately, prove that a single meaningful History would emerge from the innumerable human acts that constitute it. Since Sartre had said that this proof would be the subject of the second volume, which did not appear in his lifetime, many reviewers had withheld judgment on this point. Aron, however, intuiting the difficulties his former friend would have on this score, declared the project impossible. Anticipating in some ways—albeit from a different perspective— Louis Althusser's criticism of any form of humanist Marxism, and repeating many of the points already made by Lévi-Strauss in *The Savage Mind*, Aron noted,

> To establish a radical opposition between analytical and dialectical reason, between the natural and the human sciences, between the intelligibility of natural phenomena and the intrinsic intelligibility of history—this is not only to break with the Marxism of Lenin or Engels, it is also to break with that of Marx.[12]

---

11   J. S., "Sartre et les communistes," *La Cité*, August 11, 1960. The PCF only adopted a policy of outright support for Algerian independence in 1961, according to Danièle Joly; until then, Joly argues that "the Party's analysis of the Algerian nation, designed to include the settlers, supported its policy against Algerian independence because it pointed to a continued relationship between Algeria and France." Joly concludes, "During the Algerian war, for the first time, a large movement developed on the left beyond the control of the PCF, mainly amongst young people. This may be considered a precursor of May 1968." Danièle Joly, *The French Communist Party and the Algerian War* (London: Macmillan, 1991), 51, 98, 148.

12   Raymond Aron, "Sartre et le marxisme," *Le Figaro littéraire*, October 29, 1964, 6–9. In his 1973 full-length treatment of the *Critique*, however, he does devote a chapter to the question of Sartre and revolutionary violence, trying to make sense of Sartre's claims in the preface to *Wretched*. Raymond Aron, *Histoire et dialectique de la violence* (Paris: Gallimard, 1973). See also Raymond Aron, "Le serment et le contrat," *Contrepoint* 5 (Winter 1971), 51–9.

Always an astute observer, Aron carefully set out the stakes of the debate between Sartre and the communists. But on the subjects of colonialism and Algeria, and their significance to the intellectual context of the *Critique*, he wrote nothing.

One of the few reviews to take note of the *Critique*'s treatment of colonialism appeared in the journal *La Revue des deux mondes*. The author, Paul Sérant, criticized Sartre's depiction of colonialism on the same grounds that Sartre himself had criticized the Marxists: he said that Sartre imposed a schematic theory on a set of diverse facts for which the theory cannot hope to account:

> Sartre only wants to see it [colonialism] as a phenomenon of oppression, as a cruel plundering of the colonized by the colonizers. He thus falls into the attitude that he reproaches in bourgeois liberalism; that is, he reasons in the name of an abstract humanity without taking into account religious, ethnic, and sociological differences.[13]

Sérant's judgment is perceptive, and it calls into question the wisdom of choosing a particularly extreme example in order to illustrate a general point—in this case, about the operation of violence in history once it has been "petrified" in institutions, thoughts, and values. Though Sartre probably did not intend his account of colonialism in Algeria to be exhaustive, Sérant's criticism underscores the fact that, as we have already seen, Sartre did not seem to take much care in depicting Algerians as more than half-starved wretches bent on destruction. No doubt there were many Algerians who would not have recognized themselves in such a picture.

George Lichtheim took a rather different view of Sartre's project and his use of colonialism in his 1963 review in the English-language journal *History and Theory*, which I note here only because it sets into relief some interesting omissions by French commentators. Averring (like many others) that the most fruitful theoretical aspects of the *Critique* are to be found in the "Questions of Method," Lichtheim noted that the central point of the book is to demonstrate that there is nothing "behind" History, neither God nor Nature, and that historical materialism can thus never be grounded in dialectical materialism. Central to the *Critique*'s conception of History is the notion of the Other—not in the abstract, as Sartre had it in *Being and Nothingness*, but in contingent, concrete relations of alterity. Lichtheim wrote, "It is only because

---

13 Paul Sérant, "L'Existentialisme de Jean-Paul Sartre et le thomisme d'Etienne Gilson," *La Revue des deux mondes*, October 15, 1960, 729–30.

everyone sees in his neighbor primarily *the Other* that History has developed as it has."[14]

Pursuing this theme, Lichtheim made one of the most striking points of any of Sartre's critics. He noted that Sartre's description of relations of alterity as constituted by competition for scarce resources "bears a marked resemblance to a concentration camp." Lichtheim believed that Stalin's *univers concentrationnaire* was thus not just the spur for Sartre's criticism of dialectical materialism, but also the very model for his anthropology, and he questioned on these grounds the utility of such a description for all human interactions. He then observed, somewhat paradoxically, "It is probably no accident that Sartre wrote this during the years of the Algerian conflict … which has clearly inspired his lengthy—and often very acute—analyses of colonialism in the later sections of the *Critique*."[15] On the one hand, Lichtheim cast suspicion on Sartre's anthropological assumptions; on the other, he acknowledged some of their truth. Perhaps this contradiction can be chalked up to the fact that Sartre's conception of alterity, as a bond of serial relations, applies *only* to serial relations—of which the systems of both colonialism and Stalinism were extreme examples. What is most important here—and what was oddly missed by the French critics—is that Lichtheim pointed out the *Critique*'s function as an attack on "totalitarianism" of all varieties. That is, his review highlighted the relationship between colonialism and totalitarianism, particularly in the extreme case of a settler colony such as Algeria.[16] Totalitarianism, it might be said, is seriality taken to its limit, when other-directedness becomes the norm for all human behavior.

Indeed, this linkage between critiques of Stalinism and of colonialism as different, but related, phenomena, was made by Sartre himself on more than one occasion in this period. Significantly, one of those occasions was his 1961 eulogy of Merleau-Ponty, "Merleau-Ponty *vivant*," in the pages of *Les Temps Modernes*. In recounting the events that led to the decision by him and Merleau-Ponty to publish a dossier on the Soviet camps in 1950, he noted in passing that Merleau had suggested that "Our colonies are—*mutatis mutandis*—our slave labor camps."[17] This view of the postwar era as a set of

14   George Lichtheim, "Sartre, Marxism, and History," *History and Theory* 3, no. 2 (1963), 245.

15   Ibid., 236.

16   Hannah Arendt also posited a strong historical correlation between settler colonies (her primary case was South Africa), racist value systems, and totalitarianism in *The Origins of Totalitarianism* (New York: Harcourt, Brace, 1951).

17   Jean-Paul Sartre, "Merleau-Ponty *vivant*," in Stewart, ed., *The Debate Between Sartre and Merleau-Ponty*, 588.

perverse linkages between the *univers concentrationnaire* and the violence of colonialism also made its appearance in his June 1961 interview in another English-language publication, the *Observer*. While discussing the role of contemporary political events in the development of his ideas for theater, Sartre returned to his 1959 play about torture, the *Condemned of Altona*. In spite of the Nazi context of the play, Sartre omitted mention of Nazism altogether as the motive for its writing: "For me, *Altona* is tied up with the whole evolution of Europe since 1945, as much with the Soviet concentration camps as with the war in Algeria."[18]

In a certain way, there is little that is surprising in the reception of the *Critique of Dialectical Reason*. The communist Left was predictably hostile; Garaudy's attack, for example, seemed to be a simple rehashing of an old debate.[19] The noncommunist Left (represented by *Esprit* and *Le Combat*) was positive and even cautiously laudatory.[20] The professional philosophers typically wrote short, neutral summaries of the book that kept a respectful distance from the ideological stakes of the debate. The Right (represented by *Le Figaro*) dismissed the enterprise as a whole, sometimes with ironic jabs at every aspect of the work—its weight, density, vocabulary, and incomprehensibility.

What is surprising is that, in spite of Sartre's own activism and political writing, very few of these contemporary commentators linked the contents of the book to the most significant event of that era: the war in Algeria. There seemed to be a broad will to separate the *Critique* from colonialism, even though, as Denis de Rougemont pointed out in early 1962, Sartre was by that time inseparable from radical anticolonialism in the public sphere: "Sartre evolves inside an intellectual village and projects provincial hatred onto Europe. When he writes the word 'Europe,' he only thinks of France, and when he thinks of France, he sees only the Algerian tragedy."[21]

Even the appearance of Sartre's preface to *The Wretched of the Earth* shortly thereafter did not cause critics to comment seriously on Sartre's analysis of colonialism in the *Critique*. Jean-Marie Domenach, editor of *Esprit*, gave a particularly forceful example of this lapse in his 1962 review of Fanon's book.

---

18   Kenneth Tynan interview with Jean-Paul Sartre, "Sartre Talks to Tynan," *Observer*, June 18 and June 25, 1961—quoted in Contat and Rybalka, *The Writings of Jean-Paul Sartre*, 404.

19   See also Lucien Sève's scathing review, "Jean-Paul Sartre et la dialectique en 1960," *Nouvelle Critique* (1960), 78–100.

20   See Duranteau, "Review of *La Critique de la raison dialectique*"; and Mikel Dufrenne, "La critique de la raison dialectique," *Esprit* (April 1961), 671–92.

21   Denis de Rougemont, "Sartre contre l'Europe," *Arts*, January 17, 1962—cited in Jean-Marie Domenach, "*Les damnés de la terre* (I)," *Esprit* 30 (March 1962), 457.

Domenach divided his commentary into two separate essays, published in the March and April editions, the first of which treated Sartre's preface on its own, the second of which treated the text written by Fanon.[22] The picture of Sartre that Domenach sketched fit very well with the radical, Manichean, self-immolating European anticolonialist that formed the basis for the stereotypical image of his Third Worldism—one in which Sartre's "rages take the gods by the throat."[23] In Domenach's depiction, Sartre's view of history is overly simplistic and moves in a (Hegelian) dialectical progression; his comments in favor of decolonization show that he has been behind the curve, as decolonization has already taken place in many places by the end of 1961; the only communication possible in Sartrean existentialism is violence; Sartre's call for "new men" to be created through revolution dangerously ignores the horrors of Stalinism. In short, Domenach displayed a complete lack of knowledge of the contents of the *Critique of Dialectical Reason*: Sartre's rejection of the Hegelian dialectic; his treatment of colonialism that built on his 1956 speech "Colonialism Is a System"; his attempts to theorize common action and reciprocity as modes of communication among humans; and—perhaps most striking—the function of the *Critique* as a criticism of Stalinism (as well as of totalitarianism in general).

It would appear that Domenach had not read the *Critique*. No doubt he was not alone. The book did not restore Sartre to the prominence in the intellectual field that he had gained after the appearance of *Being and Nothingness*, although it did maintain him in tension with other already prominent intellectuals (such as Lévi-Strauss, who thought the *Critique* was important enough to respond to, thus giving it a certain legitimacy) and up-and-comers (such as Foucault, who was about to publish *Madness and Civilization*, and who would establish a certain activist relationship with Sartre in the 1970s). Sartre's position in the intellectual field was still strong enough to spark debate; one in particular would provide the context for competing strategies and positions in the field devoted to dealing with the broad theme of cultural Otherness: anthropology.

---

22   Domenach, "*Les damnés de la terre* (I)," 454–63; and Jean-Marie Domenach, "*Les damnés de la terre* (II)," *Esprit* 30 (April 1962), 634–45. The dates of the two essays are significant, as they overlapped with the French Assembly's debate on the Evian accords, which set up the referenda in France and Algeria to end the war officially.

23   Domenach, "*Les damnés de la terre* (I)," 455.

TWO TRAJECTORIES: LÉVI-STRAUSS AND BALANDIER

In 1950 anthropologist and *Les Temps Modernes* collaborator Michel Leiris published an article that threw down the gauntlet to the discipline of anthropology. In it, he claimed that anthropologists and the knowledge they produced had provided crucial support to the colonialist enterprise and were continuing to do so. In questioning the practice of anthropology thus, Leiris not only challenged the ethics of producing anthropological knowledge, but also its intrinsic value as a discipline.[24]

Leiris's challenge came during a period of radical change in the field of anthropology in France, as has been well documented.[25] Lévi-Strauss had published *The Elementary Structures of Kinship* to professional acclaim in 1949, and with his 1955 travel narrative, *Tristes Tropiques*, he became known to the public at large. Lévi-Strauss's search for universal constants among the innumerable permutations of events that constitute culture was the key to his claim that anthropology could be a science. It also implicitly placed the structuralist method above the epiphenomena of political contest and change.

In his *History of Structuralism*, François Dosse argues that there was a fundamental cleavage in the field of anthropology, beginning in the 1950s, between a structuralist method represented by Lévi-Strauss, and a method emphasizing dynamic processes represented by Georges Balandier.[26] For Dosse, the significant divergence between Lévi-Strauss and Balandier resided in the fact that they studied different geographical areas—the Americas for Lévi-Strauss, and Africa for Balandier. Although Dosse explains important biographical differences between the two—unlike Lévi-Strauss, Balandier had been a student of Leiris, a postwar existentialist, and a well-known Third Worldist activist—he seems to suggest that there is something about Africa that did not lend itself easily to structuralist analysis. He writes,

---

24   Michel Leiris, "L'Ethnographe devant le colonialisme," *Les Temps Modernes* 58 (August 1950), 356–74.

25   See François Dosse, *The History of Structuralism*, two vols, trans. Deborah Glassman (Minneapolis: University of Minnesota Press, 1997); Pascal Ory and Jean-François Sirinelli, *Les Intellectuels en France, de l'affaire Dreyfus à nos jours* (Paris: Armand Colin, 1996); Vincent Descombes, *Modern French Philosophy*, trans. L. Scott-Fox and J.M. Harding (New York: Cambridge University Press, 1980); Edith Kurzweil, *The Age of Structuralism: Lévi-Strauss to Foucault* (New York: Columbia University Press, 1980).

26   Dosse, "Africa: The Continental Divide of Structuralism," in *History of Structuralism, Vol. I: The Rising Sign*.

Not only did researchers [in Africa] need to work on populations larger than those small Indian communities that had escaped genocide, but the inter-weaving of beliefs and local customs together with colonial institutions also led to phenomena of acculturation that made it rather difficult to reduce African social organization to binary oppositions; geographically, the area to which the structural paradigm could be applied was therefore rather limited.[27]

But, as Dosse himself notes, there were indeed Africanists who were structuralists, so it is difficult to defend the argument that it was in fact geography that made the crucial difference in these two schools of anthropology.

Instead, the key seems to lie rather in the weight given to politics and dynamic processes in each method. And here it is interesting to find that Balandier credited Sartre's *Critique* as providing many of the philosophical and methodological foundations for his own "political anthropology"—thus reproducing in the field of anthropology the split that existed in the larger intellectual field between Sartre and Lévi-Strauss. As Pierre Nora notes in his 2002 interview with Balandier in *Le Débat*, his 1967 theoretical work, *Political Anthropology*, was an example of "engaged anthropology" and "a bible for generations of students."[28] In particular, Balandier cited the influence of the *Critique* concerning "the continuous production of the social rather than its reproduction, the emphasizing of the incompleteness of every society, the impossibility of an end to History."[29]

Thus, I would argue that the contest between Lévi-Strauss and Balandier had less to do with Africa as a "continental divide," and much more to do with competition within the field of French anthropology itself. The axes of conflict in the 1950s and 1960s were multiple, revolving mainly around the role of the intellectual in political life and the new claims of anthropology to scientificity. Both of these axes were related to the process of decolonization. In the first case, figures such as Balandier, who had been directly influenced by Sartre's theory of intellectual engagement, thought that political activism was the only way out of the dilemma posed by Leiris's essay. If the practice of anthropology was tainted by its use as a tool of domination, this thinking went, then

27   Ibid., 264.

28   Pierre Nora interview with Georges Balandier, *Le Débat* 118 (January/February 2002), reprinted in Georges Balandier, *Civilisés, dit-on* (Paris: Presses Universitaires de France, 2003), 89. See Georges Balandier, *Political Anthropology*, trans. A.M. Sheridan Smith (New York: Pantheon Books, 1970). For another serious consideration of political anthropology that takes a rather different view, see Pierre Clastres's 1974 book, *Society Against the State: Essays in Political Anthropology*, trans. Robert Hurley in collaboration with Abe Stein (Cambridge: MIT Press, 1987).

29   Balandier, *Civilisés, dit-on*, 26.

anthropologists must actively and consciously work against this usage. In the second case, the claim to scientificity can be viewed as a way of simply sidestepping the dilemma to which Leiris had pointed. In the case of Lévi-Strauss, his choice of objects of study—untouched Amerindian tribes—meant that the political question of the anthropologist's relationship to the process of decolonization was basically moot.

It would seem wrong, however, to consider Lévi-Strauss as utterly unengaged, even as structuralism lent itself to a certain apoliticism. Like Sartre, Lévi-Strauss had taken an interest in combating racism and offered some compelling analyses of his own on the issue. In the early 1950s, Lévi-Strauss was the secretary-general of the International Council for the Social Sciences, associated with UNESCO. Under its auspices, he wrote a small book, *Race and History*, published by UNESCO in 1952 as part of its series on the question of racism. This much-overlooked essay is one of the most succinct pieces of writing on race to appear in the immediate postwar era. Eschewing—for obvious reasons, given his methodological predilections—the strategy of applying psychological schemas to the facts of racism, Lévi-Strauss argued for a tempered relativism toward the diversity of cultures, and set out numerous arguments to reject the category of race as useful in any way for scientific analysis. He opened with criticism of Gobineau:

> The original sin of anthropology ... consists in its confusion of the idea of race, in the purely biological sense (assuming that there is any factual basis for the idea, even in this limited field—which is disputed by modern genetics), with the sociological and psychological productions of human civilization. Once he had made this mistake, Gobineau was inevitably committed to the path leading from an honest intellectual error to the unintentional justification of all forms of discrimination and exploitation.[30]

Lévi-Strauss's took his task to be to show "the contributions of different races of men to civilization,"[31] and to argue that the perspective of social evolutionism can lead to unjustifiable conclusions about innate natures.

According to Lévi-Strauss, one of the most pernicious illusions of racial thinking is the idea that progress is easily measured. He noted that the story scholars told of "man's advance" fifty years earlier ("the old stone age, the new

---

30 Claude Lévi-Strauss, *Race and History* (Paris: UNESCO, 1952), 5. Other titles in the UNESCO series include *Race and Biology* by Leslie C. Dunn, *Race and Psychology* by Otto Klineberg, and *Race and Society* by Kenneth Little. See UNESCO human rights publications since 1949 at <www.unesco.org>.

31 Ibid., 6.

stone age, the copper, bronze and iron ages") was far too simple to represent what had in fact been an irregular and discontinuous series of events. He says that progress is

> neither continuous nor inevitable; its course consists in a series of leaps and bounds, or, as the biologists would say, mutations ... Advancing humanity can hardly be likened to a person climbing stairs and, with each movement, adding a new step to all those he has already mounted.[32]

Lévi-Strauss accepted the idea that history may be cumulative, but rejected the idea that it must be so.

He then considered a possible distinction between two types of history—cumulative and stationary—and asked whether such a distinction is valid, the two representing divergent intrinsic natures, or whether the distinction is invalid because it can only be adopted from a point of view of ethnocentrism. On this latter view, which Lévi-Strauss thought to be the correct one, other cultures would only be designated "stationary" because "the line of their development has no meaning for us, and cannot be measured in terms of the criteria we employ."[33] Using the metaphor of visual perspective that he would return to in his collection of essays, *A View from Afar* (1983), Lévi-Strauss argued that the perception of speed is relative to one's position, or to "a difference of focus."[34] Ultimately, such distinctions are hopelessly subjective, as "wherever we go, we are bound to carry this system of criteria with us, and external cultural phenomena can be observed only through this distorting glass it interposes, even when it does not prevent us from seeing anything at all."[35] As for progress, it "never represents anything more than the maximum progress in a given direction, pre-determined by the interests of the observer."[36]

Given this disposition toward relativism, it is striking that Lévi-Strauss argued later in the essay for the possibility of a "world civilization." Since, however, he took part in the UNESCO series, it would seem uncontroversial to say that he placed some value on the institution and the project of the newly created United Nations—whose goal was, at a minimum, to maintain peaceful relations among states through the development of a body of international law and mechanisms to regulate conflict. This minimal account of a kind of "world civilization" fit nicely with Lévi-Strauss's description of it as a "limiting

---

32   Ibid., 21–2.
33   Ibid., 24.
34   Ibid., 25.
35   Ibid.
36   Ibid., 40.

concept": "There is not, and can never be, a world civilization in the absolute sense in which that term is often used, since civilization implies, and indeed consists in, the coexistence of cultures exhibiting the maximum possible diversities."[37]

Significantly, this is where imperialism and colonialism come into the historical picture for Lévi-Strauss. He asserted that there is a paradox in the history of humanity, his conception of which, incidentally, seems somewhat indebted to Gobineau: as civilizations build themselves, they turn diversity into uniformity; in order to sustain themselves, however, they require the constant introduction of diversity. This struggle between uniformity and diversity had also been, according to Lévi-Strauss, at work in European imperialism. "The colonial expansion of the nineteenth century," he wrote, "gave industrial Europe a fresh impetus (which admittedly benefited other parts of the world as well) whereas, but for the introduction of colonial peoples, the momentum might have been lost much sooner." For Lévi-Strauss, colonialism was a process driven by the functional need of Europe to acquire diversity (to adopt his somewhat vague language), or, as he also put it, a matter of "broadening the coalition, either by increasing internal diversity or by admitting new partners; in fact, the problem is always to increase the number of players or, in other words, to restore the complexity and diversity of the original situation." In spite of colonialism's apparently beneficial effects for all "partners" of the "coalition," even as it simultaneously (and also perhaps beneficially—here Lévi-Strauss is ambiguous) introduces inequality and exploitation among these partners, Lévi-Strauss did see the inexorable necessity of its ending:

> This process is illustrated by the social improvements that are being brought about and the gradual attainment of independence by the colonial peoples; although we have still far to go in both these directions, we must know that the trend of developments is inevitable.[38]

Absent from this discussion is any concept of power. Lévi-Strauss naturalized the conceptual categories of international relations such as "imperialism" and "colonialism"; he reduced them to the play of natural forces. It would seem from this conclusion that Lévi-Strauss's relativism with respect to the value of different cultures was in some tension with a notion of history that valorized liberal imperialism. That is, he had difficulty in this text in sorting out how his relativism might fit in practice with politics, and specifically with the key issue

---

37 Ibid., 45.
38 Ibid., 47.

of decolonization. This is not surprising, since, ultimately, talking politics means taking a position—the very thing that the structural anthropologist strives not to do. To be sure, the structural anthropologist would not say that "we still have far to go" to achieve a desired outcome, or that a certain "trend of developments is inevitable"—but a citizen might. Lévi-Strauss himself later noted that he had "overstated" his point "in order to serve the international institutions."[39] When UNESCO asked him to revisit his views for a conference in 1971, the resulting text, "Race and Culture," omitted any mention of a world civilization or of colonialism. Instead, he pushed even further his wish to direct the discussion on race toward genetics, in order to understand scientifically the creation of diversity in terms of populations defined genetically, and not in terms of psychological phenomena or essential traits—an apparently scandalous idea for his UNESCO auditors, who tried to censor his remarks.[40]

I would suggest, then, that *Race and History* demonstrates quite neatly the limits of structuralism—which, of course, should not be taken as a total worldview, but rather as a method claiming scientificity for its results; and Lévi-Strauss's own backtracking concerning the more political aspects of his essay would seem to corroborate this assertion. In the study of culture, its proponents averred, only structuralism could provide the observer with the epistemological break necessary to produce knowledge about other cultures— indeed, only structuralism could erase the observer altogether from the position of observing. But, as *Race and History* shows, when it comes to describing the phenomenon of decolonization, taking no position was extremely difficult, if not impossible. Considering his strong criticisms of dialectical reason and his denigration of history in *The Savage Mind*, it is striking that, in this particular text, ten years earlier, Lévi-Strauss had argued for a rather schematic, liberal imperialist interpretation of the phenomena of colonialism and decolonization. It is also striking, though unsurprising, that in revisiting these views some twenty years later, Lévi-Strauss dropped the word "history" from its title, replacing it with "culture."[41] Indeed, Lévi-Strauss cannot be taken as a friend of

39   Claude Lévi-Strauss, "Preface," in *The View from Afar*, trans. Joachim Neugroschel and Phoebe Hoss (New York: Basic Books, 1985), xiii. Lévi-Strauss pulled no punches in his criticism of the "contradictory assertions" of "UNESCO ideology" on race that advocated the simultaneous affirmation both of one's own identity and of another's identity (xv), and the fact that the UNESCO "catechism … had allowed them [UNESCO staff] to move from modest jobs in developing countries to sanctified positions as executives in an international institution" (xiii). In general, Lévi-Strauss viewed UNESCO as a dangerously homogenizing force that had, nonetheless, not reduced the incidence of racism in the world.
40   Ibid., xiii.
41   See Claude Lévi-Strauss, "Race and Culture," in *The View from Afar*, 3–24.

colonialism or of a civilizing mission, which is what makes his early remarks in *Race and History* appear so incongruous, and which perhaps accounts for his rethinking of them in "Race and Culture."

In contrast to Lévi-Strauss's approach, Georges Balandier's was to argue that it is impossible for the anthropologist observing the "Third World" to erase politics from the horizon of his work. Balandier began his career as an anthropologist under the guidance of Leiris just after the end of World War II.[42] He went to Senegal in the summer of 1946 to do fieldwork, where he immediately met up with Alioune Diop, the future founder of *Présence Africaine*, who Balandier had first encountered in Paris at Leiris's home. Diop invited him to live with his family in Dakar and, through his political connections (Diop was in the employ of Governor-General Barthes), helped integrate him into elite cadres there.[43] "It was with Alioune Diop that I began to meet Senghor and the young Senegalese politicians," Balandier recounted. "It was with Alioune Diop that I was associated from the beginning with the journal *Présence Africaine*, of which I was coeditor-in-chief with Bernard Dadié, the writer from the Ivory Coast."[44]

Also just after the war, Leiris introduced Balandier into Sartre's "entourage"—thus, as he recounted, he was there to witness the birth of *Les Temps Modernes*. A little later, Bataille asked him to collaborate with him on his journal, *Critique*. But it was only with the founding of *Présence Africaine* that he found his real home at a journal—one that was "incomparable to all the others."[45] In 1954 he joined the Ecole Pratique des Hautes Etudes as a specialist in African sociology, with the support of Lucien Febvre and Fernand Braudel. He also worked for Lévi-Strauss as a researcher when he was secretary-general of the International Council for the Social Sciences.[46]

Though the details of the relationship between Balandier and Lévi-Strauss in the 1950s remain a little murky (Dosse relates that the two were "close friends" until Lévi-Strauss heard second-hand a joke Balandier had told about him; the rupture was then sealed with a rather nasty footnote criticizing Balandier in *The Savage Mind*[47]), there is no doubt that their intellectual debts

---

42 On his relationship with Leiris, see Georges Balandier, *Histoire d'Autres* (Paris: Stock, 1977), 148–53.

43 Ibid., 47–51.

44 Yoram Mouchenik interview with Georges Balandier, *L'autre* 3 (December 2002), reprinted in Balandier, *Civilisés, dit-on*, 46.

45 Balandier, *Histoire d'Autres*, 151, 157–8.

46 Ibid., 182, 239.

47 See Dosse, *History of Structuralism, Vol. I*, 265; and Lévi-Strauss, *The Savage Mind*, 234–35fn.

and orientations were very different. This contention is only accentuated by the fact that Balandier, unlike Lévi-Strauss, found in the *Critique* the theoretical basis for an anthropological method. "As soon as Sartre published the *Critique of Dialectical Reason*, I seized on the book," he wrote in his memoir. "Against an anthropology of the timeless, I invoked the sociology of the here-and-now; against fixed structures and universals, I evoked dynamic processes and the continuous generation of humanity and society."[48] Like Sartre, Balandier thought that the structuralist method was useful, but only within certain limits. He argued that it was not adequate to the task of accounting for diachronic movement because he believed, like Sartre, that history is something that "makes itself without end."[49]

In *Political Anthropology*, Balandier placed an analysis of power squarely at the center of his method, and he took as his object societies that might be called political, but that were foreign to Western history. Building on the work of British anthropologists such as Max Gluckman and Edmund Leach, one of the key aims of the work was to show how "urgent it has become to dissociate political theory from the theory of the State"—even if one cannot elude the state altogether. To this end, his method tried to "envisage the relationship of power to the elementary structures that furnish it with its fundamental basis, to the types of social stratification that render it necessary, to the rituals that assure its rootedness in the sacred and intervene in its strategies." Taking as his implicit target an ethnocentrism that would define politics as a product of European history, Balandier averred that "*all* human societies produce politics and they are *all* open to the vicissitudes of history."[50] Balandier then set out a definition of power that made coercion only one among a number of elements that also included imaginary and symbolic practices. Allying himself with Ernst Kantorowicz's analysis in *The King's Two Bodies*, he wrote, "Rituals, ceremonies, or procedures assuring periodic or occasional renewal of society are, just as much as sovereigns and their bureaucracies, instruments of political action thus understood."[51] Balandier also placed political power at the heart even of

48   Balandier, *L'Histoire d'Autres*, 255.
49   Balandier, *Civilisés, dit-on*, 63.
50   Georges Balandier, *Anthropologie Politique* (Paris: PUF, 1967), 2 (emphasis in original). Clastres went even further than (and implicitly argued against) Balandier in this respect, claiming not only that there are political societies without states, but also that there are political societies without power—power defined here as relations of command and obedience. See Clastres, *Society Against the State*, 16. Though Clastres noted the belated emergence of a "political" anthropology, he does not contextualize its appearance against the backdrop of decolonization.
51   Balandier, *Anthropologie Politique*, 44. Balandier recounted elsewhere how this emphasis on the ubiquity of political power raised the ire of Louis Dumont, the

kinship systems; in a direct challenge to Lévi-Strauss, he devoted an entire chapter to kinship and power, which stood, he argued, in a dialectical relationship to one another.

Returning to the essay by Leiris, it is thus possible to view Lévi-Strauss and Balandier as poles within the field of anthropology precisely in relation to Leiris's challenge—that is, as representatives of competing solutions to the crisis that decolonization had induced in the field. Lévi-Strauss's focus on unconscious structures claimed to reduce, or even to negate, the ethnocentric perspective that had been central to the anthropological project since Jean de Léry's voyage to Brazil in the sixteenth century. "From the moment of departure in Geneva a language sets out to find a world," Michel de Certeau wrote of Léry's trip, which he viewed as the paradigmatic example of a discourse producing an object, "the Savage," while simultaneously keeping its referent silent.[52] Against this ethnocentrism that was built into the discipline, V.Y. Mudimbe has noted that Lévi-Strauss "thought that studying a diversity of cultures reduced the weight of ideology and allowed anthropologists to fight such falsehoods as those about the natural superiority of some races and traditions over others."[53] Meanwhile, Balandier tried to meet the exigencies of the Third Worldist movement by attempting to legitimize non-Western understandings of politics and authority. In a decolonizing world in which communities were achieving statehood by the dozen, integrating themselves into the international order initially established by the European great powers, Balandier lent support to Third Worldist claims that, though Europeans might have invented the system, they did not own politics broadly conceived—nor, in this dynamic system, could they prevent its change. While one tried to show how the observer might be erased (even as he subverted this contention in his discussion of colonialism in *Race and History*), the other tried to show such erasure to be impossible.

THE ENDS OF ANTICOLONIALISM

This excursus on Lévi-Strauss and Balandier helps sum up some of the difficulties concerning the production of knowledge in the postcolonial era. On the

---

anthropologist of the Indian caste system who significantly influenced the so-called New Philosophers. See Balandier, *Civilisés, dit-on*, 92.

52   Michel de Certeau, "Ethno-Graphy: Speech, or the Space of the Other: Jean de Léry," in de Certeau, ed., *The Writing of History*, trans. Tom Conley (New York: Columbia University Press, 1988), 224.

53   Mudimbe, *The Invention of Africa*, 19.

one hand, there is recognition of an intellectual indebtedness both to Marxism and to structuralism as tools of demystification—whether of systems of economic oppression or of ethnocentric value schemes.[54] Yet, on the other, Marxism too often falls into the trap of Eurocentrism by relying on preset developmental narratives that ignore or minimize the significance of negative or irredeemable moments, whereas structuralism seems politically useless because of its relativism and inherent quietism. Analogous remarks have been made of anticolonialism and Third Worldism: their function as movements against European hegemony were ultimately subverted by impulses from within—in particular, by native elites' reliance on overt European support, or on existing economic and political structures in their ascension to power— which often led to the replacement of colonialist with neocolonialist arrangements.

These tensions, inherently political, also go straight to the heart of the notion of the "cultural Other"—of the possibility of knowledge of such an Other, or even the possibility of theorizing it in any coherent way. The concept of the Other as developed in the phenomenological tradition simply does not fit easily with either Marxism or structuralism, both of which, in the 1950s at least, typically avoided and even derided the language of phenomenology (or, as in Sartre's case, existential phenomenology).

In my discussions so far of Sartre, colonialism, and the concept of the Other, I have tried to set forth some claims concerning how a critique of colonialism (and, more broadly, of racism and oppression) might have given rise to an understanding of the Other that goes beyond its strict definition as an existential relation between individuals. That is, I have tried to make some determinations concerning the applicability of the concept of the Other to groups—and, conversely, concerning the mechanisms by which, according to Sartre, collectively created structures (including thoughts and language, which he takes some care to distinguish from each other) influence definitions of "self" and "Other" for individual beings. Generally, I have tried to show that Sartre's resistance to colonialism was a potent catalyst (though certainly not the only catalyst) for rethinking the limits of any person's freedom and of the range of projects from which she might choose. Toward this goal, I have placed great weight on Sartre's explanation of how perceptual groups of "humans" and "subhumans" are created; how definitions of the social being of colonizer

---

54   For an evaluation of those debts, see Gayatri Chakravorty Spivak, *A Critique of Postcolonial Reason: Toward a History of the Vanishing Present* (Cambridge: Harvard University Press, 1999).

and colonized operate, particularly through the work of racism and the dynamic process of violence/counter-violence; and how revolutionary action provides a fleeting glimpse of genuine reciprocity and group cohesion among people.

Despite the importance of the critique of colonialism to Sartre's own political and philosophical projects, there is certainly a sense in which Sartre showed little concern for Leiris's question of whether or not knowledge of a *cultural* "Other" was valuable, or even possible. For example, though Sartre did not entirely ignore the colonized as a category in his discussion of colonialism in the *Critique*, his consistent focus was on the practices and the social being of the colonizer. Though this is perhaps understandable (Sartre was a French man who tried to speak to French people in order to effect change in his own country more than in others), it is regrettable that Sartre did not devote more of his text to an equally serious consideration of the status of the native, for there are a number of suggestive elements in his discussion that would complicate the rather schematic picture of the violent, half-starved oppressed with which the reader is often left. For example, Sartre might have developed further an idea that would seem to anticipate the efforts of contemporary Subaltern Studies:

> An army may annihilate an enemy army and entirely occupy the defeated country. But in so far as this *objectification* is ultimately an inert object and an individual reality within the developing totalisation, it is necessarily appropriated and alienated. Even defeated groups in the practical field can manipulate this field itself, and endow it with a real polyvalence which deprives the object of any univocal, uncontested signification.[55]

Failure, defeat, polyvalence, and contested meanings, Sartre might well have admitted, do a lot more work on the level of practice than his theoretical depiction in the *Critique* might lead the reader to believe. In the case of colonialism, his determined effort to demystify this "infernal machine," which incessantly churns out ever-more alienated persons both colonized and colonizing, which inserts alterity in its most "hardened" form into human relationships, might simply reinforce a notion of cultural "Otherness" that allows little or no room for communication between individuals belonging to antagonistic groups. That is, much like Octave Mannoni had argued in *Prospero and Caliban*, it seems to suggest that the psychological model of a person's relationship to the interpersonal Other might indeed be appropriately applied to a person's

---

55 Sartre, *Critique*, 665.

relationship to a cultural Other (whether it be one of sadism, masochism, Adlerian dependence, or some other relationship).

To come to this conclusion would be an error. It is true that anti-colonialism prompted a wave of books and essays on the general subject of the construction of the self as a member of an oppressed racial/ethnic group by such authors as Mannoni, Fanon, Memmi, and even Sartre. More generally, it provoked a political discussion in France, beginning in the 1950s, about the politics of cultural difference.[56] But it would be inconsistent with Sartre's methodological individualism, still in force in the *Critique*, to presume that the Other could ever be coherently collectivized into discrete groups that act as singular agents. In short, the Other, for Sartre, remained primarily the pre-numerical not-me. Any attempt to give it properties like "Algerian," "black," or "woman," would reduce its status of Otherness—which is perhaps why he largely avoided using the language of Otherness in works like *Anti-Semite and Jew* and "Black Orpheus." In spite of its usefulness as a metaphor, there is just no simple correspondence between the power of the Other to induce shame through her *look* (as described by Sartre in *Being and Nothingness*, and which presumably still held by the time he wrote the *Critique*), and the power of the colonizer to induce a similar feeling in the colonized. The latter situation cannot rely upon an interpersonal psychology for its explanation: this is the general claim that the *Critique* as a whole represents through its description of seriality, alterity, and the formation of collectives and groups.

What the *Critique* makes clear is that "cultural" Otherness must be viewed primarily through the lens of social relationships, not existential or psychological ones—that is, it calls into question the validity of the paradigm of "the Other" in describing and accounting for intercultural relationships. This has a very important consequence for how Sartre talked about cultural difference: that difference is never absolute or insurmountable, even in the extreme case of that between the colonizer and the colonized, who are locked into a relationship of alterity that continually produces violence and counter-violence. Though, it seems, Sartre would still have held that the interpersonal Other is, on the existential level, an "ex-centric limit" of my being, whose existence I can be sure of *only* because of the affect (shame, for example) he induces in me through his look, but about whose subjectivity I can *know* nothing, and so on,[57] it would not follow that Sartre believed that a non-Western "Other"

---

56   See James D. Le Sueur, *Uncivil War: Intellectuals and Identity Politics during the Decolonization of Algeria* (Philadelphia: University of Pennsylvania Press, 2001).
57   Sartre, *Being and Nothingness*, 330.

would then constitute an "ex-centric limit" to a Western "self"; nor would it even follow that he believed it was coherent to say that there are non-Western Others and Western selves, although he did sometimes slip into this kind of language. In the *Critique*, the dialectic between self and Other that was so important in his discussion of the look in *Being and Nothingness* is sidelined in favor of a dialectic between practical organisms and the practico-inert. In effect, it is the quasi-human practico-inert that takes on the role of the Other in this particular work, as Sartre focuses his attention on alterity-constituting structures and practices, rather than on affect.

This explains—perhaps as much as Sartre's political beliefs—why Sartre might have wanted to write a preface to Fanon's *The Wretched of the Earth*. After all, from *Black Skin, White Masks* to *Wretched*, Fanon had moved from a psychological description of the affective relations between blacks and whites in a particular colonial situation (Martinique) to an examination of dynamic social processes (the Algerian war and revolution). That is, Fanon moved from a treatment of "black" and "white" as homogenous categories that *themselves* regulated and produced predictable affective reactions to an analysis of the affective consequences of certain social processes—typically, traumatic ones like the rape, torture, and murder that were part of the process (the "infernal machine") of the war for independence.

Yet, even as Sartre focused attention on the production and reproduction of serial collectivities bonded by alterity, he ultimately pointed beyond them, to the identifiable yet irreducible core of those processes, which is the self-producing individual, perpetually struggling against her own unavoidable objectification by others, the predictable yet unpredictable spontaneity of human negation of the world, similar in some ways to what Pierre Bourdieu would term the "habitus"—a structured structuring of human practice.[58] On this point, it is perhaps best to refer to Sartre's treatments of individual literary figures—of himself, first of all, in *The Words* (1964), and also of Flaubert in the multi-volume, unfinished *The Family Idiot*—than it is to consult the *Critique*. Fredric Jameson described Sartre's method for the work on Flaubert as a

---

58 Bourdieu placed his own work in the context of a critique of both Sartre and Lévi-Strauss, though his description of Sartre's views correlates more closely with the existentialism of *Being and Nothingness* than the existential Marxism of the *Critique*. Whatever similarities there may appear to be between Sartre's concepts of praxis and the practico-inert and Bourdieu's concepts of habitus and field, these may be due in part to both of their readings of Merleau-Ponty. Nonetheless, these similarities may be superficial, as Bourdieu rejected the core Sartrean belief in human freedom, however constrained Sartre may have seen this freedom as being in the *Critique*. See Pierre Bourdieu, *The Logic of Practice*, trans. Richard Nice (Stanford: Stanford University Press, 1990).

dialectic between two interpretations: "a psychoanalytic one, centered on the family and on his childhood, and a Marxist one, whose guiding themes are the status of the artist in Flaubert's period and the historical and ideological contradictions faced by his social class, the bourgeoisie."[59] In spite of Sartre's commitment in the *Critique* to the possibility of free, spontaneous group action, one easily loses sight of his lifelong theme of individual revolt; indeed, the weight of the practico-inert makes it difficult to discern how individual revolt (such as Fanon's) might be possible, or what forms it might take. *The Words* and *The Family Idiot* thus deal with both the conditions and, especially, the limits of revolt by a lone person—a fascinating subject that is unfortunately beyond the scope of this book.

Starting at the end of World War II, and in connection with the development of his theory of intellectual engagement, Sartre's awareness of and fight against colonialism raised issues that should be distinguished from the problems posed by his concerns for social justice in France. Though freedom remained the cornerstone of all of his work—that is, theorizing both its possibility and the obstacles to achieving it—the relationship between the existential and social aspects of freedom, he noted, was different depending on one's situation, whether that of colonial subject, worker, black poet, woman, Jew, and so on. To the extent that colonialism and its demise forced serious thinking about cultural identity and difference, Sartre tried to meet the expectations of anticolonial elite intellectuals such as Diop, Senghor, Fanon, and Memmi by adapting his theory of radical freedom to the exigencies of membership in groups that are racially or culturally defined in texts like "Black Orpheus," his prefaces to Memmi and Fanon, and the *Critique*. Moreover, it seems clear that Sartre's engagement with Third World liberation movements was a significant factor in extending his intellectual influence past the early 1960s, when structuralism became a defining academic and cultural force. For that reason alone, it should be distinguished—though not completely separated—from his engagement with Marxism. A strong case could be made for the argument that Sartre's positions with respect to Third World liberation movements helped him maintain an avant-gardism necessary to his continuing relevance for political protest from the events of May 1968 to the post-'68 interest in issues such as racism and immigration.

---

59   Fredric Jameson, "Sartre in Search of Flaubert," *New York Times*, December 27, 1981, section 7, p. 5. For another point of comparison between the work of Sartre and of Bourdieu, see Bourdieu's own interpretation of Flaubert in *Rules of Art: Genesis and Structure of the Literary Field*, trans. Susan Emanuel (Stanford: Stanford University Press, 1996).

That is, I think that the case of Jean-Paul Sartre demonstrates both the limits and the possibilities of intellectual anticolonialism during the era of decolonization, particularly when such anticolonialism is taken as part of broader body of work. An interpretation that takes Sartre strictly as an "anti"-colonialist would view his thinking and his politics concerning colonialism and its legacy as oppositional, and thus in some sense unable to escape old, colonialist categories (for example, the distinction between "primitive" and "civilized" mentalities in *Anti-Semite and Jew*). But I think that Sartre's work, when seen from a comprehensive perspective, and also in relationship to other thinkers treating similar issues, leads to an alternative interpretation: that there is more openness in Sartre's conceptions of history, subjectivity, identity (whether spoken of in terms of facticity or in terms of the practico-inert), and the possibility for new relations among human beings in the postcolonial era than this first interpretation suggests—as I hope the last two chapters have demonstrated. I think these nuances have been lost from the historical record as French intellectuals since the 1970s have defined themselves in the intellectual field against a somewhat caricatured version of his voluminous work and extensive position-taking—a fact that some, such as (perhaps surprisingly) Bernard-Henri Lévy, have sought to correct very recently.[60] This second interpretation also gives cause for historians to re-examine anticolonialism as an intellectual movement, as a few already have, in order to discern relations between its various forms and the events of May '68 and post-'68 politics in France and elsewhere.

---

60   See Lévy, *Le siècle de Sartre.*

PART III

FAR AWAY, SO CLOSE: THE THIRD WORLD,
NEOCOLONIALISM, AND THE ETHICS OF
GLOBAL RESPONSIBILITY, 1962–1968

CHAPTER SEVEN

The Turn toward Third Worldism:
On the Assassination of Lumumba

Morality is everywhere. Injustice presents itself as justice, crime as obligation.[1]

The years between 1962 and 1968 were a "dead period" in French history, at least from the perspective of many on the Left.[2] Between the end of the French-Algerian War and the events of the student-worker revolt, the French public turned toward private concerns. "The conclusion of the cease-fire negotiations had speeded the decline of the French people toward complete political apathy," Simone de Beauvoir lamented—an observation amply illustrated by experimental filmmaker Chris Marker, who roamed the streets of Paris with a camera in May 1962, capturing with an urgent irony the return to "normalcy" of passersby, workers, Algerian immigrants, stockbrokers, shopkeepers, engineers, and a student from Dahomey (now the Republic of Benin).[3] These years are often treated as a gap separating discrete historical moments, especially in the literature on the origins of the May 1968 upheaval. The logic behind narrating events this way is to argue for the significance of a generational shift, whether on the level of changes in cultural practices or on the level of demographics—a logic that treats these years as a break with 1962 and a period of preparation for 1968, effectively minimizing the influence of the French-Algerian War on later events.

---

1 Jean-Paul Sartre, "Notes for Gramsci Lecture, Rome 1964 (typed manuscript corrected by Sartre)," The Beinecke Rare Book & Manuscript Library, John Gerassi Collection of Jean-Paul Sartre, GEN MSS 411, Series II: "Other Papers," Box 4, Folder 57, 70—hereafter referred to as "Rome Lecture Typed Manuscript."

2 Francis Jeanson, in John Gerassi's interview with him, Yale University Archives, John Gerassi Collection of Jean-Paul Sartre, GEN MSS 411, Box 3, Folder 44, "Interview with Francis Jeanson, November 13–14, 1973."

3 Simone de Beauvoir, *Force of Circumstance, Vol. II: Hard Times*, trans. Richard Howard (New York: Paragon House, 1992), 344; Chris Marker, *Le Joli Mai* (Paris: Sofracima, 1963).

THE LEFT AND THE RISE OF THIRD WORLDISM

This logic is persuasive to a certain extent, if one's aim is to make certain causal claims only about the student revolt—a narrow aim, indeed. As Kristin Ross has pointed out, public representations of "May 1968" (which often exclude the workers' strikes in June) have been dominated by those participants in the events who went on to become successful media intellectuals, beginning in the mid-to-late 1970s. One of the conditions for their success, she argues, was their willingness to see those events in a certain self-critical light, thus casting the goals of May 1968 in terms of personal egotism and the satisfaction of individual desires.[4] That is, in her account, they pulled the political teeth out of 1968—something that is all the more easily done when the period 1962–68 appears as a historical void.[5]

Perhaps one of the key consequences of the ongoing debate on the meaning of the 1968 crisis is that it keeps the famous events of May squarely in the center of postwar historiographical concerns. As one story goes concerning the evolution of the Left: after the liberation, the PCF was the largest political party in France, boosted by its active participation in the Resistance; after 1968, the possibility of revolution once promised by that dominance was forever gone. Yet there is something puzzling about making 1968 the crucial moment in this story of failure. By 1968, though still an important force, the PCF was no longer the vanguard of left-wing politics in France. It had been "overtaken" on the Left, as many historians have noted, during the French-Algerian War, when it only belatedly supported independence for Algeria—in fact, when that independence was already certain to come about. By 1968, the PCF was a firm

---

4   See Kristin Ross, *May '68 and Its Afterlives* (Chicago: University of Chicago Press, 2002). Ross's arguments against the so-called New Philosophers are compelling, but I cannot follow her so far as to condemn the "policing" function of the sociological literature on the student revolts. It seems uncontroversial that demographic expansion and change were important historical factors in the events of 1968.

5   David Drake's survey of intellectuals and politics from 1945 forward devotes fewer than two pages to the years 1962–68, in which he focuses on de Gaulle and increasing prosperity. Drake, *Intellectuals and Politics in Post-War France* (London: Palgrave, 2002), 128–30. Jean-François Sirinelli views the gap, particularly among intellectuals, as of somewhat shorter duration—from 1962 until 1965, which is for him the key turning point. The first French manifesto denouncing US action in Vietnam appeared in February 1965; starting then, the Vietnam war "went on to reactivate intellectual intervention, notably for the branch on the extreme left. For them as well, even before 1968, 1965 is a turning point." Jean-François Sirinelli, *Intellectuels et passions françaises, Manifestes et pétitions au XXe siècle* (Paris: Fayard, 1990), 368. Nonetheless, he views the years immediately after 1962 as a dead period (367). See also Ory and Sirinelli, *Les Intellectuels en France*, esp. 212–13. In this book, although the authors argue that 1965 marked the significant shift before the events of 1968, they unfortunately devote little exposition to the conditions of its occurrence.

participant in the electoral politics of the Republic, which hardly put it in a revolutionary position, as its members realized: according to a poll conducted for *Le Nouvel Observateur* in early 1968, only 26 percent of Communist Party voters surveyed wished it to gain full power; 57 percent preferred the idea that it share power in a left-wing federation.[6] Sartre's own take on the history of the Party, which he offered in conversation with Philippe Gavi and Pierre Victor (Benny Lévy) in 1972, expresses a particularly damning opinion:

> What has been the role of the PCF since it became, beginning in 1945, a great national party? What has it done? Did it ameliorate working conditions? Did it prevent de Gaulle from taking power? Did it put an end to the war in Indochina or in Algeria? It let all the bourgeois governments do what they wanted. It voted for giving special powers to Guy Mollet.[7]

In light of this comment, which Sartre concludes with a reference to the PCF's objective support for the pacification in Algeria in March 1956, it might be more pertinent to speak of an earlier failure of the radical Left—that of 1956–62. In such a story, clearly the PCF was the first casualty. Fearful of supporting the adventurism of groups it did not control, such as the FLN, the PCF renounced its claim to being the official source of radical activity—displaced by such efforts as the *porteurs de valises* of the Jeanson Network and the signatories to the Manifesto of the 121. With the return of de Gaulle, whose magnetism for working people handed it several significant electoral defeats, the PCF also saw its membership decline.[8]

But it was not only the PCF that lost during the Algerian war. Radical anticolonialists such as Jean-Paul Sartre and Francis Jeanson saw their efforts to rally the French public around the justice of the Algerians' cause overtaken by a man they publicly despised. In editorials throughout 1962 and early 1963, the editors at *Les Temps Modernes* lamented the demise of the Left and its consequences: specifically, neocolonialism pursued unchecked as a policy.[9]

---

6   "Comment les communistes veulent gouverner," *Le Nouvel Observateur* 171, February 21–27, 6.

7   Philippe Gavi, Jean-Paul Sartre, and Pierre Victor, *On a raison de se révolter* (Paris: Gallimard, 1974), 50.

8   Sudhir Hazareesingh, *Intellectuals and the French Communist Party: Disillusion and Decline* (Oxford: Clarendon Press, 1991), 142–3, 164.

9   T.M., "Demain comme hier," *Les Temps Modernes* 194 (July 1962), 2. See also T.M., "La gauche française et le F.L.N.," *Les Temps Modernes* 167–168 (February/March 1960), 1,169–73; the section, "La gauche respecteuse," *Les Temps Modernes* 169–170 (April/May 1960), 1512–34; and Sartre's editorial, "Les somnambules," *Les Temps Modernes* 191 (April 1962), 1,397–1,401, translated as "The Sleepwalkers," in Sartre, *Colonialism and Neocolonialism*, 131–5.

Charles de Gaulle had won credit for mastering the settler lobby and ending the war, effectively co-opting the radical Left's most potent political issue—and short-circuiting any idea that colonial war might turn into class war. Moreover, through negotiation he was able to maintain French ownership of oil and gas exploration rights and secure usage of the Mers el-Kebir naval station for fifteen years[10]—hence, whither the Algerian revolution they had hoped for? Indeed, throughout the 1960s de Gaulle continued to poach issues from the Left—for example, breaking with NATO and establishing diplomatic ties with China. And as Michel-Antoine Burnier noted in a 1965 essay in *Les Temps Modernes*, the Left's continued fragmentation had permitted de Gaulle to position himself as the champion of anti-Americanism.[11] The outcome of the French-Algerian War for the Left was, in general, disastrous, inaugurating two decades of right-wing dominance in electoral politics.[12]

Outside of France, however, the Algerian revolution held enormous prestige among the newly independent nations. The symbolic fruits of this prestige for French intellectuals who had supported the independence movement should not be discounted—nor should the effect that that prestige might have had on young radicals back in France. In the best recent book on Third Worldism, *The Call from Algeria: Third Worldism, Revolution, and the Turn to Islam*, Robert Malley argues that the various forms of Third Worldism were products of the encounter between South and North and the cultural exchange that took place mainly in the capitals of metropoles, particularly during the interwar era.[13] This exchange resulted not just in Third Worldism, but also some of its offshoots: "the concept of cultural revolution, renewed emphasis on the state as autonomous actor, and the search for new social foundations for the revolutionary project—the lumpen-proletariat, the socially-excluded, and

---

10   Keith Panter-Brick, "Independence, French-Style," in Prosser Gifford and William Roger Louis, eds, *Decolonization and African Independence: The Transfer of Power, 1960–1980* (New Haven: Yale University Press, 1988), 99–100.

11   Michel-Antoine Burnier, "Un coup pour rien," *Les Temps Modernes* 232 (August 1965), 201.

12   De Gaulle's actions during the French-Algerian War continue to be a matter of vigorous debate. Irwin Wall has argued, based on evidence in diplomatic archives, that de Gaulle did not intend to grant Algeria independence during the years 1958–59, instead imagining it as the jewel in the crown of a federation he called "Eurafrique." Militarily, he would win the war against the ALN (Army of National Liberation); but diplomatically, he was losing a fight with the United States, whose pressure on the French government was, in Wall's view, the greatest factor in de Gaulle's change of position. Irwin Wall, *France, the United States, and the Algerian War* (Berkeley: University of California Press, 2001).

13   Robert Malley, *The Call from Algeria: Third Worldism, Revolution, and the Turn to Islam* (Berkeley: University of California Press, 1996).

THE TURN TOWARD THIRD WORLDISM 125

what many tellingly dubbed the 'Third World within the First.' "[14] He admirably details the component parts of the ideology in the Algerian case, which was a mix of assimilationism, traditionalism, and socialism. Since his focus is on Algeria, not on France, his strength lies in showing how the FLN successfully represented itself as a rupture with past political movements, and how it created a self-legitimizing ideology of national continuity by developing a narrative of Algerian history that culminated with the birth of the FLN. By showing how the FLN relied on some traditional modes of authority, Malley also makes the important point that Third Worldism as practiced in Third World countries cannot be viewed as simply a Western import, which is how it is often summarily dismissed today. He emphasizes that Third Worldism was an ideology both *of* and *about* the Third World.

Malley leaves this crucial distinction unexplored, however. The fact is that French Third Worldists—a broad rubric under which may be categorized people supporting socialist revolutions in Third World countries—possessed different interests in defending Third World revolutions than did the revolutionaries themselves. Though many among them, such as Georges Balandier, René Dumont, or Gérard Chaliand (a former *porteur de valise*),[15] had similar credentials as scholar-activists, there is not a coherence of doctrine strong enough to call Third Worldism an "ideology" in France, as it might legitimately have been in Algeria—in spite of some scholars' schematic treatment of it as such.[16] Nonetheless, after the successes of Cuba and Algeria, many French intellectuals developed an intense interest in Third World countries. The peculiar meeting of North and South among these intellectuals was profoundly shaped, I would argue, by the failure of the radical Left to obtain any real results of their own from their engagement with the cause for Algerian independence. The Algerian revolutionaries actually held power in Algeria; their French counterparts held nothing and could claim parenthood of no substantive changes in French domestic politics. The turn of many radical intellectuals, Jean-Paul

---

14   Ibid., 28.

15   Hervé Hamon and Patrick Rotman, *Génération, Vol. I: Les années de rêve* (Paris: Editions du Seuil, 1987), 96.

16   Ory and Sirinelli provide an example of this, rendering Third Worldism simply as the belief that "the Third World is revolutionary because it is composed of 'proletarian' nations, and the proletariat conserves its redemptive role." Of course, few (if any) intellectual Third Worldists—who were often specialists in a non-European region of the world—were as homogenizing as Ory and Sirinelli are here. Their characterization also completely misses one of the key components of Third Worldism, which was the theorization of the potential revolutionary role of the peasantry, not the "proletariat." Ory and Sirinelli, *Les intellectuels en France*, 211.

Sartre above all, toward international events ought to be understood in this light: impotence at home, potent symbolic capital abroad. Take, for example, Sartre's reception in Cuba, where his support for Castro could be translated into support for revolutionary movements beginning to stir throughout Latin America, but where he had also influenced Ernesto "Che" Guevara, who had enthusiastically read Sartre's famous existentialist texts as a student.[17]

Thus, these meetings took place not only in the metropoles, but, as Hervé Hamon and Pierre Rotman describe, in Havana and Algiers, as young communists such as Bernard Kouchner (who is, as of this writing, the French foreign minister in the right-wing government of Nicolas Sarkozy) and Alain Krivine, disillusioned with the line the PCF had taken in Algeria, began to look elsewhere for leadership. In Génération, Hamon and Rotman describe the role in the early 1960s of the Union des Étudiants Communistes (UEC) and its organ, Clarté (where Kouchner, for one, cut his intellectual teeth) in supporting Third World liberation movements—which ultimately caused enough friction with the PCF central committee to lead to an open break in 1965.[18] Importantly, they are thus able to show that 1965 was not so much a turning point from left-wing apathy to politicization, but rather a bridge between two related moments:

> Under the leadership of Laurent Schwartz [who founded the Comité Vietnam National (CVN) in November 1967], the militants of the end of the Algerian war, having broken with the UEC, once again took up service: Burnier, [Pierre] Kahn, Kouchner, Krivine, [Jean-Louis] Péninou, [Jean] Schalit, and many others [joined the committee].[19]

A discussion of the turn toward Third Worldism among the radical French Left in the early 1960s does not exhaust the motivations at work in the critique of neocolonialism. One of the significant trends among not just intellectuals but the larger French population was the growth of anti-American sentiment and the broad perception that the United States represented imperialist ambitions—a perception that crystallized in protest against the war in Vietnam, starting in 1965.[20] Although de Gaulle's development of a nuclear arsenal in his *force de frappe* was one of the most direct challenges to US dominance and

---

17   Jon Lee Anderson, *Che Guevara: A Revolutionary Life* (New York: Grove Press, 1998), 38, 468.

18   In January 1961, as the upshot of the first significant conflict with the central committee, the young leader of the UEC, Jean Piel, tearfully read an autocritique accusing the group of adventurism. Hamon and Rotman, *Génération, Vol. I*, 68.

19   Ibid., 367.

20   For a long-range history of this sentiment, see Jean-Pierre Mathy, *Extrême-Occident: French Intellectuals and America* (Chicago: University of Chicago Press, 1993).

the Atlanticism of NATO, and he was the only Western leader to condemn the war in Vietnam forcefully, the radical Left was still able to leverage anti-imperialism—which often just meant anti-Americanism—to its own ends, particularly among French youth, whose experience, paradoxically, as Marker demonstrated in *Le Joli Mai*, was becoming increasingly saturated with American culture.[21] "Children of Marx and Coca-Cola," Richard Kuisel reminds us, was a popular catchphrase for the generation of 1968. Indeed, the intellectual vilification of American-style consumer society in 1960s France by the likes of Henri Lefebvre, Jean Baudrillard, Bertrand de Jouvenel, and Alain Touraine that Kuisel points out ought to be read as a sign of the level of its penetration.[22]

But students in the *lycées* and the universities did not, as a widespread phenomenon, create committees and action groups specifically to condemn the culture of consumption: they did so to condemn American intervention in Vietnam. In February 1967, French students organized *comités de base* for Vietnam—local action committees that, Kristin Ross argues, provided a new set of practices for the anti-authority engagements of May 1968.[23] As the May 22 Movement at Nanterre, one of the new universities on the outskirts of Paris, was to prove, however, these committees did not have a monopoly on anti-imperialist fervor. Indeed, that movement demonstrated the evident power of anti-imperialism to bind together a heterogeneous set of highly motivated radicals—whatever else their motives and claims were, or were to become—by taking the lead in what would snowball into the events of May. The initial uprising, which involved the occupation of the administration building at Nanterre, was spurred by the arrest of militants of the *comités de base* and the Comité Vietnam National, following the bombings of the offices of the US-owned businesses American Express, Bank of America, and TWA.[24] Daniel Cohn-Bendit and other activists organized a meeting of between 600 and 700

---

21   As de Gaulle's criticism demonstrates, it was not only the radical Left that mobilized against US intervention in Vietnam. Gaullists such as François Mauriac and David Rousset also signed petitions against the war. Bernard Droz, "Vietnam (guerre du)," *Dictionnaire des intellectuels français: les personnes, les lieux, les moments*, Jacques Julliard and Michel Winock, eds (Paris: Editions du Seuil, 2002, new edn), 1409.

22   Richard Kuisel, *Seducing the French: The Dilemma of Americanization* (Berkeley: University of California Press, 1993), 190, 188.

23   Ross, *May '68 and Its Afterlives*, 92–4. A more complete description of the emergence of the *comités de base* can be found in Hamon and Rotman, *Génération, Vol. I*, Ch. 10, esp. 338–9.

24   Hamon and Rotman, *Génération, Vol. I*, 425–7. For examples of news reports, see René Backmann, "Action et contestation," *Le Nouvel Observateur* 176, March 27–April 2, pp. 8–9; and René Backmann, "La percée des cent quarante-deux," *Le Nouvel Observateur* 178, April 3–9, pp. 18–19.

students to discuss "what we can do against such a threatening, repressive maneuver." The cohesion of the movement, the members said, centered on a single commitment: "You were with the March 22 Movement if you were anti-imperialist, whether you were CVN, *comité de base*, pro-Chinese or whatever else."[25]

There were two major conjunctures at work: first, the domestic weakness and international prestige of left-wing French intellectuals after the success of the Algerian struggle; and, second, the powerful affective force of anti-Americanism, crystallized in anti-imperialism, to help drive left-wing organization.[26] I do not, however, wish to argue that the 1960s turn toward international concerns was purely instrumental. Judging from the firmly held commitments during the French-Algerian War, in which some intellectuals actually put themselves in harm's way, one cannot discount the fact that such commitments might shape the orientation and the contents of intellectual production.

One of the deepest representations of the merging of these currents of political expediency and new intellectual commitments was the Manifesto of the 121, which appeared (or did not appear, as it could not be printed without being seized by the government) in the fall of 1960. The manifesto, entitled "The Declaration on the Right to Resist in the Algerian War," is often cited by historians as evidence of a particular radicalization not only of intellectuals but of the conflict in general.[27] Though Jean-François Sirinelli points to the Manifesto of the 121 as "one of the most famous intellectual texts of the postwar era,"[28] historians tend to treat it as a document without a legacy.

I think there are important reasons for viewing the Manifesto of the 121 as the opening salvo in a new set of intellectual engagements and practices that came to re-examine the relationship between individual freedom and social equality on a global scale. "A very important movement is developing in France," the document opens,

---

25   Emile Copfermann, ed., *Mouvement du 22 mars, Ce n'est qu'un début continuons le combat* (Paris: La Découverte, 2001 [Maspéro, 1968]), 15–17. They are also critical of a "veritable psychosis created by the pro-Chinese people of the *comités Viêtnam*," which reigned over the students by early May. Ibid., 20.

26   For another take on the links between the domestic and the international in the 1960s, see Jeremi Suri, *Power and Protest: Global Revolution and the Rise of Détente* (Cambridge: Harvard University Press, 2003).

27   See Paul Clay Sorum, *Intellectuals and Decolonization in France* (Chapel Hill: University of North Carolina Press, 1977), 174–8; and Cohen-Solal, *Sartre*, 423–6.

28   Jean-François Sirinelli, *Intellectuels et passions françaises*, 211.

and it is necessary that French and international opinion is better informed about it, at the moment when the new turn in the Algerian war leads us to see, not to forget, the depth of the crisis that began six years ago. Becoming more and more numerous, French people are pursued, imprisoned, and condemned for having refused to participate in this war.[29]

With these words, anticolonial intellectuals linked the fate of the freedom of individual French people to that of people of another nation (or nation-to-be). The vision offered in the Manifesto of the 121 of a simultaneous domestication and internationalization of the conflict formed the touchstone for subsequent political actions among many leftist intellectuals in the 1960s.

In this and the following two chapters, I turn again to the example of Jean-Paul Sartre to examine aspects of this historical shift among certain leftist intellectuals. Though Sartre's power in the intellectual field was being eroded by the methodological challenges of Lévi-Strauss's structuralist anthropology and Althusser's structuralist Marxism, his continuing unification of literary and philosophical projects with his positions on behalf of Algerian independence had made him a significant, and divisive, figure in public perceptions of left-wing radicalism—perceptions that were perhaps bolstered by the fact that the Organisation Armée Secrète had attempted to assassinate him.[30] Denis Bertholet notes that, in 1960, "Sartre is omnipresent on the intellectual and literary scene": he had just published his "appeal to youth," gaining a new audience with his preface to Paul Nizan's *Aden Arabie*; there was the *Critique* and "innumerable interviews on Cuba"; and the *Condemned of Altona* continued to play.[31] That Sartre is a representative intellectual of this turn seems uncontroversial, given his prefaces for Fanon and Lumumba, his intervention on behalf of the theorist of armed revolution, Régis Debray (captured in Bolivia after meeting with Che Guevara), his participation in the Russell Tribunal, his visits to Egypt and Israel on the eve of the 1967 Six Day War, and *Les Temps Modernes*'s myriad of articles analyzing events in the Congo, Portuguese

---

29   Ibid.
30   See Cohen-Solal's description of the hatred directed at him, as well as the assassination attempts in *Sartre*, 426–30, 440. See also the chapter " 'Kill Sartre' " in Ronald Hayman, *Sartre: A Life* (New York: Simon & Schuster, 1987), 381–92.
31   Denis Bertholet, *Sartre* (Paris: Plon, 2000), 425. Patrick McCarthy sets the Nizan preface in the context of the French-Algerian War and Sartre's growing interest in liberation movements in his essay, "Sartre, Nizan and the Dilemmas of Political Commitment," *Yale French Studies* 68: *Sartre after Sartre* (1985), 191–205. McCarthy argues that "Nizan is the model whom Sartre offers to the youth of 1960: a heretical Marxist rather than a perfect or ex-communist," describing the preface as "Sartre's attempt to resurrect Nizan as an elder brother of the young Cubans" (202, 203).

Guinea, South Africa, Rwanda, Angola, the United States (in particular, the Civil Rights and Black Power movements), China, India, Laos, Vietnam, Egypt, Algeria, the Antilles, the Dominican Republic, Latin America (treated as a whole), Brazil, Cuba, Guatemala, and Tahiti—all before the events of 1968.

Following the previous chapters' close examination of the relationship between Sartre's anticolonial engagements and his philosophical concerns, I focus in Part III on three moments in his work that clearly link thinking and practice: his 1963 preface to the political writings of Patrice Lumumba, who had been assassinated by Belgian- and US-backed Congolese foes in 1961 (this chapter); his 1964 lecture on ethics at the Gramsci Institute in Rome—often called simply as the "Rome Lecture" (Chapter 8); and his executive presidency of the International War Crimes Tribunal, nominally organized by British philosopher Bertrand Russell in 1967, and the text he contributed to the Tribunal's final report, "On Genocide" (Chapter 9). These texts (and actions), widely varied in their method of argumentation and their intended audiences, demonstrate an evolving set of concerns centered on *justice* and *ethics*—the justice of relations between peoples and the specifically normative grounds for ethical conduct, including when that conduct is violent. The Rome Lecture is of particular importance in this context. As Robert Stone and Elizabeth Bowman, who have established themselves as the preeminent commentators on Sartre's "dialectical" or "second" ethics, note,

> This work will recall the 60s, an era, preeminently, of the moral. Beneath all economic and citizenly doings there existed a space—the moral domain—in which those injured in various ways by the system could nevertheless recognize each other and immediately cooperate in constructing means for altering the system.[32]

My intention in Part III is to examine the historical weight of this claim, and to use Sartre's texts as a sign of the emerging intersection of private and international concerns, of the tricky negotiation involved in viewing oneself as a real participant in distant conflicts—not just as a matter of imagination, but as a matter of fact.

By looking at these three moments, I hope to offer a window on to the broader critique of neocolonialist arrangements and US imperialism, which

---

32 Robert V. Stone, in collaboration with Elizabeth A. Bowman, "Dialectical Ethics: A First Look at Sartre's Unpublished 1964 Rome Lecture Notes," *Social Text* 13–14 (Winter/Spring 1986), 213. The "first" ethics is Sartre's *Notebooks for an Ethics*; the "third" was projected in his work with Benny Lévy in the late 1970s.

represents an important—even seismic—shift in how the consequences of individual actions are viewed. By considering the political efforts of radical left-ists such as Sartre alongside the critique of neocolonialism, I point toward the emergence of a new understanding of personal responsibility that was based on the idea that, in an increasingly interconnected world, people's actions can have distant consequences. Through the Rome Lecture, I believe that Sartre above all offered a significant attempt in this era to provide an ethics that could be mobilized for a critique of neocolonialism. Through my discussion, I hope to show that naming as "masochism" Europeans' criticism of European actions is too simplistic, because it fails to take account of the development of this new discourse on responsibility—which was evinced anecdotally by 1968 slogans such as "Vietnam is in our factories," and by the fact that the March 22 Move-ment took the inspiration for its name from Castro's July 26 Movement, but which was also provided with a deeper philosophical content through Sartre's efforts.[33] Finally, after describing the emergence of the intellectual battle against neocolonialism as a key site of moral and political struggle in the 1960s, I will also show how Sartre attempted to join the debate with structuralism through precisely these angles of ethics and responsibility.

LUMUMBA—REVOLUTIONARY WITHOUT A REVOLUTION

"Lumumba and Fanon"—Sartre wrote in 1963—"these two great dead men represent Africa."[34] Sartre's passionate preface to *The Political Thought of Patrice Lumumba* expresses both outrage and disappointment: outrage at the objective conditions that, Sartre argued, sabotaged Lumumba's efforts to unify his country, and disappointment at Lumumba's own failings, in spite of his great gifts as a leader. But why these two people? On a personal level, it could be that Fanon's own feelings for Lumumba colored his choice. "Fanon often talked to me about Lumumba," Sartre wrote; and, "I remember that Fanon in Rome was devastated by [his death]."[35] As Sartre made clear, however, his

---

33   Kristin Ross, *May '68 and Its Afterlives*, 80, 91. I noted in Chapter 3 that François Mauriac was one of the first to use the charge of masochism against the more radical anticolonialists in 1947, but it was really Pascal Bruckner who struck a public chord in his 1983 book, *The Tears of the White Man: Compassion as Contempt*, trans. William R. Beer (New York: Free Press, 1986).

34   Jean-Paul Sartre, "The Political Thought of Patrice Lumumba," in *Colonialism and Neocolonialism*, 156. The editors misidentify the original French publication as "preface to *Discours de Lumumba*." Strangely, his biographer Denis Bertholet also misidentifies the book, this time as *Ecrits de Lumumba* (Bertholet, *Sartre*, 456). In fact, the original book was *La Pensée politique de Patrice Lumumba* (Paris: Présence Africaine Editions, 1963).

35   Sartre, *La Pensée politique de Patrice Lumumba*, 157, 200. Fanon was actually in the

choice had higher theoretical stakes than a simple sorting out of emotions. Sartre set up the two as representative of opposite revolutionary choices: Fanon was the man of violence, Lumumba the man of nonviolence. Though each was strongly critical of the continuation of colonialism through neocolonialist arrangements, Sartre argued that Lumumba's almost immediate political failure and eventual murder provided evidence that only the unifying acts of armed revolution could be powerful enough to reshape economic and social foundations, thereby preventing the installation of a neocolonialist regime.

The preface is a somewhat surprising piece of writing. First, it demonstrates an impressive knowledge of Lumumba and the events that led to his arrest and assassination—all the more impressive as it seems outside the sights of both Sartre and *Les Temps Modernes*, which did not cover the crisis in the Congo in depth until Third Worldist activist Jean Ziegler's March 1963 article, "The White Army in Africa."[36] But this knowledge is perhaps not so surprising if one accepts that this was one of the major world events of 1960–61. It involved the first United Nations–led intervention in a sovereign country, and a controversial one at that, since many observers thought the UN to be actively abetting the secessionist claims of the resource-rich province of Katanga and its Belgian-backed governor, Moïse Tshombe.[37] The assassination of Patrice Lumumba was viewed as the opening shot in the war to maintain "neocolonialist" power in the recently independent nations—the herald of future strategies; indeed, it put neocolonialism on the map, both figuratively and literally.

Second, it is interesting because, at forty-five pages in length, it was not a short text, and it came at a time when Sartre was also putting the finishing touches to his autobiographical masterpiece, *The Words*, first published in *Les Temps Modernes* in late 1963. Indeed, Sartre employed many of the tools of biography he had used in writing about Mallarmé, Genet, Tintoretto, Flaubert,

Congo for a Pan-African Congress during the crisis. See David Macey, *Frantz Fanon: A Biography* (New York: Picador, 2002), 434–5.

36   Jean Ziegler, "L'armée blanche en Afrique," *Les Temps Modernes* 203 (April 1963), 1,848–58. It was, however, mentioned in the "Cours des Choses" section, which dealt with contemporary news, in March 1962; Jacques-Laurent Bost, "Le Cours des choses," *Les Temps Modernes* 190 (March 1962), 1,389. For a contemporary description of the history of colonization in the Congo, see a later article: Renée Saurel, "L'edelweiss aux Indes noires," *Les Temps Modernes* 226 (March 1965), 1,624–42.

37   Sartre held this view. See Sartre, "The Political Thought of Patrice Lumumba," in *Colonialism and Neocolonialism*, 198. The debate on responsibility for Lumumba's assassination and the role of the UN in the Congo was restarted in recent years. See Ludo De Witte, *The Assassination of Lumumba*, trans. Ann Wright and Renée Fenby (New York: Verso, 2001). De Witte's interpretation of Lumumba as a Jacobin may be indebted to Sartre's 1963 essay.

and himself in describing the social forces he believed to have shaped Lumumba's destiny as a failed leader. For Sartre, Lumumba's education by well-meaning whites as a child in missionary school, and his later position as a government-employed black man (a postal worker) clearly indebted him to a system that, at the same time, refused to grant him anything near full equality of opportunity. The result was a duality of lived experience: "When he reveals now one, now the other of the two opposing conceptions of Belgium's 'civilizing' work," Sartre noted, "it is because they coexist within him and translate the profound contradiction of what can only be called his class."[38] The class in question here was that of European-trained African *évolués* ("evolved ones," or those Africans who had "evolved" through education and assimilation).

Though they remain murky, it is possible that one of Sartre's reasons for undertaking this project was that it offered attractive material for stepping back and assessing his own stand on independence movements and their prospects for "genuine" socialist revolution. He had already employed a more cautious tone in discussing the situations in both Cuba and in Algeria, even as he remained a partisan of what he took to be their overall projects. In addition, *Les Temps Modernes* had also begun publishing and covering the work of Pierre Bourdieu on the Algerian peasantry, which cast significant doubt on quasi-Marxist theories of the revolutionary peasant.[39] In conjunction with these turns, Sartre seemed to have been taking a more critical attitude toward revolutionary activity and its outcomes, particularly after having been burned by the Soviet Union's invasion of Hungary—even if a text such as his preface to *Wretched* made him appear to be an overenthusiastic supporter.

Another of his reasons may have been to apply the ideas developed in the *Critique of Dialectical Reason* to yet another historical situation, and one that was rapidly becoming a hot political issue—that of neocolonialism. Two of Sartre's long-term associates at *Les Temps Modernes*, André Gorz and Francis Jeanson, had already described their views on the definition of and conditions for neocolonialism.[40] Like Jeanson, Gorz, and other sympathetic observers,

---

38   Sartre, "The Political Thought of Patrice Lumumba," 159.
39   See, for example, Pierre Bourdieu, "Les relations entre les sexes dans la société paysanne," *Les Temps Modernes* 195 (August 1962), 307–31; and Pierre Bourdieu, "Les sous-prolétaires algériens," *Les Temps Modernes* 199 (December 1962), 1,030–51.
40   Francis Jeanson, *L'Algérie hors la loi* (Paris: Editions du Seuil, 1955), Part II, Ch. III; and André Gorz, "Gaullisme et néo-colonialisme (A propos du Plan de Constantine)," *Les Temps Modernes* 179 (March 1961), 1,150–71. Jeanson's book was published before his break with Sartre over Sartre's denunciation of the Soviet invasion of Hungary. His rapprochement with Sartre began with the 1959 interview in Francis Jeanson, "Interview de Sartre," *Vérités pour...* 9 (June 2, 1959), 14–7, and he rejoined the review in 1962, after Marcel Péju was kicked out.

Sartre feared the consequences of a purely political—not socialist—revolution in the newly independent countries. Unlike Jeanson and Gorz, however, Sartre typically did not rely primarily on economic data to make his arguments. Instead, he appealed to concepts developed in his own philosophy and on the basis of historical analogies, usually with the events of the French Revolution. In the case of the Congo, Sartre argued, the logical (and practical) outcome of aiming only for political revolution was neocolonialism. In an inventive, though debatable, move, Sartre linked the fate of the revolution to the fate of a single *évolué*, Lumumba, whom he considered to be a "black Robespierre," trying to show how this particular man both lived and represented the contradictions of a country riven by ethnic and economic divisions. Though at certain points Sartre attempted to show how the outcome of the Congo crisis might have been different, his unwavering focus on Lumumba's impotence in the face of enemies coming from all angles makes it hard to see how Sartre thought any alternative path might actually have been taken.

Sartre's argument runs as follows: in order for real, not sham, independence to have succeeded in the Congo, the post-independence leadership had to find a way to unite from within a country that had until then been united from without by colonial rule. Referring to terms defined in the *Critique*, Sartre asserted that colonial rule had atomized the existing society by reducing or replacing its internal bonds with the external bond of subjectship under the Belgian king. The problem, according to Sartre, was that producing such post-independence national cohesion through a process of centralization was difficult in a society in which the political leaders represented particular constituencies or interests. Lumumba was the only Congolese leader with any power to have tried to make claims to universality—to have tried aggressively to put into action a plan for the centralization of authority, rather than the federalism desired by competing politicians. But Lumumba's claim to universality was only a fiction of his class, the educated *évolués* who were in fact petty-bourgeois functionaries intent on replacing colonial power with their own. "The abject and very skillfully chosen word *évolué*," he wrote,

> hid the truth: a small privileged class regarded itself as the vanguard of the colonized ... In the light of events, we now see that it was an abstract entente: the indigenous masses were proud of their *évolués* who proved *for everyone* that blacks, provided they were given the opportunity, could equal or surpass whites.[41]

---

41   Sartre, "The Political Thought of Patrice Lumumba," 169.

Here Sartre's argument is tricky, because he wanted to argue not only that the future leaders of the Congo were picked from among the class of *évolués* in the European capitals, but also that somehow Lumumba was able to transcend his class, even as he attempted to realize its universal ambitions—to become, in effect, the *évolués'* martyr in their eventual accession to power. This is the weakest link in Sartre's argument: How did Lumumba distinguish himself? Why did his actions diverge from those of the other *évolués*? Why did he live his contradictions in a way that led simultaneously to his own death and to the triumph of his class—indeed, the necessity of his death for the triumph of his class? Sometimes Sartre chalked this up to Lumumba's naïveté about the real desires of his cohort; he could not conceive of any other enemy than "old colonialism." At other times Sartre seems simply to have wanted to stress the mystery of Lumumba's transcendence of his social being, through his belief in pan-African unity and his drive to unify his country: "What Lumumba hinted at—but as we know, he understood it immediately—was that Congolese independence was not an end in itself but the beginning of a struggle to the death to win national sovereignty [throughout Africa]."[42] Lumumba's function in the text as a "singular universal"—a term that Sartre would theorize at great length in his study of Flaubert, which he had already begun to write—remains too schematic here to be convincing.

Sartre did not say why this insight was immediate for Lumumba but not for other *évolués*, but he did try to explain why, for the neocolonialist project to triumph, Lumumba had to die. Interestingly, he turned to the basic themes of existentialism—shame and anxiety—married to the idea of the Other as mediator of human relations in the field of the practico-inert, the external element that gives meaning to any binary relationship. "The alive and captive Lumumba," Sartre wrote, "was the shame and the rage of an entire continent: he was present for everyone as a demand which they could neither fulfill nor remove; *in him*, everyone recognized the power and the ferocity of neocolonial trickery."[43] Removing that demand was the only solution for supporters of neocolonialism.

Thus, the thrust of Sartre's argument is that Lumumba had the right idea (centralization), but the wrong method (nonviolent politics) to achieve it—the latter fact oddly calling into question Sartre's analogy between Lumumba and Robespierre. He held out hope for a "Congolese Castro"[44]—thus avoiding the

---

42 Ibid., 174.
43 Ibid., 199.
44 Ibid., 200.

endgame of a Congolese Napoleon in his French Revolutionary analogy, which after Mobutu's coup may have been closer to the mark (if the analogy itself were accepted). He emphasized that cohesion is best formed by risking one's own life, or placing one's life in the hands of others, and that the fact that independence was granted, not taken, was perhaps the single most important factor in Lumumba's failure. In spite of the Lumumbists' deep rejection of colonialism, "The fact remains, however, that circumstances did not allow or demand recourse to *organized* struggle. In Vietnam, in Angola, and in Algeria, the organizations were armed, they were people's wars." For a situation such as the Congo's, Sartre wrote, "independence granted is merely a variation on servitude."[45]

With this last assertion, Sartre indicated once again the central theme that underlay his writings in support of liberation movements: the linkage between freedom and revolt. For Raymond Aron, it was precisely this linkage, which he interpreted as a necessary one in Sartre's thought, that led Sartre uncritically to support violence as a means of advancing liberation movements. In fact, Sartre's philosophy, from *Being and Nothingness* to the *Critique* and beyond, represented "the systematic choice of violence or of Revolution," Aron wrote. "I see two principal reasons for this [choice]: the absolutist conception of freedom (or of negation), and the refusal to accept the inevitable socialization of *praxis*."[46]

Aron's conclusion certainly highlights one of the (often noticed) great tensions in Sartre's work. Yet it may be challenged on two counts. First, the notion that violence is always a default choice in Sartre's philosophy wrongly equates violence with negation, which takes an infinite number of forms, each dependent on the situation to be negated and the person doing the negating: negation may or may not be violent. Second, Aron's conclusion seems to lose all sight of one of Sartre's other key ideas, that of situation. Aron was right that, in the case of Third World liberation movements, Sartre readily adopted violence as the most "progressive" form of negation—and is liable to criticism on those grounds; but it would not be correct to assume that Sartre thus considered violence to be the best means of change in every given circumstance.

---

45   Ibid., 181. This statement strongly echoes Fanon. As Fredric Jameson notes, "The African states had to face the crippling effects of what Fanon prophetically warned them against—to receive independence is not the same as to take it, since it is in the revolutionary struggle itself that new social relationships and a new consciousness is developed." Fredric Jameson, "Third-World Literature in the Era of Multinational Capitalism," *Social Text* 15 (Fall 1986), 81.

46   Aron, *Histoire et dialectique de la violence*, 222.

Finally, Aron seems to have raised to an imperative or norm what, for Sartre, was in fact only a means. Violence and terror are means of modifying both praxis and the practico-inert—and, again, are liable to criticism on those grounds—but they are not the only means; they reply to the exigencies of particular circumstances. It is simply not justifiable to say that, for Sartre, violence is undertaken "in and for itself," as Aron asserted.[47]

Still, Aron—himself no pacifist—was right to be critical, since Sartre never really described what imperative or norm (if any at all) violence ought to be called upon to defend. In the *Critique*, violence appeared to be causally related to systems of alienation, rather than being a tool of specifically moral action. Such a description might have been expected in the long-awaited book on ethics that Sartre had promised since the end of *Being and Nothingness*—but this book never appeared. Apparently, the only sustained argument on the ethics of violent action he ever made to the public occurred on May 23, 1964, in a lecture he gave at the Gramsci Institute in Rome. The notes for the lecture, though written in clear prose until the final section, which was left in rough-draft form, were never published. Unsurprisingly, one of the central examples he chose to illustrate his argument was the armed liberation struggle that had recently ended in Algeria.

---

47   Ibid., 218.

CHAPTER EIGHT

The Ethics of Global Responsibility: The 1964 "Rome Lecture"

"If Sartre, in *Critique of Dialectical Reason*," Elizabeth Stone and Robert Bowman note,

> traces the structures of history back to the praxis of the common individual, then in the Rome Lecture Notes he does the same for the structures of morality. Against the post-structuralist current of our times, he places morality back in the hands of free practical agents.[1]

Just as Sartre had argued in the *Critique* that dialectical materialism was an idealist philosophy that ignored the fact that history could only be made through the actions of individuals, in the Rome Lecture he said that dialectical materialism's focus on modifying things as the basis for modifying persons was nothing less than "putting morality on vacation."[2] As Thomas C. Anderson, who has also commented on the Rome Lecture in his book on Sartre's ethics, aptly writes, "Those who reduce norms to facts also reduce all history to the evolution of practico-inert systems, Sartre complains. In doing so, they eliminate human agents and their praxes."[3] Taken as a moment in his massive body of work, the Rome Lecture represented a crucial endeavor to shore up the old existentialist contention that our acts are freely chosen, after the *Critique* had argued so strongly for the weight of structures and other-direction in affecting those acts. Anderson makes the point that during the 1950s, Sartre became a political realist—which had the effect of explaining (or even explaining away) Stalin's horrific acts. "Though he was uneasy with this position," Anderson writes, "he says that he held it until the 1960s."[4]

In my discussion of the Rome Lecture, I will focus on Sartre's description of and justification for the actions of Algerian revolutionaries, about which he wrote in the longest section of the manuscript, entitled "The Roots of the

---

1   Stone and Bowman, "Dialectical Ethics," 211.
2   Sartre, "Rome Lecture Typed Manuscript," 1.
3   Thomas C. Anderson, *Sartre's Two Ethics: From Authenticity to Integral Humanity* (Chicago: Open Court, 1993), 116.
4   Ibid., 111.

Ethical." I take this approach for two reasons—one that is internal to the body of his work, another that aims to contextualize it in the broader current of critiques of colonialism and neocolonialism. First, I wish to supplement my earlier discussion of the *Critique* by describing precisely what was left out of that book's depiction of colonialism and racism—what Sartre took to be the means of combating them. Although, just as in the *Critique*, racism and colonialism are used as extreme examples demonstrating a more general process of alienation and collective serialization, I wish to take seriously the fact that he chose these particular examples, and not some other examples, to demonstrate "the roots of the ethical." They seem to have been meaningful for him in more than a simply instrumental way. Second, I wish to fold Sartre's arguments into the broader process of the critique of neocolonialism in the 1960s and what I argue was a new set of intellectual engagements, whose justification was grounded in an enlarged, cosmopolitan understanding of personal responsibility.

THE ONTOLOGICAL STRUCTURE OF THE NORM AND THE ROOTS OF THE ETHICAL

The broad purpose of the lecture was to discover "the ontological structure of the norm when it is purified of the system's inertia,"[5] and ultimately to argue for a minimally universalist basis for ethical action once this structure had been revealed. To do this, Sartre began by examining everyday ethical experience through a discussion of how people individually enact (or, as he terms it later in the lecture, "incarnate") norms, imperatives, and values.[6] This he did in direct debate with the positivist understanding of norms as facts, which has the effect of marginalizing the meaning of their perception by any individual agent. Though he seems to have agreed with much of the picture given by positivists —indeed, with the view that specific norms are created through repetition over time—he argued that this gave only a partial picture. Instead, the objective character of the norm is that it is "given as *my* possibility," which is "objective" for Sartre because it is at the same time the possibility of another. Thus, he replaced the repetition of the positivist with his own concept of seriality, developed in the *Critique*. Though given, any particular norm is given only insofar as it "designates me as the possible subject of my act." No matter what its

---

5   Sartre, "Rome Lecture Typed Manuscript," 47.

6   Anderson points out that these terms are not interchangeable, and that "norms" is the generic term. Following him, I will focus in these comments, as Sartre does, on "the norm." See Anderson, *Sartre's Two Ethics*, 114.

content—again, Sartre was trying to discern its ontological structure—the norm is *my possibility of producing myself as a subject.*[7] In a striking conclusion to the section, Sartre asserted that "morality and praxis are one"[8]—that all action is moral in character, although there are different kinds of morality, as he would soon explain. In making this claim, he once again foregrounded the temporal character of specifically human activity: as in *Being and Nothingness*, every act is in some way a choice of a future. "The normative," he wrote, "is thus in principle the temporalization of praxis beginning with its unconditional end"—the unconditional end here meaning the possibility of producing oneself as an unalienated, whole human being. "But this structure," he continued, "is not necessarily given in its purity. It appears in times of insurrection."[9]

It is in the second section of the lecture, "The Roots of the Ethical," that Sartre developed this relationship between the "purified" norm—which aims at producing the "integral human"[10]—and revolutionary action. He began by substantially summarizing his discussion in the *Critique* of colonialism both as a historical process and as a set of everyday practices that continuously reproduce structures of alienation and serial collectivities. Yet there is a marked difference here in the way that he talked about the production of values. Recall that, in the *Critique*, Sartre described colonial racism as a "system of other values, entirely governed by alterity,"[11] that arose under the very particular circumstances of the colonization of Algeria, and that was intimately linked with the need for cheap labor and the institution of a regime of "super-exploitation." There is the implication that a new set of values—indeed, not just new, but *better*—might be produced if the circumstances were right. Obviously, if the mode of production were to change, these values would also change. But what precisely is involved in changing the mode of production? Or, to follow Bowman and Stone, if we accept the claim that colonialism as a system is so

7   Sartre, "Rome Lecture Typed Manuscript," 12.
8   Ibid., 50.
9   Ibid., 50–1. For a fuller picture of Sartre's arguments, see the excellent summary in Elizabeth A. Bowman and Robert V. Stone, " 'Socialist Morality' in Sartre's Unpublished *1964 Rome Lecture*: A Summary and Commentary," in William L. McBride, ed., *Existentialist Ethics* (New York: Routledge, 1996); and Robert V. Stone and Elizabeth A. Bowman, "Sartre's *Morality and History*: A First Look at the Notes for the Unpublished 1965 Cornell Lectures," in Ronald Aronson and Adrian van den Hoven, eds, *Sartre Alive* (Detroit: Wayne State University Press, 1991), 53–82.
10   Anderson's comments on "integral humanity" as the goal of Sartre's ethics are especially illuminating. See Anderson, *Sartre's Two Ethics*, Chs 7 and 8.
11   Sartre, *Critique*, 720.

anti-human "as to require all humans to seek [its] overthrow as a matter of moral priority, in favor of some more human future, then how can this task be accomplished in an effective and morally defensible manner?"[12] And is there an easy correspondence between changes in the mode of production and the invention of new values? After all, values can be remarkably persistent things.

In the Rome Lecture, Sartre moved away from pure description of the production of values, which perhaps left the impression that he believed them to be mere effects of a system, toward prescription—a move he had to make in order to avoid his own charge of positivism. Yet, again, it must be stressed that he did not appear to have rejected all the claims of the positivist approach: the contents of norms are indeed multiple, derived from history and situation. Where Sartre differed was in ascribing an ontological structure to the norm: it always aims at the creation of the integral human. Unfortunately for humanity, however, in giving this norm specific form in concrete circumstances, individuals mostly misfire in their determination to "incarnate" this ontological structure. This is what Sartre called "alienated" morality—a prescriptive function that, in its aim of creating conditions for people to lead freer, more human lives, instead produces alienating structures that dominate them. For Sartre, colonialism as a system represented an alienated morality—but, importantly, a morality nonetheless. Sartre insisted that the colonizer was a moral agent just as all humans are, and that all his actions aimed at creating integral man—it is just that "his ethics consists not in defending man in the immediate, but in aiming at him through a system."[13] Under colonialism, individuals' moral intentions were misdirected because of the mystification involved in being part of the process of colonization.

This seems like a return to the old definition of bad faith—the colonizer may "mean well" in her harmful acts; but, in contrast with his earlier defense of radical freedom, Sartre placed great obstacles in the way of overcoming it. A moral agent who is situated in a position of domination can only gain clarity on the "real" consequences of her actions by extreme measures—siding with Algerian revolutionaries against her own government, for example. Still, for most among the colonizers this may be nearly impossible; Sartre held out more hope only for those in the metropole, who, though implicated, were not direct participants in the "infernal machine." Unfortunately, colonizers lived an impossible ethical contradiction: their praxis, like all human praxis, must make

---

12   Bowman and Stone, " 'Socialist Morality,' " 166. In their essay, they cite capitalism and bureaucratic socialism as the anti-human systems requiring overthrow.

13   Sartre, "Rome Lecture Typed Manuscript," 67.

"integral man" its meaning and its goal; and yet, "the basis on which he makes history commands him, *in his very praxis*, to reduce historical future to his own private future."[14] Thus, the ethics of the colonizer represented an extreme alienation, bordering on the positivist definition of it: "The ethics of the colonizer is an *ethics of repetition*. This is in contrast with the ethics of the metropolitan citizen, who maintains at least an abstract future conceived through the form of a slow evolution."[15] Still, Republican claims of "liberty, fraternity, and equality" could only take people in the metropole so far—even though they may be admirable and ultimately desirable goals—since they were at this point in history quite contentless, because their implementation through colonialism had had the effect of creating their opposite. Recasting Kantian ethics, Sartre wrote of colonialist morality,

> The first characteristic of these [colonialist] norms, is that the subhumanity of the *indigène* is not an objectively detectable fact, but a value to be maintained. And super-exploitation … is a categorical imperative: "Act in such a way that you always treat the *indigène* as an inessential means and never as an end."[16]

In this way, Sartre dispensed with the alienated moralities (both colonizer and metropolitan) of the most favored—but how did he justify his claim that the morality of the "least favored"[17] (the colonized, in this case) is closer to the purified ontological structure of the norm? Why is their morality not also alienated? Indeed, he argued that it, too, represented at that moment in time an alienated morality. It was in the context of their activity, however, that Sartre finally set forth his ideas on the possibility of resistance and on the criteria for right action. He did so by returning obliquely to the central anthropological motor of the *Critique*—scarcity; that is, by introducing need as the authentic basis of morality, as the "root of the ethical." Need, in Sartre's view, is what helps us decide correctly between conflicting imperatives in order to "[defend] man in the immediate"—and not just in the abstract.

Identifying need as the key criterion for an authentic ethics allowed Sartre to do several things. First, it gave him a prime mover for revolutionary action, and in this case for anticolonial resistance in Algeria. "It is a question," he wrote,

---

14   Ibid., 73.
15   Ibid., 72.
16   Ibid., 63.
17   I use the single term "least favored" throughout, because I think it captures best Sartre's intent. His description of conflict in the Rome Lecture refers to *classes défavorisées/exploitées/opprimées* (often switching between these three—and almost always plural) versus a *classe dominante* or, infrequently, *classes dominantes*.

of a counter-violence that is directly linked to the material structure of the *indigène*. However, it cannot release itself without making itself normative, because it proclaims the end of the subhumanity of man. It is the very root of the ethical, its eruption at the deepest level of materiality. In considering the Algerian struggle, we see that the anticipating movement took root *in need*.[18]

Second, it allowed him to separate individuals from the systems that create them—for Sartre did indeed hold that individuals are the products of systems, but that each person incarnates the world individually (as a "singular universal"). Yet the fact that the human organism has any needs at all proves, in Sartre's eyes, that it is to some degree independent of the practico-inert; no matter how restricted the circumstances, need shows an organism to be self-producing: "Through need, the organism has to remake itself in *remaking* the world around it: illuminated by the possible beyond the impossible, the environment becomes the *practical field*."[19]

In short, need "is the first rudiment of a dialectical future, the first praxis of the negation of a negation, the first unconditioned end, the first normative structure." From this, Sartre said, "We say that the colonized has as an unconditioned end the realization in his person of integral man. Simply because he claims, through the system and against it, the possibility of reproducing his *bare life* [*sa vie nue*]."[20] Importantly, needs are not blind givens, but rather felt exigencies. They include freedom (of course) and bodily requirements to sustain life (nourishment, protein), but, as Anderson points out, Sartre ultimately went further, including "our need for others, in particular for their love and valuation. He refers to our need for knowledge, for a meaningful life, and for culture, and insists that without the latter we would not become human."[21] He then aimed to show concretely, using the example of resistance to colonialism in Algeria, "the dialectic through which impossibility changes itself, in and through need itself, into the possibility of man beyond all systems."[22]

---

18   Ibid., 76–7.
19   Ibid., 79. Bowman and Stone make the important definitional point: " 'Humanity' is a rich concept designating a multi-faceted entity. Humanity's root is in need. Need is not reducible to preference (as liberal economic theory would have it); rather it posits a future satisfaction, and, thereby, continued life." Bowman and Stone, " 'Socialist Morality,' " 170.
20   Sartre, "Rome Lecture Typed Manuscript," 76.
21   Anderson, *Sartre's Two Ethics*, 148–9.
22   Sartre, "Rome Lecture Typed Manuscript," 80, 81.

THE THREE PHASES OF RESISTANCE

It is at this point that Sartre's ideas on revolutionary action and ethics coalesce
—around a discussion of the history (in three "phases") of resistance to colonialism and revolution in Algeria and the actions of both its leaders and the
broader populace. In this sense, it serves as a nice counterbalance to the
Critique's treatment of colonialism almost exclusively from the point of view of
the colonizers; it reintroduces in a serious way the agency of subject peoples
and the historical significance of failed efforts that one might intuit were necessary to a full account on Sartre's model, but that are so sorely lacking in that
text. It may also be true that much of what Sartre wrote in this section was an
attempt to justify philosophically both his and Fanon's views in *The Wretched
of the Earth*. But instead of embarking on a headlong rush into proclaiming the
existence, and hence necessity, of violence, Sartre aimed squarely at establishing the ethical content and the limits of violent action.

In the three phases of anticolonial resistance Sartre described, individual
anticolonial praxis passed from a purely negative struggle for restitution of the
precolonial ways of life to an alienated consciousness that aimed toward an
impossible (because structurally disallowed) assimilation to the colonizer's
culture and values, and finally to the recognition of the failure of assimilation
and the simultaneous grasping of the colonized's true position in a system of
domination. This schematic (and by the 1960s, perhaps banal) interpretation
of events is accompanied by a more novel and interesting set of arguments
concerning the morality associated with each phase. Throughout the discussion, Sartre kept his focus trained on an element of particular significance: the
willingness—the choice—to put one's own life at risk as both evidence of and
part of the very logic of the normative response to colonialism, or any other
inhuman system. He wanted to argue that each phase involved a refusal which
was in principle the same, but different in content each time: the refusal of a
conditioning that restricted the colonized's possibilities to live humanly—that
is, to live in such a way that their needs might (one day) be satisfied. In short, it
was the closing down of that future possibility through the denial of autonomy
that prompted the colonized's refusals. Sartre was on delicate ground here, as
he did not want to say that Algerians' ways of life during the time of Abd al-
Kader already represented the possibility of humanity; in fact, this was a case of
competition between two alienated moralities, two moralities "of repetition."
Rather, his view was that, had autonomy been maintained, the Algerians'
future would have remained perhaps more open toward this possibility. The
aim of the system of colonialism, he argued, was to make the humanity of the

colonized "rigorously impossible." But the very fact of living, breathing, needing *indigènes*, gave the lie to the system, demonstrating instead the "normative impossibility of not being human."[23] This fundamental contradiction was the ethical basis of resistance from 1830 up to 1962, taking different objective forms along the way, until finally the entire system itself became the target.

The role that risking one's own life played in this struggle was absolutely crucial: it was only in risking life that those who had nothing could oppose concretely the set of values of those who dominated them. To the dominant "bourgeois" values that said "Life at all costs," the values of the least favored said, "Not *this* life." It was only in this naked refusal, the most fundamental form of refusal possible, that a system as powerful as colonialism began to totter, because "the force of a system, whichever it may be, is that it is maintained by human agents who want above all to live." In grim, even grisly terms, he continued, "Through their only real refusal, which is assumed risk of death, the agents once again become subjects in so far as they produce their own death … and at the same moment the system once again becomes an exterior object."[24] Interestingly, this conclusion concerning the effect of putting one's life at risk is different from Sartre's conclusions in the text on Lumumba, and also rather different from the *Critique*. In those works, he emphasized the role of risk-taking in the creation of bonds of reciprocity. That is, it is through both risking my life and putting my life in the hands of my fellows that common action can truly be forged. By contrast, in the Rome Lecture he talked of resistance from the perspective of atomized individuals grasping at the only means at their disposal to refuse; this was morality lived individually, first and foremost. At this level, it was still a desperate refusal and not, as it was in the preface to *Wretched*, a triumphant and quasi-messianic one.

This was a significant change in tone, and it can perhaps be accounted for if we take into consideration the failures, the disappointments, and the ambiguities of the end of colonialism that were already in evidence by 1964—and that were amply demonstrated by the events in the Congo in 1960–61. In the Rome Lecture, messianic rhetoric is absent; Sartre does not optimistically announce the invention of new men, as both he and Fanon had, in vague terms, in 1961. Instead, just as in his text on Lumumba, he recognized the force of a new set of arrangements:

---

23   Ibid., 102.
24   Ibid., 105.

The transformation of colonialism into neocolonialism (that is, into imperialism: a nation is ruled from outside by keeping a tight grip on its economy, while at the same time according it the appearance of sovereignty) is lived ethically as the reintegration of the future into morality.

The subhuman is human in power: he becomes human through a long evolution, with which the neocolonialists offer to help him.

This new ethics is an effective illusion because it presents humans as the future of subhumans and places their autonomy at the end of a long development:

This means that one proposes that they restart the mystification of the preceding phase and that they alienate themselves in an ethics that consecrates their inferiority.

...

The evolution predicted by neocolonialist ethics consists in *the anticipated reification of future man.*

The subhuman thus defined is deprived by definition of praxis.

He does not have *to make himself* human, but to let it happen.

What is rejected here, and which is the deepest exigency of ethics, is the emancipation of subhumans by themselves.[25]

Consistently returning to the themes of self-production, autonomy, and the possibility of freedom, Sartre's ethics captured all of the early concerns evinced in texts like *Being and Nothingness*, "Black Orpheus," "Présence noire," and the *Notebooks*, recasting them for contemporary usage.

THE DIFFICULTIES OF SARTRE'S ETHICS: THE CASE OF THE ARAB-ISRAELI CONFLICT

Yet it is still hard to see how Sartre's ethics would help defend in all cases the values (and the potential human futures) of the least favored. Surely there must be cases in which the values of different groups of the least favored themselves conflict—then decidability would become very difficult, prompting questions such as: "Whose human needs are most demanding of satisfaction?" This conflict was perhaps most acutely "incarnated" for Sartre in the 1967 Six-Day War. "The Left is divided: How could I blame it, me who—like so many others —feel the Judeo-Arab conflict as a personal tragedy?" was the title of his

---

25 Ibid., 107–8. Sartre may well have been replying to Aron's *La tragédie algérienne* when he noted that the argument that "capitalism can bear the costs of decolonization much more easily than those of colonial warfare" represents just this transformation of colonialism into neocolonialism (107).

contribution to the special issue of *Le Nouvel Observateur* on the war.[26] Sartre had been a supporter of Israel since its foundation in 1948. As Jonathan Judaken notes, in "What Is Literature?" Sartre seemed to support the move-ment for an independent Palestine as a national liberation movement against British rule. Moreover, like many on the French Left, especially up to the Suez crisis in 1956, Israel was viewed not as an instance of colonialism, but rather as a place of refuge for a people who had suffered the worst form of tragedy during World War II. The tide began to turn around Suez, according to Judaken, "when Israelis were now coming to the aid of the French parachutists of Guy Mollet's Socialist government. Now Israel was no longer the humiliated but the humiliator, no longer the victim but the perpetrator."[27] Sartre's consistent defense of Israel's right to exist became a source of deep consternation to Arab intellectuals in the 1960s. Many had expected Sartre to be favorable to their cause based on his support for the FLN, as evinced in his preface to *The Wretched of the Earth*, and they were scandalized when he did not condemn what they saw as Israeli aggression in 1967.[28] By the time of the Six-Day War, when Sartre tried to straddle both sides of the conflict, Frantz Fanon's widow, Josie, was so infuriated by his attempts at neutrality that she requested that his preface be struck from all future editions of *Wretched*.[29]

Sartre's article in *Le Nouvel Observateur* was a reprint of his editorial from the massive June 1967 issue of *Les Temps Modernes* about Israel and the Arab states, which was finished just before the outbreak of the war. As Judaken tells it, Sartre began to take a greater interest in the Arab-Israeli conflict around 1965, "when he determined that Gamal Abdel Nasser's politics were beginning to develop in a revolutionary direction. In this context he sought to open a

26   Jean-Paul Sartre, " 'La gauche est divisée: Comment pourrais-je l'en blamer, moi qui—comme tant d'autres—ressens le conflit judéo-arabe comme un drame personnel?' " *Le Nouvel Observateur*, June 14–20, 1967.

27   Jonathan Judaken, *Jean-Paul Sartre and the Jewish Question: Anti-antisemitism and the Politics of the French Intellectual* (Lincoln: University of Nebraska Press, 2006), 198; see also 187–8.

28   In interviews with *Al-Ahram* journalist Lutfi El-Khori that year, Sartre appeared to try to take a Camusian position of silence on the conflict between Israelis and Arabs. The reaction in Egypt was not positive. Sartre was so concerned that Egyptians did not under-stand his support for the plight of the Palestinians that he called El-Khori to try to help correct the record, to little avail. See Amina Elbendary, "Of Words and Echoes," *Al-Ahram Weekly* 477 (April 13–19, 2000), available at <weekly.ahram.org>. Elbendary's article is based on El-Khori's book, *Bertrand Russell and Sartre* (1968), which contains the interviews with Sartre, and which has never been translated from Arabic. Another strong voice of ambiva-lence concerning Sartre is that of Edward Said in "Sartre and the Arabs: a footnote," *Al-Ahram Weekly* 482 (May 18–24, 2000), available at <weekly.ahram.org >.

29   Judaken, *Jean-Paul Sartre and the Jewish Question*, 196.

dialogue between the Egyptian Left and the Israeli Left."[30] Toward the end of the year, he granted an interview to the Egyptian newspaper *Al-Ahram* in which he announced his intention to publish the special issue on the Arab-Israeli conflict, which was intended to represent both sides from a politically neutral perspective.

As part of the preparation for the special issue, Sartre and Beauvoir traveled to the Middle East on a three-week journey through Egypt and Israel in early 1967. In each country, he met with prominent academics, journalists, artists, and politicians, including Nasser. At his final news conference, he maintained his position of neutrality on the conflict, much to the dismay of his Arab interlocutors. Adding to the frustration, on the eve of the war, Sartre signed a manifesto circulated among French intellectuals that again attempted to straddle the fence, and which stressed Israelis' and Arabs' "rigorously incompatible" views of the conflict.[31]

Indeed, Sartre was not able to resolve the struggle within himself regarding his support for—and perhaps also his disagreement with—these two "rigorously incompatible" views. As Judaken tells it, Sartre continued in his efforts to take a balanced view, and "to recommend changes in the positions of both sides." For example,

> He suggested that Israel should evacuate the occupied territories, give the Palestinians sovereignty, and ensure equality between Arab and Israeli citizens. At the same time, he spurred the Palestinians to recognize the right of Israel to exist and to accept the right of every Jew … to have the right to immigrate to Israel.[32]

In Judaken's judgment, Sartre's positions were more balanced than those of most of the French Left, which had turned sharply against Israel in the wake of the Six-Day War, viewing the Palestinians as the new Algerian cause.

The possibility of conflicts among groups of the "least favored" raises a number of other significant problems. "The Corrèze before Zambezi," wrote journalist Raymond Cartier in *Paris-Match* in 1956, giving birth to the important doctrine that came to be known as Cartierism, in which domestic concerns are given priority over foreign ones by default.[33] Whatever Cartier's own

30   Judaken, *Jean-Paul Sartre and the Jewish Question*, 190–1.
31   Ibid., 191–5.
32   Ibid., 199.
33   See Yves Lacoste, *Contre les anti-tiers-mondistes, et contre certain tiers-mondistes* (Paris: Editions de la Découverte, 1985), 14–15; and Wall, *France, the United States, and the Algerian War*, 195. The French formulation is more graceful: *La Corrèze avant le Zambèze*.

motives may have been in formulating his maxim, not only did it have a significant influence on French foreign policy—it also represented two challenges to
the views under discussion here. First, it expressed for the domain of foreign
policy the values of patriotism so important to the Gaullist era: I should interest
myself in the least favored of my own community before the least favored of
those outside of my community. Second, by noting the plurality of groups
of disfavored people, no matter what borders divide them, it gave rise to
the insight that even outside my community, the "least favored" are a highly
heterogeneous lot, with varying and possibly conflicting needs. To the first
objection, Sartre might have replied that the norm to help people create their
own human futures should not lead to a conflict about whether to prioritize
Corrèze or Zambezi—both could be attended to. Though this is not really
a reply to patriotism as a value, it is an effective way of sidestepping it. On a
deeper level, however, it is clear that, for Sartre, the equation of the national
community with a moral community represented an "alienated" morality.
Sartre always condemned French patriotism, particularly in his attacks on de
Gaulle, yet his frequent references to the French Revolution and support for
national liberation movements make it clear that the establishment of national
communities did play an important historical role in creating the possibility of
an "unconditioned end," if only a limited one. Ultimately, however, his universalist emphasis on *human* needs as the "roots of the ethical" explicitly negated
the value of the national community as an absolute basis for the evaluation of
moral claims. The second objection is far trickier, because navigating it necessarily depends upon extensive knowledge and evaluation of local situations.
The norm itself is vague enough that it might be invoked by competing sides—
in a civil war, for example, or in the case of the conflicting claims of Israelis and
Palestinians. On the issue of evaluating competing claims based on genuine
human need, it is difficult to guess how Sartre might have replied.

Another problem with Sartre's account of ethics, particularly as an expression of its era, is that it did not explicitly address the legitimacy or illegitimacy
of terrorist action, defined as the targeting of civilians for political ends—one
of the most controversial issues of his day, as Aron's and others' criticisms
demonstrated. Sartre addressed violence, in particular revolutionary violence,
both as a legitimate response to systems of oppression and as a means of liberation, but he seems to have been speaking generally about wars of liberation and,
specifically, guerilla wars, such as the ones undertaken in Algeria and Cuba. He
generally avoided the question of whether progressive revolutionary violence
may include, for example, killing teenagers in a bar, as had also occurred in
Algeria. This is an important distinction to make, because many commentators

on Sartre's "Third Worldist" texts—such as Aron—appear to have made the assumption that by "violence" he meant terrorism thus defined. This is perhaps because of the famous sentence in his preface to *Wretched*:

> To shoot down a European is to kill two birds with one stone, to destroy an oppressor and the man he oppresses at the same time: there remain a dead man and a free man; the survivor, for the first time, feels a *national* soil under his foot.[34]

Yet even here, it is unclear that Sartre was advocating as a rule the murder of noncombatants—as it is also unclear who would be considered a noncombatant in a situation in which physical violence or its threat were common enough among civilians. The text itself is ambiguous.[35]

One instance in which he did reveal his thoughts on the deliberate targeting of civilians concerns the Palestinian Liberation Organization's (PLO) massacre of Israeli athletes at the Olympics in Munich in 1972. Sartre defended the PLO's actions—and was one of the few French intellectuals to do so. His defense was partly motivated by consistency—based on the fact that he had defended the actions of the FLN, and this act was similar to some of the attacks on civilians they had undertaken. He also believed them to have been a "terrible" and "horrible" necessity, as he put it at the time.[36] Presumably, on his view, they were a necessary consequence of a deeply alienated morality produced by deeply alienating conditions of life—and an attempt to refuse that life. But the form of the refusal was "horrible" and "terrible" to him. Assassinating innocent athletes was an inhuman act, even if it was a necessary one in his view—a view that set him against many of his friends on the Left, including some of his colleagues at *La Cause du Peuple*.

I would suggest, from my reading of the *Critique* and the Rome Lecture, that there is a distinction between violence as a war of liberation and violence as terrorism (as defined above) in those texts—but a rather fine one that is often difficult to tease out. In the end, as his comments on the PLO's massacre show, Sartre did justify both, though for different reasons. Violence undertaken as guerilla action in a war of liberation represented for Sartre that norm of aiming toward an integral humanity quite unequivocally, since it aims at destroying

---

34   Jean-Paul Sartre, "Preface to *The Wretched of the Earth*," in *Colonialism and Neocolonialism*, 148.

35   For two reassessments of Sartre and violence, see Ronald E. Santorini, *Sartre on Violence: Curiously Ambivalent* (University Park: Pennsylvania State University Press, 2003); and Aronson, *Camus and Sartre*.

36   See the account in Judaken, *Jean-Paul Sartre and the Jewish Question*, 201.

the systems that prevent that humanity from appearing. As for terrorism, it seems in Sartre's account to be an alienated, atomistic response to intolerable conditions of life experienced by the least favored in an inhuman system; it is serialized "counter-violence." It represents itself an alienated morality, but one that is directly produced by the inhuman system imposed on the colonized: "It [terror] springs from the masses, and the leaders must take it back in their turn. But in taking it back, they have to denounce it and define its character." Specifically, they have to prevent such actions from institutionalizing themselves, from forming a system. If that were to happen, if terrorists began to invent morals "of suspicion (vigilance), denunciation, lies (publicized optimism, hidden truth) ... [m]anicheism ... [i]deology of socialism in a single country," or if terror were to "*make men* ... the instruments of terror and the objects of terror," then the hoped-for end would be lost.[37] If the means change the end, Sartre emphasized, then the means must be disallowed. Drawing such a fine distinction between armed struggle and terrorism certainly would not have satisfied critics such as Aron—had they known about it. Nonetheless, the fact that there is a distinction demonstrates at the very least an awareness that terrorism was an extremely thorny issue, and one to be taken seriously.

Finally, one could make the objection that Sartre's ethics give no clear reasons why a person who has no contact with the "oppressed" should care about the claims of these least-favored human beings. Why not just leave them alone—in effect, give them the autonomy Sartre said everyone desires? This was perhaps one of the central issues of French radical activity in the 1960s, fixed as it was on revolutions and personal heroes in far-away countries. Sartre might reply that, given increasing global interdependence, there was no longer any space in which to "leave people alone." Beyond this, however, he made a more dramatic and fundamental case: acting in accordance with the ontological structure of the norm amounts to exactly the same thing as supporting the claims of the least favored in situations of oppression. My acts, were they to discount the needful claims of the least favored, would contradict the norm; this is precisely what alienated moralities allow us to do. To cast it in the old terms, this is bad faith. Thus, there seem to be two levels of argument: on one level, Sartre seems to have argued that "connectedness" may do much to account for our responsibility; yet on another, our responsibility is defined simply by our belonging to a species that aims to "become" human.

Though Sartre provided only broad arcs and minimal clues to follow in order to enact the norm for producing integral humans in an increasingly

---

37   Sartre, "Rome Lecture Typed Manuscript," 134.

interconnected world filled with multiple alienated moralities, his Rome Lecture itself followed the arcs and clues of contemporary critiques of neocolonialism (or, in his own equation, imperialism), attempting to give them some much-needed ethical support. Stone and Bowman summarize this with their characteristic succinctness:

> We will look in vain among Sartre's dialectical ethics for general rules or principles of right action. Clearly for Sartre, no such positive norm is required to justify revolutionary praxis. If "need is its satisfaction's own justification," then the moral burden of proof lies not on those who want reliably to satisfy their hunger and thirst, but instead on any who would allow systematic denial of these and other needs.[38]

Such is the moral basis for a broad individual responsibility to support the claims of those who experience extreme poverty, systemic violence, lack of real political self-determination, and other limitations on freedom. Since, however, the contents of the Rome Lecture were not diffused widely, it was left to a more mediatized event to publicize his views. As the 1960s progressed, Sartre found —along with a host of activists, young and old alike—a new cause célèbre: the war in Vietnam.

---

38   Stone and Bowman, "Dialectical Ethics," 209.

CHAPTER NINE

Vietnam and Bolivia:
Two Battles, Two Intellectuals

After he delivered his address on ethics to the Gramsci Institute in May 1964, Sartre accepted an invitation from Cornell University to give a series of lectures the following year. He intended to talk about his views on ethics and the ongoing project on Flaubert. But the lectures never took place. In the intervening time, the US Congress had passed the Gulf of Tonkin resolution, the US military had begun extensive bombing campaigns, and Sartre cancelled his plans in protest at US escalation of the war in Vietnam.[1]

Sartre's interest in Vietnam found its way into many of his works from 1965 onward, beginning with his lectures given in Tokyo and Kyoto in the fall of 1965, later published as *A Plea for the Intellectuals*. But his knowledge of events there likely preceded that time. *Les Temps Modernes*'s first salvo in the fight against escalation came in the form of Hugh Deane's November 1963 essay, "The War in Vietnam," which opened with a quote from none other than Bertrand Russell: "The United States government is conducting a war of annihilation in Vietnam."[2] In May 1965, André Gorz announced: "The American aggression is a crime."[3] In *A Plea for the Intellectuals*, Sartre outlined his views on the duties of the intellectual, often making reference to the events unfolding in Vietnam. He defined the intellectual as a technician of practical knowledge who exits her own domain in order to comment on matters that do not concern her. Just as he indicated in the Rome Lecture, there is no ideal theory to guide her: she applies her position by "feeling it out ... she undertakes a practical activity of discovery."[4] To be a true intellectual, one must lend one's voice and one's symbolic capital to the least favored. Because there is no

---

1 See Jean-Paul Sartre (interview), "Il n'y a plus de dialogue possible," *Le Nouvel Observateur*, April 1, 1965, reprinted in Sartre, *Situations, VIII, Autour de 68* (Paris: Gallimard, 1972). A large sheaf of handwritten notes for the lecture can be found at the Beinecke Rare Book & Manuscript Library, John Gerassi Collection of Jean-Paul Sartre, GEN MSS 411, Series II: "Other Papers," Box 4.

2 Hugh Deane, "La guerre au Vietnam," *Les Temps Modernes* 210 (November 1963), 934.

3 André Gorz, "Le test vietnamien," *Les Temps Modernes* 228 (May 1965), 1924, reprinted in Gorz, *Le socialisme difficile* (Paris: Editions du Seuil, 1967).

4 Jean-Paul Sartre, *Plaidoyer pour les intellectuels* (Paris: Gallimard, 1972), 58.

universal perspective one can take to have knowledge of the society in which one lives, since all perspectives are particularistic, Sartre said—perhaps surprisingly, as he had not used this argument before—that the intellectual must adopt the perspective of the least favored because they are the "*immense majority*, particularized by oppression and exploitation."[5] The intellectual should not do this uncritically, however. As a technician of practical knowledge, she has certain tools at her disposal: historical method, the analysis of structures, and "the dialectic" are the examples Sartre gave.[6] In short, the intellectual does not give directions, but rather makes distinctions, provides clarity; she follows popular intuitions, but she refines them, sometimes criticizing them.

THE RUSSELL INTERNATIONAL WAR CRIMES TRIBUNAL

This is the role that Sartre aimed to play in investing more than one year of his time in the Russell Tribunal.[7] In his activism against the war in Vietnam, Sartre seemed to find a clear-cut case of "least favored" peoples obliging intellectuals to lend them their support through determined fact-finding, clarification of the issues, and critical assessment. At the conclusion of the Tribunal, he described the US intervention in the starkest possible terms—"It is the greatest power on earth against a poor peasant people"[8]—and argued that the massive imbalance of power and the methods of war represented nothing less than a genocidal intent on the part of the US government—an intent that followed directly from the fact of an industrialized nation making war on an unindustrialized one.[9] It can be debated, as it was vigorously at the time, whether or not the Tribunal succeeded in achieving Sartre's intellectual goal of providing clarity on the myriad of issues involved in the war. Nonetheless, the diversity of the witnesses (from American ex-soldiers, to historians of Asia, to academics

---

5   Ibid., 61.

6   Ibid., 69.

7   Judaken argues that Sartre also applied this new model of intellectual activity to the Arab-Israeli conflict. See Judaken, *Jean-Paul Sartre and the Jewish Question*, 191. For a survey of peoples' tribunals that also gives an account of the Russell Tribunal, see Arthur Jay Klinghoffer and Judith Apter Klinghoffer, *International Citizens' Tribunals: Mobilizing Public Opinion to Advance Human Rights* (New York: Palgrave, 2002).

8   Jean-Paul Sartre, "On Genocide," in John Duffett, ed., *Against the Crime of Silence: Proceedings of the Russell International War Crimes Tribunal* (New York: Bertrand Russell Peace Foundation, 1968), 625.

9   For an assessment of Sartre's claims of genocidal intent, see Lawrence J. LeBlanc, "The Intent to Destroy Groups in the Genocide Convention: The Proposed US Understanding," *American Journal of International Law* 78, No. 2 (April 1984), 381–2.

sent to the field to gain knowledge of events "on the ground"), along with the orchestrated publicity, indicated that one of the main goals of the endeavor was public education. As Sartre put it, "What we wish is to maintain, thanks to the collaboration of the press, a constant contact between ourselves and the masses who in all parts of the world are living and suffering the tragedy of Vietnam."[10]

Moreover, Sartre seems to have considered the Russell Tribunal a forum for putting political morality into practice—necessary since it had been "put on vacation," to borrow the terms of the Rome Lecture, by de Gaulle's regime. De Gaulle, though critical of the US war in Vietnam, opposed having the Tribunal meet on French soil and denied an entry visa to its Yugoslavian chairman, Vladimir Dedijer. Sartre then wrote a letter to the president, asking him both to admit Dedijier and to permit the meeting of the Tribunal, by invoking the rights to free speech and to association. In his response, de Gaulle argued that, since justice could emanate from no other entity than the state, the purported "justice" to be dispensed by any independent tribunal would be "acting against that very thing which it is seeking to uphold."[11] Sartre, now replying to de Gaulle, seized upon this equation of justice with the state to condemn, as he had been doing since 1958, what he took to be the general's anti-democratic conception of politics, by which he placed himself and the state at a remove from the French people. For de Gaulle, it was the leader's responsibility—and his alone—to criticize the actions of another government.

Sartre also made a rather different—and significant—argument here. "I want to emphasize this point," he wrote.

> In forbidding us to meet, de Gaulle invokes among other things the 'traditional friendship' linking us to the United States. That clearly means … that as soon as it becomes a question of making a moral judgment, governments pull back. There is a widespread attempt to suppress the idea of political morality.[12]

Académie Française member, long-time anti-communist, and *Le Figaro* columnist Thierry Maulnier thought that, whatever evidence was presented at the Tribunal, its undertaking was too "political" to be "moral." Upon the opening

---

10   Jean-Paul Sartre, "Inaugural Statement to the Tribunal," in Duffett, *Against the Crime of Silence*, 44.

11   "Letter from de Gaulle to Sartre," in Duffett, *Against the Crime of Silence*, 28. In a perhaps more convincing and eloquent argument, de Gaulle wrote, "Let me add that to the extent that some of those allied with Lord Russell represent a moral value outside the public legal machinery, it does not seem to me that they add to that value or to the weight of their arguments by assuming robes borrowed for the occasion." (Ibid.)

12   Jean-Paul Sartre, "Answer and Commentary to de Gaulle's Letter Banning the Tribunal from France," in Duffett, *Against the Crime of Silence*, 35.

of the first session of the Tribunal, *Le Figaro* published Maulnier's front-page disquisition on the morality of the Tribunal's undertaking, which cited Sartre's contention on "political morality."[13] (Maulnier also hosted a public debate, sponsored by the Mouvement Fédéraliste Français, on the Tribunal and Sartre's "operation of psychological warfare.")[14] For Maulnier, such a declaration had no meaning coming from Sartre, whom he believed to be a hypocrite. According to Maulnier, a true morality must regard equally the crimes of both sides in a fight. A tribunal that refused to make the methods of the Vietcong part of its inquiry, or that, Maulnier guessed, would never sit in judgment on the crimes of Egyptian-backed forces in Yemen, could not render justice, because "it cannot situate itself at the same time at the heart of the battle and above the battle."[15] This argument from hypocrisy may have had broad appeal, as it resonated with the arguments of many during the French-Algerian War who condemned the methods of both sides—what Sartre referred to as the "respectful Left" (even if, in this case, Maulnier was not a man of the Left). But, of course, it also avoided the larger question, broached by Sartre, of why there was indeed no such standing tribunal to hold to account actors who violate international humanitarian law, why the "law of the jungle" prevailed instead of "ethical and juridical rules"[16]—why there was no independent international criminal court, in effect; which, Sartre argued, was because the European powers did not want to be held to account for their actions in the wars of colonialism and decolonization. "The Nuremberg Tribunal," Sartre wrote,

> was still fresh in people's minds when the French massacred forty-five thousand Algerians at Sétif, as an "example," but this sort of thing was so commonplace that no one even thought to condemn the French government in the same terms as they did the Nazis.[17]

---

13   Thierry Maulnier, "Violence et conscience: Un tribunal de combat," *Le Figaro*, May 2, 1967, 1, 28. Maulnier had also commented on Sartre's involvement with the case of Henri Martin. See Thierry Maulnier, "Henri Martin et Jean-Paul Sartre," *La Table Ronde* 72 (December 1953), 29–39. *La Table Ronde* was founded by Maulnier and François Mauriac after World War II.

14   "Un débat sur le 'tribunal' Bertrand Russel [*sic*]—Jean-Paul Sartre," *Le Figaro*, May 15, 1967, 4.

15   Maulnier, "Violence et conscience," 28.

16   Sartre, "Inaugural Statement to the Tribunal," 43.

17   Sartre, "On Genocide," 615. Indeed, when the French law on crimes against humanity was passed in 1964, it was written so as to make the only people punishable under it Germans who had participated in World War II. See Henry Rousso, *The Vichy Syndrome: History and Memory in France since 1944*, trans. Arthur Goldhammer (Cambridge: Harvard University Press, 1991); and Richard J. Golsan, ed., *The Papon Affair: Memory and Justice on Trial* (New York: Routledge, 2000).

Still, in the end, Maulnier essentially agreed with Sartre that the goal of the Tribunal was to open up the debate on morality—but for Maulnier, Sartre wished to "confuse" rather than to enlighten minds. To that end, nothing helped him more than the fact that the Tribunal was a "fiction," a "theatrical" spectacle aiming at a "psychological" effect—claims that Sartre the playwright might have appreciated. Maulnier might have noted here, though he did not, that the Tribunal's aims were only abetted by the subsequent denials of many heads of state to permit this "theater" on their soil, thus lending it the very legitimacy it lacked. Maulnier himself, in even discussing the legitimacy of the Tribunal, fell into the trap of taking seriously something he wished to describe as unserious. On these two points, Maulnier effectively summed up the main thrust of the arguments against the Russell Tribunal: justice that chooses a side cannot be justice; a tribunal that is outside the law is a sham, yet it seems to present a threat to the law real enough to require it to be banned.

With Maulnier's (correct) charge of partiality in mind, I would like to look at the Tribunal in this light: as a practical exercise in Sartre's ethics of a future integral humanity, as developed in the Rome Lecture. What, in this context of 1960s French protest against US imperialism, did engaging the "idea of political morality" mean? This might perhaps be summed up by a discussion of Sartre's essay "On Genocide." Unsurprisingly, the themes of that work resonate strongly with his other texts from the early-to-mid 1960s. In addition to references to the 1948 Geneva Convention, Sartre's description of the genocide he claimed the United States to be perpetrating on the Vietnamese relies heavily on his analysis of colonialism in the *Critique*. We find the same vocabulary of alienation and the same focus on super-exploitation, subhumanity, and the emphasis on racism as a set of values undergirding a process that involves, among other things, killing. Referring repeatedly to the history of colonization in Algeria, he argued that the overwhelming military superiority of the colonizing state put into motion a dialectic of repression and resistance, leading to massacres that, based on the 1948 Convention, he declared acts of genocide. But there are two key differences with the *Critique*. First is the fact that here Sartre made greater room for the introduction of the other side of the process: how the least favored could create the conditions of their own liberation. Second, Sartre gave the struggle an ethical dimension lacking in the *Critique*. Both of these "new" elements follow from his thinking in the Rome Lecture.

On the first point, Sartre placed the actions of Ho Chi Minh and the Vietcong—which he viewed as representatives of the will of the Vietnamese people, and not as one side in a civil war—in the framework of a refusal of intolerable options. Again, legitimately or not, he did this in the starkest terms possible: the

Vietnamese faced the choice of either submitting to US authority or being eliminated as a people. What is significant here is that he re-emphasized the willingness to risk life as the fundamental basis of that refusal. In this context, the role of guerrilla warfare was of key importance: "On Genocide" was an explicit justification of guerrilla tactics as the only response with any chance of success against overwhelming military superiority. The only thing a population as poor as the Vietnamese had going for it, on his account, was its sheer numbers—and, as a corollary, the willingness of many to choose death as a possibility.

On a deeper level, however, this justification of guerrilla warfare went beyond political realism. It also expressed the idea that, in Sartre's view, the guerrillas fought not just for their own lives, but for the existence of their community and for the possibility of creating an integral humanity through liberation struggles throughout the world. For Sartre, the "logical" response to guerrilla tactics was the very genocide he took the Americans to be conducting. "The Americans want to show others that guerrilla war does not pay," he wrote.

> They want to show all the oppressed ... in short, they want to show Latin America first of all, and more generally, all of the Third World. To Che Guevara who said, "We need several Vietnams," the American government answers, "They will all be crushed the way we are crushing the first."[18]

Thus, the structure of Sartre's argument leads to a justification of his support for the least favored: people who are the beneficiaries in a system of domination will stop at nothing—not even genocide—to maintain their hegemonic status. The United States could not act otherwise than it was acting at this particular moment, given its complex history of racism. "This racism—anti-black, anti-Asiatic, anti-Mexican—is a basic American attitude with deep historical roots and which existed, latently and overtly, well before the Vietnamese conflict," he claimed—glossing over the fact, of which he was well aware, that African- and Mexican-Americans also participated in the war. And, "Since 1966, the racism of Yankee soldiers, from Saigon to the 17th parallel, has become more and more marked."[19] The reason? Again, Sartre returned to guerrilla warfare, in which every Vietnamese becomes suspect as a possible abettor of the enemy, arguing,

---

18   Sartre, "On Genocide," 619.
19   Ibid., 623, 624. On his awareness of the disproportionate use of African-American soldiers in combat in Vietnam, see his questions to David Kenneth Tuck, an African-American ex-soldier who testified before the Tribunal. Duffett, *Against the Crime of Silence*, 415–16.

"From the neo-colonialists' point of view, this is true. They vaguely understand that in a people's war, civilians are the only visible enemies."[20] Thus, the population as a whole became the target, and the only way to free Vietnam was, in effect, to free it of the Vietnamese.[21] Hence, revolt was justified, and putting life in danger was the only true method of revolt under these particular circumstances. Although this line of reasoning did little to bring to light the complexities of the war in Vietnam, Sartre's emphasis on the function of risking one's life set into sharp relief the differences between it and the Congo: the Congo, which had no armed liberation struggle, was beholden to the very neocolonialist pressures that Vietnam was attempting to escape.

The centrality of putting one's life at risk in Sartre's argument dovetails with the second difference with the *Critique*—namely, the emphasis on determining the specifically ethical content of both the acts of Vietnamese revolt and of non-Vietnamese support for that revolt. As we have seen in the Rome Lecture, putting one's life at risk in a situation in which the possibility of satisfying basic organic, psychological, and social needs is being forcibly restricted is seen as an act that signifies a rejection of "*this* life." It forms the basis for the morality of the least favored, and it is the reason why everyone, no matter what their social position, should endeavor to help them—because it better expresses the norm of aiming toward an integral humanity than do the imperatives of one's own deeply alienated moralities. It is precisely this point that Sartre tried to bring to the fore in "On Genocide," by broadening the claim that the Vietnamese fought to preserve themselves and to establish the basis for a more human future to the claim that they were fighting for "all of us." This particular argument relies on two propositions. First, referring to geopolitics, Sartre said that, in fighting the war in Vietnam, the United States was attempting to establish a global hegemony, a "One World" as a form of globally integrated capitalism. The second is that, in resisting the United States, Vietnam was resisting the imposition, and thus the inexorability of the future possibility, of a "One World"—which, it goes without saying, was for Sartre

---

20   Sartre, "On Genocide," 624.

21   This claim about the war in Vietnam chillingly resurfaced in a series of Pulitzer Prize–winning articles about war crimes committed in 1967 by a US special forces team called the Tiger Force. Their efforts to clear a free-fire zone of Vietnamese farmers by relocating them to refugee camps turned into "emptying" the zone by killing the hundreds (no one really knows how many in all) of residents who refused to leave. Although the army investigated the team extensively and found evidence of war crimes, no one was ever charged. Of course, whether or not such acts can be cited as evidence of "genocidal intent" is another question. See Michael D. Sallah, Mitch Weiss, and Joe Mahr, "Buried Secrets, Brutal Truths," *Toledo Blade*, October 20, 2003, 1.

a system that aimed to constrain human freedom. Thus, in somewhat over-wrought terms, he wrote,

> The ties of the "One World," on which the United States wants to impose its hegemony, have grown tighter and tighter. For this reason, as the American government very well knows, the current genocide is conceived as an answer to people's war and perpetrated in Vietnam not against the Vietnamese alone, but against humanity.
>
> When a peasant falls in his rice paddy, mowed down by a machine gun, every one of us is hit. The Vietnamese fight for all men and the American forces against all. Neither figuratively nor abstractly.
>
> ...
>
> The group which the United States wants to intimidate and terrorize by way of the Vietnamese nation is the human group in its entirety.[22]

Here, in sweeping and unequivocal terms, Sartre captured the essence of the ethics he had described in the Rome Lecture.

As he had during the French-Algerian War, Sartre suggested that everyone was implicated to some degree, everyone bore some responsibility. In his articles on Algeria in the 1950s, Sartre claimed that, by not speaking out against abuses, French people were giving moral aid to the abusers. In the case of Vietnam, the stakes had apparently increased, and Sartre's claims had been correspondingly strengthened: since the ontological structure of the norm was to aim toward integral humanity, all people now were obliged in all their actions to strive toward that end. Doing so, on Sartre's account of ethics, implied recognizing the claims of the least favored, not as a matter of some form of collective guilt or compassionate identification, but as part of one's *own* process of leading a moral life that aims toward the norm itself. A negative "do no harm" is replaced by a more robust—though ill-defined—obligation to strive (as well as one can, given all the resistances of the practico-inert) toward integral humanity in all of one's actions. Building on the Rome Lecture, in "On Genocide," Sartre opposed a species-centered morality that required the denunciation of oppressive regimes to the alienated morality of the Americans' "One World," which aimed to extend an oppressive regime, in this case through armed invasion and massive bombing.

Although the organizers of the Tribunal feared a press boycott, there was worldwide newspaper, radio, and television coverage of the event—some of it in considerable depth, some of it superficial. As the interviewer from *Le Nouvel*

---

22   Sartre, "On Genocide," 626. He also seems to recast here an old claim of *Anti-Semite and Jew*: that the anti-Semite has a hatred of humanity.

Observateur politely put it in a conversation with Sartre, "Concerning the war in Vietnam, we had the impression that we already knew what we needed to know [before the Tribunal]."[23] "On Genocide" tapped into a great number of the contested issues of the period, typically concerning the power of the United States: mostly worries over the effect of such a concentration of military and economic might. These worries appear to fit with, or were even displacements of, other, more quotidian concerns over the modernization of French society and the changes in cultural products and social norms—all thought by contemporary observers to be strongly influenced by American-style consumer culture. Thus read, French anti-imperialism regarding US actions in Vietnam was, just as Sartre had indicated, itself an expression of a rejection of a "One World." This claim is made only elliptically in "On Genocide," but it is a claim he had stated forcefully a year earlier, on the occasion of the "Six Hours for Vietnam" protest marking the foundation of the Comité Vietnam National in November 1966—at which he received a standing ovation in recognition of having just signed on to the Russell Tribunal. In that speech he said, "We must show solidarity with the Vietnamese people because their fight is ours. It is the fight against American hegemony. Vietnam fights for us."[24]

But had the Russell Tribunal and Sartre's polemical closing argument changed the terms of the debate on Vietnam and anti-imperialism in France? Had Sartre's attempt to put morality back at the center of political conversation, at least on this particular issue, succeeded? Clearly, by casting US actions as genocide, perhaps one of the most ethically freighted words to have gained a lexical foothold in the postwar era, Sartre was throwing down the gauntlet of responsibility to the European and American publics—especially to the Americans, of whom he demanded that they oppose the actions of their government. This was, in effect, a reprise of the demand of the Manifesto of the 121: resist this unjust war, even if it is waged by your own government.[25]

---

23   Jean-Paul Sartre (interviewed by Serge Lafaurie), "Le génocide," *Le Nouvel Observateur*, December 6–12, 1967, 25.

24   Cited in Hamon and Rotman, *Génération, Vol. I*, 309.

25   Sartre makes explicit parallels between Algeria and Vietnam in "On Genocide." Surprisingly, however, David Schalk does not mention the Russell Tribunal in his study of French and US antiwar intellectuals, despite the participation of high-profile figures such as Stokely Carmichael and James Baldwin. He does note, however, that the American petition, "Call to Resist Illegitimate Authority," which he describes as "the single most influential petition of the Vietnam era," was directly inspired by the Manifesto of the 121. See David L. Schalk, *War and the Ivory Tower: Algeria and Vietnam* (New York: Oxford University Press, 1991), 44, 122–4.

If the aim of the Tribunal was to be a sort of "theater" in which the dialogue between witnesses and judges might force its audience to action, as Maulnier had claimed, the question remains what impact it really had in France. As a "show trial," did it create a new narrative on the war in Vietnam? Like the reporter from *Le Nouvel Observateur*, there is cause to take a skeptical view about effects—if only for the reason that many, if not most, French were already convinced of the injustice of the war. *Le Figaro*, aside from Maulnier's essay, devoted brief reports of the Tribunal's sessions in May and November, and simply ignored Sartre's final statement on genocide. *L'Express* did not report the sessions at all, although it ran a story announcing the Tribunal and describing de Gaulle's rejection of its meeting in France. *Le Monde* reported daily or every other day from the Tribunal, using a special reporter, Camille Olsen, for the second session, who described Sartre as reading "On Genocide" with "rigor and brio."[26] And, of course, *Le Nouvel Observateur* covered both sessions using both reporting and the interviews and texts of Sartre's. *L'Humanité* went from very little coverage during the first session to fuller coverage during the second.

In keeping with its coverage of the Tribunal, the French press was also fairly nonplussed by "On Genocide." The claim of US genocidal intent did not provoke any real debate in France; most observers may have taken the same view as the reporter from *Le Nouvel Observateur*, who pushed Sartre on the difference between the war the United States was conducting and other "total wars,"[27] indicating that he doubted there was a difference, and who also suggested to Sartre that, if it really were genocide, the US military presence would have been escalated much more rapidly than it had.

Indeed, one of the few voices to take serious note of the genocide argument was the official Communist Party newspaper, *L'Humanité*. Before the Tribunal had even heard evidence on the issue of genocide, René Piquet wrote in a front-page story, "The imperialists want to practice genocide [in Vietnam]. It is a whole people, their life, their work, they seek to destroy."[28] Indeed, *L'Humanité*'s—and the PCF's—positions regarding the Tribunal were curious. *Le Monde* reported that "lively debates" had taken place in the central committee before the PCF decided to permit its members to participate. *L'Humanité*'s reporting of the Tribunal demonstrated a marked change from a

---

26   Camille Olsen, "Le 'tribunal Russell' conclut à la culpabilité du gouvernement américain," *Le Monde*, December 3–4, 1967, 2.

27   Jean-Paul Sartre (interviewed by Serge Lafaurie), "Le génocide," 27.

28   René Piquet, "La jeunesse avec le Vietnam," *L'Humanité*, November 21, 1967, 1.

cool detachment during the May session to the colorful, engaged reporting of their *envoyé spécial*, Michel Vincent, during the November session—only four stories on the Tribunal in the first, versus twelve much longer stories in the second. Vincent, whose first article on the Tribunal used the figure of "circles of hell" to describe various situations in Vietnam, wholeheartedly confirmed that genocide had been proved even as the testimony continued to be heard. "Day after day," he wrote, "a conclusion is confirmed ... This neocolonial war [has been] undertaken with such means that a word imposes itself little by little: genocide."[29] Significantly, and in strong contrast with all of the rest of the press coverage, Sartre was barely mentioned in any of the reports, and a one-sentence description of his final statement on genocide was buried in the middle of a paragraph. In minimizing Sartre's role, it may be that the editors wished to co-opt the Tribunal's activity as much as possible—for example, by making the claim of genocide *before* the Tribunal itself had done so. Certainly by November, the PCF had seen clearly how effective the Vietnam issue was becoming in motivating and organizing the young. The main front-page story on November 27 was the anti-Vietnam protest organized by the Mouvement de la Jeunesse Communiste, which was said to have attracted 70,000 people.[30] René Piquet, in the same article that used the charge of genocide against the United States, waxed enthusiastically: "Our Party is delighted with this national demonstration of French youth for Vietnam."[31]

L'Humanité aside, this general *lack* of a debate on the claim of genocide is suggestive on two counts: first, it signals a lack of interest in genocide—in the possibility of genocide or the fact of historical genocides—in France *tout court* at this moment. It is interesting that Sartre's interview, "Le Génocide," appeared in the same issue as *Le Nouvel Observateur*'s examination of "De Gaulle et les juifs," after the general had infamously referred to Jews as "a self-assured, dominating people." In fact, in a strange visual juxtaposition, a banner announcing the interview with Sartre on genocide was set across a photomontage of de Gaulle and the flag of Israel ("De Gaulle et les juifs" was the cover story; "Le génocide" was the only other cover line). The story was written by Jean Daniel—a Jewish pied-noir and an influential editor and co-founder of *Le Nouvel Observateur* in 1964 who had also been an active anticolonialist during the struggle for Algerian independence. Daniel asserted that de Gaulle stood on

---

29 Michel Vincent, "Deux Vietnamiennes et plusieurs témoins ont décrit les tortures infligées aux femmes," *L'Humanité*, November 27, 1967, 3.
30 "Les jeunes avec le Vietnam: Plus de 70.000 manifestants à Paris à l'appel du Mouvement de la Jeunesse Communiste," *L'Humanité*, November 27, 1967, 1.
31 René Piquet, "La jeunesse avec le Vietnam," *L'Humanité*, 4.

the right side of history concerning the Dreyfus affair, but was on the wrong side concerning the Holocaust. "Contrary to his entourage," Daniel noted, "he lends no special attention to the specific Hitlerian initiative of genocide. For him, it was a slightly more barbarous war than the others." Noting that many non-Jews in de Gaulle's entourage, including his niece, had been interned in concentration camps, and emphasizing that de Gaulle's condemnation of the horrors of the camps could not be questioned, Daniel continued more precisely: "The will to exterminate the Jews appears to him only as one among the abominable acts of a horrible war." Then, significantly, relating de Gaulle's position to current events, Daniel wrote: "Just as today 'the odious Vietnam War' must not appear to him—even though he is the only Western head of state to condemn it so categorically—to have passed the threshold of genocide that Sartre denounces in this issue."[32] If Daniel's interpretation of de Gaulle's position on the Holocaust is correct, one wonders whether de Gaulle rejected the possibility of genocide altogether. In any case, though it is impossible to generalize from these comments to the public at large, I would surmise with caution that "genocide" still appeared to many to be an ambiguous concept— one that appeared to be difficult to define, and even more difficult to discern in actual events (even if it seemed so clear-cut to the editors of *L'Humanité*). And, as Sartre's "On Genocide" made clear, the definition of it in terms of intent under the 1948 Convention was so broad as to make almost any act of domination also a potential act of genocide.

The lack of debate on Sartre's essay also suggested something else: that even Sartre, a writer at the height of his polemical powers in "On Genocide," could not command public attention in the way that a subsequent generation of activist intellectuals could. It was a sign that, although still important, *writing* had been displaced as the central source of power in the intellectual field. It was perhaps no coincidence that, in an almost exact concurrence of events, from mid April to early December 1967, the Russell Tribunal was competing for news space—and losing badly—to another story about Third World revolt: the capture and trial of Régis Debray in Bolivia.[33]

---

32   Jean Daniel, "De Gaulle et les juifs," *Le Nouvel Observateur*, December 6–12, 1967, 16–17.
33   This is true of all of the publications I examined—*L'Express, Le Monde, Le Nouvel Observateur*, and *Le Figaro*—except *L'Humanité*, which is consonant with the Party's uneasiness with guerrilla movements such as Guevara's.

LIVING GLOBALLY

In his preface to Nizan's *Aden, Arabie,* Sartre had advised the young to leave a Europe compromised by colonial war and become Cuban, Russian, or Chinese—advice that had inspired Debray to go to Cuba in 1961.[34] A student of Althusser at the Ecole Normale Supérieure, Debray was critical of the theoreticism of his peers, which had left them, in his opinion, too politically unengaged. After having traveled around Latin America, he wrote a seminal article on Latin American Marxism and its possibilities for decentering Europe as the subject of history, which appeared in *Les Temps Modernes* in January 1965.[35] Guevara, apparently a reader of *Les Temps Modernes,* told Castro of Debray's article; this led to an invitation to return to Cuba and to write his guerrilla manifesto, *Revolution in the Revolution?*—first published in Cuba in early 1967.[36] That spring, Debray took a message from Castro to Guevara in Bolivia, where the latter was attempting to draw support to his guerrilla *foco,* and was arrested by Bolivian police in late April.[37] Debray's captivity, trial, sentencing to thirty years in prison, and the numerous public interventions on his behalf by prominent intellectuals of every political stripe, provided the drama for one of the biggest news stories of the year.

It was probably no accident that Debray, the careful observer of the rise of the "media intellectual" in France, was himself one of the first great instances of it—though through no plan of his own.[38] The media coverage of this lost French son's captivity was intense, and probably aided by the fact that no one was quite sure exactly what he had been doing in Bolivia, even if his political sympathies were clear. Had he been a journalist on assignment to interview Guevara? Was he really on trial for his writings in favor of the Guevarist *foco?* Intellectuals on the Left and Right flocked to the cause of saving Régis Debray from prison—or worse. *Le Nouvel Observateur* took great advantage of some pre-captivity photos of a sensitive, sun-kissed Debray in coat and tie—hardly looking like a Guevarist guerrilla—to accompany its articles on him, starting in

---

34   Cited in Donald Reid, "Régis Debray's Quest," *History of European Ideas* 14, No. 6 (November 1992), 844.

35   Régis Debray, "Le castrisme: la Longue Marche de l'Amérique Latine," *Les Temps Modernes* 224 (January 1965), 1,172–237.

36   This narrative relies on Reid, "Régis Debray's Quest," 847; and Hamon and Rotman, *Génération, Vol. I,* 288.

37   News of the arrest was sketchy at first. *L'Humanité,* for example, wrote that Debray was possibly dead. "Un Français tué en Bolivie," *L'Humanité,* April 24, 1967, 2.

38   Régis Debray, *Teachers, Writers, Celebrities: The Intellectuals of Modern France,* trans. David Macey (New York: Schocken Books, 1981).

May 1967. Indeed, the cover story of May 24–30—"Might Régis Debray be shot?"—used a montage of these images to sell its edition.

After learning of Guevara's death in Bolivia in October 1967, Debray began his own letter-writing campaign—but one directed toward the French intellectuals who had been writing to save him. Allying himself directly with Guevara and his *foco*, Debray admonished the intellectuals who had rallied around his own cause for making it into a "circus," and told them to turn their energies elsewhere: "If there still exists a 'Debray Committee,' it would be worth reducing its scope or changing its character and converting it into a committee for the [Latin] American revolution." Not wishing to renounce his complicity or wash his own dirty hands, he continued, "If writing is an act and an engagement, if Brasillach is responsible for having justified collaboration, I am responsible for having justified and advocated guerrilla warfare, and I accept this responsibility as a privilege."[39] The intellectual-turned-revolutionary, the young Frenchman fighting at the side of the mythic, post-"disappearance" Guevara, the Althusserian *really* putting theory into practice, took to a new level an action figure from the French-Algerian War—the *porteur de valise* of the Jeanson network—by fighting at the sides of non-European revolutionaries, rather than simply abetting their actions. Whether he wished it or not (and he later came to lament it), he served as a model for *gauchiste* theorization and activity back in France.[40] His friend, Bernard Kouchner, was soon to become a rather different symbol of activism. (According to Hamon and Rotman, Debray and Kouchner had gone together to the Cuban Embassy in 1961, attempting to enlist to help the Cubans fight the United States; they were turned away.[41]) After returning from a stint working as a doctor for the Red Cross in Biafra, he broke the silence required in his contract (the Red Cross wished to remain neutral in disputes) and tried to mobilize international support to end atrocities there. This initiative having failed, Kouchner and others set up Médecins Sans Frontières in 1971.[42]

---

39   Régis Debray, "Ce que je demande de mes amis," *Le Nouvel Observateur*, November 1–7, 1967, 12. On these issues, see also Jean Daniel, "Guevara et Debray," *Le Nouvel Observateur*, October 18–24, 1967, 19.

40   See Régis Debray, *A Critique of Arms, Vol. I*, trans. Rosemary Sheed (New York: Penguin, 1977).

41   Hamon and Rotman, *Génération, Vol. I*, 74.

42   See <www.msf.org>. Under their "Milestones," MSF describes one of its founding principles as follows: "The founders of MSF also distinguish themselves from other aid workers by their awareness of the role of the media in bringing the plight of [the] population to the attention of the general public."

Though there was much to separate Sartre from Debray and other younger activists who had been students not in 1968, but during the French-Algerian War, there was also much that bound them together. First, there was the tendency to view individual responsibility in a global perspective; second, there was an explicit or implied critique of structuralism; third, there was a movement toward decentering Europe in the domains of values, knowledge, and political power. I discuss each of these in turn below.

The first commonality is perhaps the most important: the tendency to view individual responsibility in a global perspective was bolstered during the 1960s not just by critiques of neocolonialism and imperialism in France, but also by the emergence of theories of economic dependency—created largely by radical economists in Latin America and the United States, whose works were swiftly being translated into French by the mid 1960s. While it is not important here to detail dependency theory in depth, it is important to note that it typically viewed the underdevelopment of some countries as the necessary effect of capitalism. In direct contrast with modernization theorists, dependency theorists argued that underdevelopment was actually a consequence of the spread of capitalism, and as such was in no danger of being eradicated by it.[43] Dependency theory would thus have been able to reinforce the view that we "here" are responsible for events "there." Perhaps not surprisingly, one of the vectors of transmission for dependency theory in France was *Les Temps Modernes*, which published articles by Fernando Hernique Cardoso (who later became president of Brazil), André Gunder Frank, and Paul Baran.[44] In fact, Sartre's influence in Latin America apparently had some effect on the development of dependency theory, as Cardoso, one of its leading lights, named him as one of his influences, and Robert Packenham notes that Cardoso's early works (1962 and 1964) "draw heavily" on a range of thinkers that included Sartre.[45] The most significant

43   For the politics of modernization theory, see Nils Gilman, *Mandarins of the Future: Modernization Theory in Cold War America* (Baltimore, Md.: Johns Hopkins University Press, 2003); and Michael E. Latham, *Modernization as Ideology: American Social Science and "Nation Building" in the Kennedy Era* (Chapel Hill: University of North Carolina Press, 2000).

44   For the articles, see Paul Baran and Eric Hobsbawm, " 'Un manifeste non-communiste,' " *Les Temps Modernes* 193 (June 1962), 1,914–27; Paul A. Baran, "Economie politique et politiques économiques," *Les Temps Modernes* 212 (January 1964), 1,226–61; Fernando Henrique Cardoso, "Hégémonie bourgeoise et indépendence économique," *Les Temps Modernes* 257 (October 1967), 650–80; and André Gunder Frank, "Qui est l'ennemi immédiat?" *Les Temps Modernes* 275 (May 1969), 1963–2008.

45   He cites Baran, Lukács, Marx, Sartre, and Sweezy. Robert A. Packenham, *The Dependency Movement: Scholarship and Politics in Development Studies* (Cambridge: Harvard University Press, 1992), 9.

vector, however, was Maspéro—the publishing house responsible for bringing the works of Mao, Guevara, Castro, Fanon, Debray, Ho Chi Minh, activist-attorney Jacques Vergès, and the French-language edition of *Tricontinental* to the French public; it also published major monographs by radical economists such as Baran, Gunder Frank, and Paul Sweezy.

This rethinking and repositioning of European countries in a world of systemic injustice was just one of many effects of decolonization on bodies of knowledge—but it was the effect that resonated perhaps most strongly with left-wing French intellectuals, as it fit with their wish to see socialism develop in post-independence countries and with their criticism of the forces, such as the United States, opposing that wish. This will, forged in deeds such as the Manifesto of the 121, to place the actions of the individual in a transnational perspective, and to generalize responsibility accordingly, was transformed during the 1960s by Sartre and others. It was the basis for the reconceptualization of a justice beyond borders that was based not on charity, aid, or a civilizing mission, but rather on systemic change—a point about the shape that Third Worldist thinking took in France that is often missed by its observers (and critics).[46]

The second important commonality between Sartre and the newer activists in the 1960s is that they each deployed in some way an implicit or explicit critique of the fetishization of theory—and, in particular, structuralist theory—while still often acknowledging its utility and influence. It became a cliché after May 1968 to say that a structure cannot descend into the streets; but many intellectuals did not need to wait for the events of May to realize that structuralism was not an effective tool when it came to devising practices of social contestation. Debray, for example, moved directly to the field of practice by inserting himself into a struggle; and Sartre, who perhaps took a greater interest in the work of Lévi-Strauss than in that of any other contemporary thinker, nonetheless, through his ruminations on morality, rejected structuralism as an all-encompassing theory of both the human being and the social field.

Significantly, in the Rome Lecture, Sartre specifically targeted structuralism as a method—as usual, he did not take care to distinguish different thinkers—that was fundamentally inadequate for grasping morality. Indeed, the Rome Lecture appears to have been one of Sartre's few extended engagements with structuralism. He never really responded to Lévi-Strauss's

---

46 One of the few people to note this distinction is Yves Lacoste, in his defense of some Third Worldists against Bruckner. Lacoste, *Contre les anti-tiers-mondistes*, 17.

criticisms of the *Critique*; instead, it was Pierre Verstraeten who published an epic-length review of *The Savage Mind* in which he defended Sartre.[47] And most observers found Sartre's comments on structuralism in the special issue of *L'Arc*, in which he lumped various people (Robbe-Grillet, Foucault) together and dismissed them, to be wholly inadequate.[48] Though Sartre seems to a large degree to have felt a blithe indifference to the criticism of others— perhaps because he was inundated by it—in the Rome Lecture, at least, he gave some reasons for preferring his own method. First, he argued, because structuralism is simply positivism: it does not take seriously the contents of the rules it is otherwise so helpful in discerning. Second, because it is concerned only with rules and their repetition, thus ignoring the lived experience of moral decision-making that often involves negotiating competing rules, structuralism is ironically unable to describe the ontological *structure* of the norm, which is the basis for rulemaking itself. Sartre believed structuralism to be fundamentally flawed because it treats humans as objects whose choices are created outside of themselves. Although this is true perhaps most of the time, Sartre admitted, there is a limit—and that limit, for him, demonstrated the structuralist view of morality to be wrong. Sartre proposed that the limit-case of risking one's life, or of choosing death as a possibility, demonstrated that moral choice is not exhausted by exterior conditioning. The fact that I can always choose death means that I can always choose my future—that it is not always determined by my past, as the structuralists might have claimed.

In Sartre's treatment of structuralism the theme of risking one's life once again resonates strongly with the armed struggle advocated and employed by many liberation movements around the world. Sartre continued to work at a remove from such examples of direct action; yet throughout the 1960s, his writings on neocolonialism and imperialism, his participation in the Russell Tribunal, and his support for the student movement situated him in a certain relationship with the extra-PCF "New Left"—one that was later to deepen, when he became a cautious defender of the Maoist Gauche Prolétarienne.

---

47 Pierre Verstraeten, "Lévi-Strauss ou la tentation du Néant," *Les Temps Modernes* 206 (July 1963), 66–109; and "Lévi-Strauss ou la tentative du Néant," *Les Temps Modernes* 207/8 (August–September 1963), 507–52. Although much has been made of Lévi-Strauss's criticism, not only was part of *The Savage Mind* published in *Les Temps Modernes*—Claude Lévi-Strauss, "Le temps retrouvé," *Les Temps Modernes* 191 (April 1962), 1,402–31—but he even continued to publish in the review. See, for example, Claude Lévi-Strauss, "Vingt ans après," *Les Temps Modernes* 256 (September 1967), 385–406.

48 For an example of this reaction, which he calls "obscurantism," see Philippe Sollers, "Un Fantasme de Sartre," *Tel Quel* 28 (Winter 1967), 84–5.

Fredric Jameson has noted that there is a certain logic fitting these various actions and engagements together:

> Sartre's *Critique*, at the beginning of the 1960s, written during the Algerian revolution and appearing simultaneously with the Cuban revolution, the radicalization of the civil rights movement in the United States, the intensification of the war in Vietnam, and the worldwide development of the student movement, therefore corresponds to a new period of revolutionary ferment.[49]

But it is also striking that there is nothing particularly Marxist about Sartre's ethics; neither his emphasis on death as a possible future nor his use of "need" as the foundation for the ethical is Marxist. He also made no use of a relationship to "the Other" in describing his views. His ethics is deeply individual, but the individual in this case has broad, cosmopolitan responsibilities. Although he criticized Kant, his ethics, like Kant's, makes a claim for universalizing the principle animating individual acts—in this case so that they aim at what Sartre takes to be the ontological structure of the norm. There are moments in which he refers to the Other, usually as the mediator of a system of inertia, or in some other negative or potentially hostile capacity—and thus in some ways reflecting both *Being and Nothingness* and the *Critique*.[50] Although it might be tempting to try to describe the relationship between colonizers and colonized, or between Americans and Vietnamese, in terms of a relationship with the Other, the fact is that, in Sartre's view, all beings are affected by inertia, not just one side in a conflict. Moreover, what Sartre was really getting at was not a conflict between a subject and an "Otherness," but rather a dialectic of individual, multiple praxes that are ranged in certain positions by the practico-inert—that is, by past praxes. In this account, the struggle for freedom thus did not involve a struggle against "the Other," but rather against the past as embedded in the structures of the present. This lack of interest in theorizing the relationship to "the Other" as a component of globalized responsibility was general in the 1960s; it was simply not a term that was frequently invoked to describe relationships obtaining between peoples, nor one that was often used to delimit the possibilities of struggle.

---

49 Fredric Jameson, *Marxism and Form: Twentieth-Century Dialectical Theories of Literature* (Princeton: Princeton University Press, 1974), 299.

50 In the first appearance of "the Other" in the text that I noted, he writes, "The ontological structure [of the norm] is manifested in its entirety. And inertia *comes from its contents*. But these *contents* are given as impossible to dissolve insofar as they are also maintained by *the Other*." Sartre, "Rome Lecture Typed Manuscript," 29.

Set in the context of global political conflict, the appeal of the Sartrean position over a structuralist one seems clear. Once again, as in the postwar era of anticolonial struggle, Sartre's continued emphasis on individual freedom, his demand that people be given the autonomy necessary to make their own decisions (and mistakes), and his more recent interest in the social conditions of freedom resonated strongly with politics in the non-European world, providing a powerful set of tools and narratives for those wishing to contest what they viewed as unjust neocolonial or imperialist aims.

The final commonality between Sartre and the activists is that each argued for a decentering of Europe in the domains of knowledge, values, and political power—however tenuous or unsuccessful such efforts might have been given the immense economic and military advantages of Europe and North America, as well as the disarray in which many new nations found themselves after independence. (Indeed, for all that has been written about the importance of the 1955 Bandung Conference as a signal of global Third World solidarity against the wealthy nations, it was really not until the advent of OPEC in 1960—and, in particular, its 1973 price shock—that such solidarity went substantially beyond the symbolic.) Sartre's continued prestige among Third World intellectuals and the noncommunist Left in France thus derived not only from the theoretical tools he may have provided, but, perhaps more importantly, from his consistent desire to take non-Western interlocutors seriously—to recognize them genuinely as subjects outright, and not as potential subjects or as victims in need of being saved. In light of this, his decision not to go to the United States in 1965 is revealing: he was concerned that "people in the Third World would condemn him," a concern that outweighed what the Americans' opinion of him might be.[51] Similarly, his ethics is one in which the claims of people in the Third World were given more weight by default than those of the wealthy or the powerful. Moreover, the efforts of Sartre and others to show a *preference* for ideas, leaders, and movements contesting the economic hegemony of the wealthiest people demonstrated a decentering of Europe in leftist narratives of global development. Sartre explicitly recognized this process of decentering in 1965:

I would like to say in a more general way that one must not take America to be the center of the world. It is the greatest power in the world? Yes. But be careful. It is far from being the center. When one is a European, one also has the duty to not take oneself as the center; one must … prove one's solidarity

---

51   Sartre (interview), "Il n'y a plus de dialogue possible," 18–19.

with all the Vietnamese, the Cubans, the Africans, all the friends of the Third World who are attaining existence and liberty, and who prove every day, precisely, that the greatest power in the world is incapable of imposing its laws. The United States will evolve, of course—slowly, very slowly—but even more so if it is resisted rather than lectured.[52]

That this decentering of Europe among left-wing intellectuals took place in precisely the same era when the Left in France was so effectively dominated by Gaullism should come as no surprise. Once again, however, I would suggest that there is no reason to take this decentering as a mere instrumentalization of the Third World. Rather, I think it signals a significant change in perspective— occurring especially during the years 1962–68—in which many left-wing intellectuals such as Sartre took stock and redefined their roles based on a new set of political circumstances. Each of the unique myriad of conjunctures—left-wing impotence at home, prestige abroad; the growing appeal of anti-Americanism making it a potent tool of leftist organization; and leftist, activist intellectuals chafing against a compelling, yet (for them) troublingly quietist structuralist thought—provided a key condition for the emerging interest of many intellectuals in Third World struggles in the 1960s. But the development of engagements and practices during the French-Algerian War, such as the efforts of the Jeanson network and the signers of the Manifesto of the 121, were signs of the seriousness of certain left-wing intellectuals' commitments—commitments that were transformed and broadened in the 1960s. Indeed, I turn in the next chapter to a discussion of how these commitments were transformed yet again, this time to develop an analysis of racism and "colonialism" in France itself. As more and more non-European immigrants moved to France; as concerns about racism became a matter of public debate; as movements for Basque and Breton autonomy picked up steam; as concerns about American imperialism persisted; and as *gauchiste* (or New Left) activist groups such as the *Gauche Prolétarienne* began taking direct action to streets and factories, Sartre and others began to refocus their analyses of colonialism and neocolonialism back to the former metropole.

---

52   Ibid.

PART IV

DECOLONIZATION ON TRIAL, 1968–1980

CHAPTER TEN

Sartre, the Left, and Identity in Postcolonial France

In 1975, I was still the same man who had been stirred by May '68 and who, basically, was trying to associate his ideas with those of the Sixty-eighters without too many contradictions. Then the international scene became what it is now—the triumph of rightist ideas, at least on the part of governments, in almost all nations.[1]

On November 6, 1973, Sartre lost a court battle to eight editors of the extreme right-wing weekly, *Minute*, who had sued him for defamation, making death threats, and justifying the crime of destruction by explosives, and he was ordered to pay each of them a 400-franc fine.[2] The reason for the conviction was an article that had appeared in the Maoist newspaper, *La Cause du peuple*, of which Sartre had become the director in May 1970 in an effort to keep the Maoist organ alive after its editors, Jean-Pierre Le Dantec and Michel Le Bris, were arrested. *Minute*, according to the article, was staffed by "the poorly purged of the Liberation and those who had been in the half-pay of the OAS"— referring to the right-wing French terrorist organization that had worked to prevent Algerian independence from France in the early 1960s. The Maoists warned

> all of the Kollaborators of this newspaper, director and editors alike, that ... we will not publish their addresses and leave to others the task of acting with our blessing. We will keep them, but we affirm that we will know how to use them if the need is felt.[3]

---

1 Jean-Paul Sartre in Sartre and Benny Lévy, *Hope Now: The 1980 Interviews*, trans. Adrian van den Hoven (Chicago: University of Chicago Press, 1996), 109.

2 "Poursuivi par huit journalistes de *Minute*, M. Jean-Paul Sartre est condamné à 400 francs d'amende," *Le Monde*, November 8, 1973. See also Simone de Beauvoir's account in *Adieux: A Farewell to Sartre*, trans. Patrick O'Brian (New York: Pantheon Books, 1984), 56–8. *Minute* was among the most important organs of the extreme right, as it was under the direction of the founding members of the Front National. Its tabloid style attracted a broader reader base than the other well-known right-wing publication, *Rivarol*.

3 Francis Cornu, "*Minute* poursuit M. Jean-Paul Sartre en correctionelle: L'accusateur accusé," *Le Monde*, October 10, 1973.

The court judged that the article's threatening words here had gone too far, and that Sartre as director was accountable: "While strongly pointing out the dangerous and illegal consequences risked by the consistently violent, not to mention hateful, style of the editors of *Minute* who are contesting him in this court today," the judge announced, "Sartre employed, for his part, in the article of June 21, 1972, a style and a vocabulary comparable in every way to theirs."[4]

This particular fight, however, was merely an extension of a series of hostile exchanges between *Minute* and *La Cause du peuple*, many of which were ideological contests over the proper contents of French nationality, and which thus made consistent reference to defining and divisive historical events such as the Algerian war for independence. The political struggle over postcolonial French identity had been joined, and Sartre would, in the early 1970s, operate both as an actor and as a symbol in the struggle's debates. *Minute* had been tracking the activities and pronouncements of Maoists and other *gauchistes*, to whom it invariably referred under various pejorative names. But it had always had a special, enduring interest in Sartre, the "pope of the Revolution," viciously reviewing his books, acerbically commenting on his political positions, and passing along gossip on his health and personal life.[5] Sartre was a convenient lightening rod for criticism of the radical Left, and an effective magnet for criticisms of Third Worldist sympathies. Thus, when *Minute*'s offices were bombed in May 1971, its editors blamed the "*gauchiste* dogs," but named Sartre on its front page: "Sartre, you are the criminal!" read the tabloid-style block type across an image of the building's damaged exterior. The hostilities escalated further the following month, when *Minute* adopted as the centerpiece of its campaign to have Sartre jailed the pronouncements of *La Cause du peuple* and other *gauchiste* publications for which Sartre had also assumed responsibility, for similar reasons, such as *Tout* and *J'accuse*. "We accuse!" and "To prison, Sartre!" its June 1971 cover lines read.[6] According to the editors of *Minute*, the authorities had been indulging Sartre's incitations to "disorder, pillage, and hatred."[7] Thus, the editors surmised, it would only be by taking matters into their own hands that Sartre might be brought to "justice." As their defense

---

4   *Le Monde*, "Poursuivi par huit journalistes de *Minute*."

5   "Sartre malade? Ce serait la raison de son étrange silence," *Minute* 598, September 26–October 2, 1973, 3.

6   "En prison Sartre!" *Minute* 479, June 16–22, 1971, 1, 6–9.

7   In fact, Sartre was charged shortly after the appearance of *Minute*'s accusations, which led Contat and Rybalka to imply a link between the two events. Substantiating such a link is, however, very difficult. See Contat and Rybalka, *Writings of Jean-Paul Sartre, Vol. I*, 579.

attorney intimated at the trial: "I am pleased to finally see M. Sartre in front of a judge, and I regret that the prosecutor did not take the initiative in this action."[8]

The court's decision was a minor censure, taken on behalf of a group of editors whose wish was to stamp out Sartre and his radical support for Third World liberation movements, immigrant workers, and cultural pluralism—as well as the democratic experimentation he and others advocated to achieve greater freedom and participation for all. As I show in this chapter, this minor censure developed over the first half of 1970s into a broader critique of such views—a critique that spanned the Right-Left divide in France, and that strongly colored debates on the inclusiveness of French democracy.

POSTCOLONIAL CULTURE WARS

The battles of extreme Right and Left between *Minute* and Sartre, whom the newspaper took as its primary *gauchiste* target, help bring into focus some of the key political contests of the early 1970s, as well as Sartre's own function in those contests, which was both active and symbolic. One of *Minute*'s central missions was to protect and foster an integralist conception of French nationality. After all, *Minute* had been founded in April 1962 by *Algérie française* supporter Jean-François Devay, and one of its key contributors was François Brigneau, a leader of the right-wing group Ordre Nouveau (banned in 1973 after an anti-immigrant protest turned violent), and a founder of the Front National in 1972. Sartre and the *gauchistes* challenged *Minute*'s mission in two crucial ways. First, they defended the place of non-European immigrants in French society. Second, they participated in the shift of regionalism away from its traditional home on the Right, and toward a radical democratic defense of cultural pluralism. On both counts, Sartre and the *gauchistes* were interested in rethinking democratic practice in France in ways they took to be more inclusive and a direct challenge to the forces of order; in doing so they relied strongly on radical critiques of colonialism developed during the era of decolonization and adapted to new social conditions.

In keeping with these aims, *gauchiste* publications such as *La Cause du peuple* had made immigrants' working and living conditions in France a staple issue in their pages. Likewise, Sartre, continuing his decades-long concern with race and racism, took an active part in bringing attention to both the social and political issues at stake in the absorption and protection of immigrants in

---

8   Cornu, "L'accusateur accusé."

French society. Although Michel Wieviorka opens his book, *La France raciste*, with the claim that "the return of the theme of racism on the political agenda dates from the 1980s and the growth of the Front National,"[9] this return really should be dated a decade earlier, making the success of the Front National partly a consequence of that return, not its cause. The fact that the French parliament passed a law against racism in 1972 for which the Mouvement Contre le Racisme et Pour l'Amitié Entre les Peuples had lobbied for thirteen years suggests the political urgency of racism in the early 1970s. The law prohibited racial discrimination in employment, housing, and services, gave the government the power to disband organizations that promoted racial hatred, and extended provisions against incitement to racial violence to include racial insults.[10]

Both Sartre and his Gauche Prolétarienne collaborators frequently invoked both historical examples (typically, that of Algeria) and theories of colonialism in their analyses and condemnations of the mistreatment of immigrants. This importation of the radical critique of colonialism back to the metropole was symptomatic of an important trend of the early 1970s, particularly among left-wing activists and intellectuals. Discussions of the "new racism" (the title of a 1972 essay by Sartre, published in both *La Cause du peuple* and *Le Nouvel Observateur*), for example, centered on the vexing problem of tolerance of significant non-European and non-Christian populations, making explicit reference to the residues of racism from the colonial era.[11] But the use of the radical critique of colonialism was also used by national minorities within Europe; it was applied to national minorities within Europe. In the case of France, the strongest regionalist movements sprang up in Brittany and Occitanie; in these cases, separatists often used the model of "internal colonialism"—an application and modification of the core-periphery model used in dependency theory—to describe what they viewed as the historical process of both cultural and economic oppression.[12]

This chapter examines Sartre's involvement in theorizing racism and collective identity, and it helps to explain the eclipse of his influence in intellectual discourse by the mid-to-late 1970s. His interventions on behalf of

---

9   Michel Wieviorka, *La France raciste* (Paris: Editions du Seuil, 1992), 25.

10   Catherine Lloyd, *Discourses of Antiracism in France* (Aldershot, UK: Ashgate, 1998), 169–70.

11   Jean-Paul Sartre, "Le Nouveau racisme," *Le Nouvel Observateur*, December 18–22, 1972.

12   For a classic historiographical work using the model of internal colonialism, see Michael Hechter, *Internal Colonialism: The Celtic Fringe in British National Development* (Berkeley: University of California Press, 1975), esp. Ch. 2.

immigrant workers and regionalist movements were, I show, linked both conceptually and politically for thinkers and activists involved with the radical noncommunist Left. For his part, like many other *gauchistes*, Sartre adapted the radical critique of colonialism and racism he had developed in the 1950s and early 1960s in response to the war in Algeria and Third World liberation movements to address social problems in France in the early 1970s. Just as he had used these earlier analyses to support liberation movements abroad, Sartre sought to find ways in the postcolonial era to deepen France's democracy by highlighting and publicizing its various exclusions, thereby supporting home-grown liberation struggles. By the mid 1970s, however, a new discourse on cultural assimilation had come to the fore, pushed mainly by the rising Socialist Party and its adherents: a new "universalism" that valued human rights over the protection of particular identities, and that tended to excoriate defenders of particularism on the Left as outmoded and perhaps "totalitarian" defenders of Third World revolutionary practices gone awry. In the wake of this shift, Sartre's model of each human being as a "singular universal"—which he used to support claims to cultural autonomy in the 1970s—was pushed aside in favor of a vision of universal tolerance fostered by supporters of the Socialist Party. I suggest that it might be worthwhile to reconsider the positions of Sartre and the *gauchistes* since, thirty years after these events, many of the same issues of identity that I discuss in this chapter remain contentious and unresolved.

"REVERSE" COLONIALISM: ANTI-IMMIGRANT RACISM AND FRENCH IDENTITARIAN CONCERNS

True to its ideological formation, *Minute*, whose editorial tone was often openly racist, vigorously denied the possibility of assimilating increasingly numerous non-European immigrants.[13] These immigrants, whose political visibility from the late 1960s onward was on the rise, had become important tokens in the struggle between Left and Right in the immediate postcolonial era. By the early 1970s, the stakes concerning immigrants from North Africa in particular began to be sharply contested. In January 1971, Algerian president Houari Boumedienne closed off French companies' access to Algerian oil, a step toward nationalizing the oil industry, which he consummated in 1973. This event led to an intensification of *Minute*'s attacks and a veritable obsession with

---

13   The number of Algerians in France doubled between 1958 and 1968; by 1972, Algerians had overtaken the Portuguese, Spanish, and Italians as the largest immigrant population, at 20 percent of all immigrants. Vincent Viet, *La France immigré: Construction d'une politique, 1914–1997* (Paris: Fayard, 1998), 262, 265.

Algerian immigrants: "Enough of Algeria!" one headline read. "They're chasing us out ... now let's chase them out!"[14] In an issue later in the same month devoted to Algerians in France, the contributors employed stereotypically racist arguments to define the "threat" that such immigrants posed: Algerians' "natural" way of life made for unsanitary living conditions; refusing to live alone, whether in order to save money or because of "racial instinct," they "reconstitute their tribes"; and they were incapable of taking care of property—for example, the lodgings given to them.[15]

But *Minute* was by no means alone in its concern with Algerian immigrants, nor in initiating a backlash against them driven by the Algerian government's nationalization of private enterprises. According to sociologists Alain Gillette and Abdelmalek Sayad, the French government's decision to reduce the number of entries granted to Algerian immigrants in 1971 (from a net total of 35,000 to 25,000) was partly motivated by its "irritation" at such economic interference.[16] By 1973, *Minute*'s descriptions of the "problem" of Algerian immigration had become even more insistent, using terms such as "invasion" and "race war."[17] (Once again, the newspaper linked its denunciation of the presence of North Africans on French soil to world events related to oil—in this case OPEC's oil shock.)[18]

Certainly, the rapid growth of the Algerian population up to the early 1970s represented the most significant shift in the demographics of the immigrant population in France, which had traditionally been dominated by Italians, Poles, and Spaniards. Other non-European populations grew as well, however, including Moroccans and Tunisians, and the sub-Saharan African population went from being negligible before decolonization to reach 65,000 by 1972. *Minute*'s and others' reactions to these changes signaled the advent of non-European immigration not just as a social, but also as a political issue in France. Jean-Marie Le Pen founded the Front National in 1972, thereby inserting the question of the protection of an "integral" French identity directly into

---

14   "Algérie ça suffit! Ils nous chassent ... chassons les!" *Minute* 470, April 14–20, 1971, 1 (cover line). See, in the same issue, François Brigneau, "Algérie ça suffit!" 11.

15   J.-P. Mefret, "Les Algériens chez nous," *Minute* 458, January 21–27, 1971, 12–13.

16   Alain Gillette and Abdelmalek Sayad, *L'immigration algérienne en France* (Paris: Editions Entente, 1976), 97.

17   See the edition—*Minute* 595, September 5–11, 1973—in which the cover lines read, "Arretez l'invasion algérienne, maintenant la cote d'alerte est dépassée" and "Ceux qui vont nous amener la guerre raciale."

18   See "L'autre guerre qui commence: Le chantage arabe au pétrole," *Minute* 602, October 24–30, 1973, 1; and "La riposte aux arabes: Oui, elle est possible! Ils veulent nous mettre à genoux avec le pétrole," *Minute* 608, December 5–11, 1973, 1.

electoral politics—though his party did not have any significant electoral success until the 1980s, partly owing to the political schism on the extreme Right between him and *Minute*'s Brigneau, beginning in 1974.

The early 1970s thus represented a conjuncture in which immigration, racism, xenophobia, and the politics of extremes intersected in many areas. Yet this conjuncture may also, in some ways, be a misleading one—as the historian of French immigration Gérard Noiriel points out—since it obscures the fact that France has had a long history of immigration, with concomitant problems of assimilation. Still, what seems unique about this particular period was the intense politicization of intellectuals on the issue of immigration, and in particular those actively doing research on it. It was in this era, Noiriel explains, that "a combination of Marxism and anticolonialism assured the fortunes of a new term, the 'immigrant worker'—little used until then. With decolonization, two previously unrelated research trends melted together: immigration studies per se and studies of the colonial world."[19]

Like *Minute*, racism was a central theme of *La Cause du peuple* in 1971, as the editors published articles calling for a "war on racism" in order to "strike back" at racists.[20] Though it is unclear what (if any) role Sartre played in the development of these articles, they nonetheless demonstrate strong affinities with his own position-taking on the issues of racism and immigration—as well as, for him, the centrality of colonialism to understanding those contemporary issues. Sartre's first attempt to help publicize the conditions of life and work for non-European immigrants came in 1970, when he spoke at an event celebrating the publication of the *Livre des travailleurs africains en France.*[21] The text of his speech, "The Third World Begins in the *Banlieue*," was published in *Tricontinental* later that year[22]—and it marked in a rather prescient way many of the issues that would dominate political discussion concerning relations with non-Western countries and peoples for the coming decade and beyond: the social, economic, and cultural problems of immigration; the contemporary conjuncture of racism with economic and demographic pressures pushing and pulling people across borders; the persistence of colonialism, whether on the

---

19 Gérard Noiriel, *The French Melting Pot: Immigration, Citizenship, and National Identity*, trans. Geoffroy de Laforcade (Minneapolis: University of Minnesota Press, 1996), 24.

20 See, among many others, "La guerre au racisme," *La Cause du peuple* 6, June 28, 1971, 16; and "Frapper le criminel raciste," *La Cause du peuple* 9, September 23, 1971, 14.

21 Union générale des travailleurs sénégalais en France, *Livre des travailleurs africains en France* (Paris: Maspéro, 1970).

22 Reprinted as Jean-Paul Sartre, "Le Tiers Monde commence en banlieue," *Situations VIII* (Paris: Gallimard, 1972).

level of economics (neocolonialism) or of ideas (as a model for social oppression and exclusion); and, finally, the possibility of freedom for the least favored of the world, beaten down in this case by poverty and exploitation, but in other cases by repressive governments in their home countries.

It seems likely that this text was influenced by the January 1970 deaths of five Malians living in an immigrants' hostel (or "vertical" *bidonville*, as such temporary quarters were sometimes called) in Aubervilliers. As was common practice, they had tried to use gas as a source of heat, and they died by asphyxiation. Sartre was among the intellectuals (including Michel Leiris and Jean Genet) who participated in the demonstrations organized around the immigrants' funerals on January 10, thereby drawing press attention to what was a persistent problem in France's growing *bidonvilles*.[23] In "The Third World Begins in the *Banlieue*," Sartre broadened the discussion beyond the *bidonvilles* themselves, insisting throughout on the necessity of understanding the position of African workers through the lens of colonialism. He argued that, in fact, colonial conditions had been reproduced in the metropole: the Malthusianism of the market (and lack of social protections), the insalubrious and overcrowded housing, the denial of training to improve skills, the systematic insecurity of jobs, the development of racism as a means of control—each of these conditions recreated, in Sartre's view, the colonial situation he had been describing since the mid 1950s, in particular in his classic 1956 essay, "Colonialism Is a System."

As the participation of Sartre and others in demonstrations against terrible living conditions in the *bidonvilles* indicates, the "war" against racism toward non-European immigrants—though actively promoted by *gauchiste* groups such as the Gauche Prolétarienne—attracted support from many different quarters, even if that support did not run very deep on either the Left or the Right.[24] Sartre and other intellectuals, such as Michel Foucault, Claude Mauriac, Gilles Deleuze, Genet, and Leiris, banded together on numerous

---

23   Roland Castro, Leiris, and Genet were all arrested when they occupied the offices of the French employers' organization as part of their protest. Castro was later prosecuted, and both Sartre and Genet testified at his trial. See "De la mort de cinq Maliens à l'occupation du CNPF: Une peine de prison ferme est requise contre un architecte inculpé de violences et rébellion," *Le Monde*, February 25, 1970; see also Beauvoir, *Adieux*, 4, 26.

24   Indeed, in their published conversations, Sartre, Pierre Victor (Benny Lévy), and Philippe Gavi talked of the difficulties of combating racism among French workers. Gavi pressed Victor on what role marginal politics (homosexual rights, immigrant rights, feminism) played in the Maoist conception of revolution, asking, "What kind of society do you want? A society in which those who control production continue to think 'filthy nigger' or 'fairy' does not interest me. I am not fighting for that." Philippe Gavi, Jean-Paul Sartre, Pierre Victor, *On a raison de se révolter* (Paris: Gallimard, 1974), 111.

occasions in order to bring public attention to police brutality, inhuman living conditions, or racist acts. On the occasion of the shooting death of a young Arab, Mohamed Diab, by a police officer in 1972, Sartre drafted the petition/ essay, "The New Racism," which was signed by 137 intellectuals.

"The New Racism" incorporated many of the old themes of Sartre's polemics from the French-Algerian War, and, like "The Third World Begins in the *Banlieue*," it set contemporary racism specifically in the context of French colonialism and decolonization. According to Sartre, the "new" racism was a direct consequence of the creation of impoverished "colonies" in the metropole. In this "reverse" colonialism, it was the "colonized" French who held the power and thus set the rules for systematic exploitation and exclusion, and it was they who this time justified their power through the invention of everyday practices and ideological categories that made the immigrant worker into a subhuman. "Thus was born a new racism," Sartre wrote, "that wanted to make the immigrants live in terror and remove their desire to protest against the conditions of life that were made for them"—echoing arguments he had employed in "Colonialism Is a System," and in a fuller form in the first volume of the *Critique of Dialectical Reason*. These somewhat sketchy ideas (in an admittedly very brief article) about reverse colonialism were not Sartre's only references in this text, however; he also made use of the memory of the French-Algerian War to argue for his point of view. "We will not accept the rebirth of this ideology of the idiotic that we knew all too well during the French-Algerian War," he wrote. "From 1956 to 1962, we struggled so that victory for the Algerians would be lasting. For them, first of all, but also for us: so that the shame of racism would disappear from French thinking."[25]

Sartre's take on the "new" racism fit in unlikely ways with that of his foes at *Minute*, as both of their discursive strategies relied upon understanding current social problems through the lens of colonialism. In their September 1973 nine-page portfolio on the Algerian "invasion," the writers reiterated a host of colonialist tropes to decry the intrusion of "medinas," "casbahs," and "souks" into French cities—all the while strongly denying that they were motivated by racism in any way.[26] For *Minute*, the integration of North Africans was impossible for the simple reason that "they don't want it"; they wanted, instead, to maintain their own culture, by frequenting cinemas in which "only Arabic language films are shown," for example.[27] Apparently another integral aspect

25 Sartre, "Le Nouveau Racisme."
26 Their defense was mounted in the editorial, "A ceux qui parlent de racisme," *Minute* 595, September 5–11, 1973, 2.
27 "Ce qui, un jour, amènera l'explosion: Ces casbahs au coeur de nos villes," *Minute* 595, September 5–11, 1973, 6–7.

of North African culture being imported to France were the diseases brought about by close and unhygienic living conditions, as well as an anti-republican political life in which "the FNL [sic] is still the boss."[28]

What is important here is not the quality of the analyses offered on the issue of non-European immigration, but rather the fact that colonialism and decolonization were themselves still powerfully in play as symbolic chips in these political debates. After all, as Noiriel has taken such pains to show in *The French Melting Pot*, contests over immigrants and assimilation were nothing new; what was new in this case was that they took place in the still-vexing shadow of decolonization. Moreover, it was those very decolonized people— and not, for example, Portuguese immigrants, who by the mid 1970s were as numerous as Algerians in France[29]—who bore the brunt of the identitarian discourse taking shape in the postcolonial era. This is perhaps why racism and anti-racism played key discursive roles in establishing the stakes of the debate, just as they had for anticolonialists when they had fought colonialism.

Take, for example, one of the central problems of the late 1960s and beyond: the provision of adequate housing for immigrants in *habitats à loyer modéré* (HLM—subsidized housing) or other dwellings, and the elimination of the *bidonvilles*. While politicians and bureaucrats struggled unsuccessfully to summon the resources and will necessary to the task of providing adequate housing under these economic conditions, *gauchistes* and Ordre Nouveau adherents effectively replayed some of the battles of the French-Algerian War by employing that era's language and tropes. In particular, there was Sartre's re-evocation of racism as a set of practices and a way of thinking that establishes the "subhuman" as a category of exclusion and a justification for exploitation.

Thus, when he protested an April 1972 police raid on an overcrowded building in Paris's 19th arrondissement during which the tenants had been evicted, Sartre emphasized the objectively racist character of the system of laws and the bureaucracy governing the lodging of immigrants.[30] Uninhabitable conditions were inextricably related to racism, on his view—especially since, as he pointed out on another occasion, there were hundreds of thousands of empty apartments in Paris. *Minute*, on the other hand, dipped into the old

---

28   See, in *Minute* 595, September 5–11, 1973, "On ne peut plus supporter cette invasion," 3–5; J.-P. M. " 'Carta Toubib Choléra,' " 5; and "Dans le medina de la Goutte d'Or, le FNL [sic] est encore le patron," 6.

29   See Maxim Silverman, *Deconstructing the Nation: Immigration, Racism and Citizenship in Modern France* (London: Routledge, 1992), 52.

30   See Mauriac, *Et comme l'espérance est violente*, 362; Contat and Rybalka, *Writings of Jean-Paul Sartre, Vol. I*, 590; and Beauvoir, *Adieux*, 30.

repository of colonialist fears of native unhealthiness, dirtiness, laziness, and disease—and the best means of managing or containing them. If North Africans lived in *bidonvilles*, this logic went, it must be because they were comfortable living there, or because this was how their "nature" had fashioned them to live. The solution, then, was not to rearrange their social environment—which could have no effect, and which they did not want in any case— but rather simply to get rid of them: "Scram!"[31]

This resurgence in the public domain of the discursive leitmotifs and arguments of colonialism and decolonization corresponded to what political scientist Catherine Wihtol de Wenden has called the emergence of immigration as a "total social phenomenon" between 1968 and 1972. After having encouraged clandestine immigration in the 1960s, the French government found itself faced with a population that could no longer be considered temporary—and, hence, with the recognition that immigration was related to, or even a cause of, structural changes in the economy as well as the social fabric. As the political stakes became clearer, and as *gauchistes* tried to organize immigrants, thus aiding the "awakening of a collective consciousness" among them in this period, as Wihtol de Wenden relates,[32] parties on both the Left and Right began rethinking and re-legislating immigration. While parties on the Right held fast to increasingly restrictive policies based on the assumption that non-European populations were unassimilable, beginning in 1972, the quickly growing Parti Socialiste (PS) began to develop a discourse on immigration that proclaimed a "right to difference" and a "new citizenship."[33] The question on the Left over the course of the decade was, on the one hand, whether this declaration of respect for difference would be enfolded into a politics of identity that positively valued the contributions of different cultures to democratic deliberation; or, on the other hand, whether "respect" for difference would ultimately entangle the Left in a perhaps Quixotic quest for a new form of universalism that could somehow be more broadly inclusive than the old universalism of the colonial *mission civilisatrice*.

---

31   "La France sans algériens: Chiche! En attendant, ils continuent à arriver à pleins bateaux" [cover line], *Minute* 598, September 26–October 2, 1973, 1.
32   Catherine Wihtol de Wenden, *Les immigrés et la politique* (Paris: Presses de la fondation nationale des sciences politiques, 1988), 147.
33   D.S. Bell and Byron Criddle, *The French Socialist Party: The Emergence of a Party of Government* (Oxford: Clarendon Press, 1988, second edn), 172.

"INTERNAL" COLONIALISM: COLLECTIVE IDENTITY AND
REGIONALIST MOVEMENTS

Debates on racism and immigration were not the only ones in which colonialism and decolonization figured prominently in the early 1970s, and in which the creation of concrete space for culturally distinct political claims was advocated as a means of fostering more inclusive and genuinely deliberative democracy. In June 1974, linguist Robert Lafont penned an article for *Le Monde diplomatique*, "Allies in the Cultural Combat against Colonialism," whose subtitle specified a somewhat surprising union: "Worker Immigrants and Regionalist Movements in France." Indeed, for many *gauchistes*—such as *La Cause du peuple* editors Jean-Pierre Le Dantec and Michel Le Bris—activism on behalf of these issues was already well established. Lafont argued for both a practical and a conceptual link between the two. "The analysis," he wrote, "of colonial or semi-colonial situations on the territory of the metropole has been developed. It forms the basis for a new struggle in which the cultural argument plays a determining role."[34]

Lafont was one of the major left-wing French theorists of regionalism. His 1967 book, *La Révolution régionaliste*, popularized the concept of "internal colonialism" for the broader French public, and his 1971 book, *Décoloniser en France: Les régions face à l'Europe*, was an explicitly political treatise in which he argued that "regional decolonization is an important form of the global struggle against imperialism."[35] Lafont's work was symbolic of an important political trend: the shift of regionalist movements from their traditional political home on the Right to one on the Left, beginning in the early 1960s.[36] As the publication date of the first book demonstrates, the attraction of regionalist movements pre-dated the events of 1968. Indeed, Lafont cited a rather different motive than young *gauchiste* activism for the resurgence of political contestation over regional cultures and autonomy: the French-Algerian War. Arguing that "the romantic opposition to national evolution" was no longer a viable political option for regionalists, and that they must instead "insert themselves into the center of French life," Lafont made the case that the revelation of *Algérie française* as a fiction forced people to start "rethinking France."

---

34   Robert Lafont, "Alliés dans un combat culturel contre le colonialisme intérieur," *Le Monde diplomatique* (June 1975).
35   Robert Lafont, *Décoloniser en France: Les régions face à l'Europe* (Paris: Gallimard, 1971), 287.
36   For a brief history of this shift, see Maryon McDonald, *"We Are Not French!": Language, Culture, and Identity in Brittany* (London: Routledge, 1989), esp. Ch. 5.

Echoing Lafont's writings, the Gauche Prolétarienne gave regionalism significant coverage in *La Cause du peuple*—not least because its editors were involved in regionalist movements, but also because regionalism of Lafont's variety represented anti-statist claims for broad access to and exercise of democracy. Both Le Dantec and Le Bris wrote books about regionalist movements, the latter writing a seminal work on the famed Larzac uprising, which spanned the decade and launched the career of "alterglobalization" activist José Bové.[37] Le Bris's and Le Dantec's works were published in a Gallimard series called *La France Sauvage* (*Savage France*), which was under Sartre's directorship.[38]

Though Sartre's intervention in debates on regionalist claims for cultural autonomy date to the era of his involvement with the Gauche Prolétarienne, his interest in them does not appear to be a direct consequence of that involvement. Rather, as his remarks in the preface to a 1971 book edited by Gisèle Halimi, *Le procès de Burgos*, suggest, there were strong conceptual and political continuities—in his mind—between regionalist movements and the national liberation movements he had supported so strongly in the past.[39] The occasion for the text was the December 1970 trial in the Spanish town of Burgos of sixteen members of the Basque nationalist movement in Spain, Euzkadi Ta Askatasuna (ETA). The trial was a major international news story, and Halimi, a lawyer who had gained fame for anticolonialist activity during the French-Algerian War, went as an observer. It was in this preface that Sartre first outlined his views on the legitimacy of ethnically based claims for autonomy, and even independence in Europe, as well as the structural parallels between European regionalist movements and non-European national independence movements.

Sartre began his essay by arguing that decolonization was one of the primary spurs to nationalist movements within European countries.[40] Like Lafont, Sartre noted the possibility for an awakening of consciousness among young men from Brittany sent to fight in Algeria—against, that is, a movement

---

37 See Herman Lebovics, *Bringing the Empire Back Home: France in the Age of Globalism* (Durham, N.C.: Duke University Press, 2004).

38 The idea for the series was Le Bris and Le Dantec's. See Beauvoir, *Adieux*, 67–8, 96.

39 Jean-Paul Sartre, "Préface," in Gisèle Halimi, *Le Procès de Burgos* (Paris: Gallimard, 1971), vii–xxx. Sartre's preface was also excerpted in *Le Nouvel Observateur*, May 24–30, 1971.

40 Marianne Heiberg confirms that Sartre's interpretation as applied to ETA was well founded. Although only a handful of ETA's leaders were Marxist, she writes that "one factor above all the others was instrumental in pushing ETA to the extreme Left—the model of the revolutionary struggle of national liberation as exemplified by Cuba, Algeria and Vietnam." Marianne Heiberg, *The Making of the Basque Nation* (Cambridge: Cambridge University Press, 1989), 111.

for national independence, only to see that movement succeed. Sartre then shifted quickly to an explanation of events that relied heavily on his own conceptual vocabulary, and in particular the term that played a key role in his work on Flaubert: the singular universal. Basque nationalism was, on this argument, a *collective* form of universalizing the singular. Indeed, the whole of the preface was geared toward explaining how a collectivity might be understood as a singular universal:

> I want to attempt here to oppose the abstract universality of bourgeois humanism to the singular universality of the Basque people, to show what circumstances have led it by an ineluctable dialectic to produce a revolutionary movement, and what theoretical consequences one might reasonably pull from the current situation—that is, what profound mutation that decentralization might bring today to a centralizing socialism.[41]

In making his case, Sartre privileged two arguments, both of which demonstrated strong continuities with a number of earlier writings—in particular "Black Orpheus." The first was that the basis for Basque unity, and thus the proof of the legitimacy of Basque claims to independence, was the historical and linguistic distinctness of the Basque language, Euzkara. The second was that group identity was reinforced through a common struggle against colonialism. The two claims were interrelated, both for Sartre and for ETA, since they took the suppression of the Basque language as the primary mode of Spanish domination, and as a sign of its intent to commit "cultural genocide." Hence, strongly echoing "Black Orpheus," Sartre held that "to speak his own language is, for a colonized person, already a revolutionary act."[42]

Sartre folded this focus on language as the carrier of the "Basque personality" into his discussion of the singular universal. Though his evocation of a "Basque personality" came perilously close to suggesting the existence of timeless group characteristics, Sartre instead wrote of the practice of being Basque, of "making oneself Basque" through the everyday act of speaking Euzkara. Being Basque and speaking the Basque language coincided "not only because he [the speaker] recoups a past that belongs only to him, but especially because he addresses himself, even when alone, to a community of those who speak Basque."[43] It was through this practice of speaking—and speaking to one another—that Basque people might come to discern what made their culture "singular," and thus combat the homogenizing and falsely universalizing force

---

41   Sartre, "Préface," in Halimi, *Procès de Burgos*, xi.
42   Ibid., xix.
43   Ibid.

of Spanish centralization which, especially under Franco, had targeted Euzkara for extinction.

Sartre did not say why he privileged linguistic practice over other practices in the Basque struggle—it could have been because the fight to speak the Basque language was already given to Sartre as the central problem. Nonetheless, it was the specificity of the language that, for him, marked the possibility for Basque people to access their history and culture as something "concrete," thus taking a step on the road toward discovering, "not man in general, but man as Basque."[44] Once this step was taken, the non-alienated political claims of free, individual Basques might come also to express universal aims. That is, only by passing through the concrete singularity of one's own culture that one could hope fully to recognize not only one's own freedom, but also that of other peoples.

Although Sartre's argument concerning language reaffirmed some of the key ideas of "Black Orpheus," his claims about collective identity appear to have directly contradicted another text from that earlier period, *Anti-Semite and Jew*. Whereas in that essay Sartre had bracketed (or, some would argue, emptied) the contents of Jewishness for Jews themselves by averring that it is the anti-Semite who creates the Jew, here Sartre invoked a minority population's singular "character" and "reality"—and not others' perceptions of it—as the foundation for identity. He even made an appeal to stable somatic markers over time as a structuring force. Indeed, there are—paradoxically—commonalities not only between the Basque of Sartre's *Burgos* essay and the Jew of *Anti-Semite and Jew* as oppressed minorities, but also between the Basque and the anti-Semite: each shares an attachment to her native soil, for example, and prioritizes the given values of community over the self-created values of the individual. In many ways, then, there was something rather arbitrary about the line that Sartre and others (Le Dantec and Le Bris, specifically) wished to draw between the reactionary and the revolutionary when it came to regionalist movements. As Pierre Bourdieu would point out just a few years later, as struggles for recognition, regionalist movements should be classed as attempts to impose a legitimate scheme of "vision and di-vision" on the social world, and as attempts to define the "law" governing that scheme in order to justify the domination of one group by another.[45] A regionalist movement's attempt to

---

44   Ibid., xx.

45   Pierre Bourdieu, "Identity and Representation: Elements for a Critical Reflection on the Idea of Region," in *Language and Symbolic Power*, trans. Matthew Adamson (Cambridge: Polity Press, 1991). Bourdieu's goal was to caution sociologists against taking too seriously the representations made by regionalist movements themselves.

gain recognition as a distinct nationality may be as much a mode of domination as is a centralizing state's denial of such nationality. This means that, in
terms of the desired goal—unification and autonomy, or independence—
there could be no easy distinction between, say, Breton regionalism and
German nationalism.

Such a homology between "revolutionary" regionalism and "reactionary"
nationalism cannot have been lost on Sartre and others, and one might surmise
that the key to maintaining this tenuous distinction lay in situating a particular
struggle in a colonialist paradigm. Reading the Burgos preface in the context of
Sartre's 1964 "Rome Lecture" on ethics, which discussed at length the normative reasoning behind revolutionary action, one could plausibly argue that, if
the imposition of a particular set of social boundaries was unjust—if it was a
"colonial" order, with all of its attendant economic and social violence—one
could find therein a clear-cut case of a "least favored" people that would then
require intellectuals' support. Moreover, in the *gauchiste* account of anticolonial struggles, the least favored held a privileged position as the suppliers of
democratic innovation.

The key here is that nationalist projects that do not seek to dominate
other nationalities—that seek democratic decentralization rather than undemocratic centralization—are the ones that may be legitimately supported. An
anticolonialist or regionalist movement that tries to impose its own order as a
matter of domination cannot be considered a liberation movement. Thus, the
most important, and classically Sartrean, argument made in favor of regionalist movements was that their left-wing emanations claimed to represent the
expansion of human freedom. In this case, Sartre's decision to use the Basque
nationalist movement as his point of public entry into debates on regionalism
was well taken since, at the time, the Basques were fighting against a reactionary
dictatorship. But freedom figured as an important normative aim of political
action for the *gauchistes* as well. In *Les fous du Larzac*, Le Bris stressed freedom
as a goal. He argued, in a strongly Sartrean vein, that the famed mid-1970s
movement of a group of 103 farmers who defied the French government's
attempt to expand a military base onto their land was necessarily guided by
freedom—by the freedom of each of its members and by the recognition of
freedom in others. This stress on freedom formed the cornerstone of Le Bris's
concluding remarks in the book, "A New Discourse on 'Revolt-Freedom,' " in
which he argued that the 103 had discovered and put into action *gauchiste* aims
better than the *gauchistes* themselves.[46]

---

46   See Michel Le Bris, *Les Fous du Larzac* (Paris: Les Presses d'aujourd'hui, 1975).

Le Bris's latter point is an important one—for regionalism, *gauchisme*, and the colonial paradigm. The Larzac revolt, along with the 1973 workers' takeover and self-management (or *autogestion*) of the Lip watch factory, were the signal events marking the fact that, for Le Bris, "Marxism is at an end, and organized *gauchisme* is moribund."[47] This conclusion that *gauchiste* groups such as the Gauche Prolétarienne were not, in fact, driving the most innovative and significant popular movements of the early 1970s forced a coming to terms with all of the old assumptions, chief among them the utility of the radical critique of colonialism for left-wing politics. Le Dantec, in his 1974 book, *Bretagne: Re-naissance d'un peuple*, cautioned those on the Left that uncritical overuse might easily lead to misuse. Brittany, after all, was *not* Algeria. *Gauchistes*—and he criticized them explicitly in the book—should not

> imagine themselves in Algeria, Vietnam, or Martinique and reinsert themselves into a model so classical as the struggle for national independence. These "solutions" have the merit of facility; unfortunately, they do not respond in the least to the questions of a real movement.[48]

THE RISE OF THE "NEW" CITIZENSHIP

The cautionary note sounded by Le Dantec concerning intellectuals' application of the radical critique of colonialism to situations not classically colonial was, moreover, general. By the mid 1970s, left-wing French intellectuals began a sweeping reconsideration of the meaning of colonialism and the process of decolonization—along with France's rightful role in them both. Radical *gauchiste* movements were confronted with the lack of success of their own tactics for fomenting revolution and seizing state power through extra-electoral and extra-legal means. At the same time, the arrival on the political scene of a consolidated and fortified Socialist Party in 1972 suddenly offered a new political option for *gauchistes* and others on the noncommunist Left who had lost enthusiasm for—and were often openly hostile to—the Communist Party. The PS quickly made the issues of the immigrant worker and the decentralization of power to regions part of their political platform, coopting two of the *gauchistes'* most significant issues.[49] This support for decentralization had

47   Ibid., 359.
48   Jean-Pierre Le Dantec, *Bretagne: Re-naissance d'un peuple* (Paris: Gallimard, 1974), 294.
49   See the party platform written by PS secretary Pierre Joxe: "The Socialist Party proposes to effect a profound decentralization at the level of communes, departments, and regions"; and "Decent living conditions will be assured for immigrant workers; parity in

immediate effects, helping the PS to extend its support in Brittany in the 1973 elections.[50] As for Larzac, it was only in 1981, with the accession to power of Socialist president François Mitterrand, that plans for the Larzac military base's expansion were canceled—in fulfillment of one of his campaign promises.[51] But this cooptation also entailed a substantial modification in the contents of political claims about identity—in effect, a shift away from a defense of cultural particularity and toward a "universal" conception of French identity that could encompass all citizens.

This shift on the Left was, additionally, a shift away from the views Sartre expressed in favor of cultural autonomy. Liberation and the self-determination of peoples could not be expected to go hand in hand. It is perhaps for this reason that Sartre's attempt to apply his concept of the "singular universal"— which was invented to describe how an individual could be an incarnation of the world—to collectivities such as the Basques raised more questions than it answered. As we have seen, his arguments in the preface to the *Procès de Burgos* were unclear: did Basques together represent a collective "person," which could be described as a singular universal, or was each individual Basque, as Basque, a singular universal whose universality was expressed in his free choice and exercise of the practices of his culture, such as speaking his own language? Indeed, were the rights of peoples and the rights of man incompatible? Back in 1953, Sartre had not thought so; he argued for the recognition of both. In an interview he gave in that year to *La République algérienne*, he declared,

> Neither the "right of peoples to decide their own fate" nor the "rights of man" formulated in 1789 have been recognized for the colonized by the colonizers. Nowhere is the exploitation of man by man more apparent; the colonizers can only justify themselves—even in their own eyes—by a racism that will finish by infecting the "metropole" itself.[52]

---

wages and rights between foreign workers and French workers will be established" as part of a "struggle against all forms of discrimination." Pierre Joxe, *Parti Socialiste* (Paris: Epi Editeurs, 1973), 79, 85.

50   Yves Rocaute, *Le Parti Socialiste* (Paris: Editions Bruno Huisman, 1983), 88.

51   Mitterrand had a troubled history with the Larzac movement—he was roughed up by *gauchiste* activists when he showed up in 1974 to lend support to the cause. See Bernard E. Brown, *Socialism of a Different Kind: Reshaping the Left in France* (Westport, Conn.: Greenwood Press, 1982), 114.

52   Interview with Jean-Paul Sartre, "Jean-Paul Sartre: 'Le problème colonial et celui de la démocratie sociale en France sont indissolublement liées," *La République algérienne*, January 16, 1953, 1.

By the mid 1970s, as Sartre's interventions in favor of immigrants and regional movements indicate, he had not moved appreciably away from this position. The French political context in which he took this position had, however, changed markedly. Against Sartre's argument that living fully one's own cultural identity was a basic freedom that ought to be defended, culture-based arguments for rights were increasingly treated as *incompatible* with the universalist-based arguments once more in vogue on the Left. Moreover, Sartre's insistence that race and other forms of identity be taken seriously as factors in systemic oppression that could not easily be solved through political means—a key claim of the radical critique of colonialism—was rejected in favor of appeals to a "new citizenship." Sartre's adaptation of the radical critique of colonialism to new social struggles in the early 1970s may not always have been convincing or scientific, yet it demonstrated a concern with the limits of the purely formal or human rights approach that the Socialists would once again champion.

CHAPTER ELEVEN

The Critique of Third Worldism
and the Human Rights Turn

In January 1970, the bloody civil war that had been waged between the Nigerian state and separatists in Biafra came to an end. It was one among many wars that took place in the aftermath of decolonization as indigenous groups fought for control of political institutions and access to valuable natural resources. For French intellectuals, however, Biafra represented a qualitatively new event—a struggle in which they found it difficult to take sides. Throughout the 1960s, left-wing intellectuals' commitment to Third World revolutions had remained fairly strong. Many, including Jean-Paul Sartre, felt obliged to criticize the paths that some of these revolutions had taken, but they nonetheless remained partisans of revolutionaries' goals in Africa, Latin America, and Southeast Asia. Biafra was different from these other struggles. It was not just the bloodiness of the events, which was so terrible that many termed it a genocide; rather, the conflict between the central government (supported by former colonizer Great Britain) and the Biafran separatists was so thorny, and seemingly so little related to the aims of socialist revolution generally supported on the Left, that the war forced a serious reckoning among left-wing intellectuals with the fact that Third World battles could not always be summed up in the stock terms of revolution versus counterrevolution.

Disillusionment with the outcomes of many Third World independence movements was nothing new. As we saw in Chapter 7, the death of Patrice Lumumba in 1961 and the subsequent rise of Mobutu Sese Seko in the Congo (later Zaïre) marked an early and important comedown for those who were hoping to see genuinely novel and independent arrangements generated in the former colonies. The Biafran War, however, evoked a new response on the Left: one that condemned, in the name of humanity rather than politics, the inaction and irresponsibility of *all* international actors in the First, Second, and Third Worlds, as they were then known, who had failed to stop the bloodshed. Bernard Kouchner—recently returned from Biafra after a stint with the International Red Cross, and soon to be the co-founder of Médecins Sans Frontières—organized a petition condemning this abdication, which was published in France's leading newspaper, *Le Monde*. Calling the inaction "a gangsterism of planetary dimensions" that had facilitated the murder of the Ibos of Biafra, the

petition was signed by (among others) Sartre, Simone de Beauvoir, Claude
Lanzmann, Jean Pouillon, Laurent Schwartz, Pierre Vidal-Naquet, as well as
Kouchner.[1]

This document marked the beginning of an important shift in French
debates on Third World conflicts—a shift that would come to define the stakes
of left-wing views on intervention in international affairs by the end of the
1970s, toward the primacy of the humanitarian over the political.[2] Rejecting
the idea that UN member-states "dying from wealth" were simply passively
complicit with the genocide that had taken place, the text argued instead that
such nations "deliberately rejected all procedures that would have permitted
saving those ethnic groups for which we already fear we must begin to mourn."
Directly implicated here were both a "pseudo-Labor" Great Britain and "pseudo-
Socialist" Soviet Union, who provided arms for the conflict, but also—and this
signals the import of this text—"almost all African and Arab States, 'Third
World' States, socialist, democratic, and fascist States," and even UN Secretary-General U Thant, who had "given his murderous blessing to the great
cause of the unity of petrol in Nigeria." With a relentless pessimism, the signers
advanced the claim that the "Biafran event" actually "totalizes" all historical
atrocities, from the slow murder of Native Americans to the "transformation of
Jews into soap and Black Sudanese into game birds," ultimately heralding "the
beginning of a decidedly new era in which any constituted nation can, in front
of any other or of all nations, brag about doing whatever it wants in the name of
any principle whatsoever."[3]

Left-wing anxiety concerning some of the results of decolonization would
only increase over the course of the 1970s, when charges of "totalitarianism"
against any (or all) socialist states became both a matter of vigorous public
debate and also a way of pillorying opponents caught on the "wrong" side of
the issue. As I turn here to one of the most important debates in the 1970s on
the Left concerning foreign policy and French responsibilities toward both its
former colonies and toward Third World countries in general, it is important

---

1   "Des personnalités de gauche dénoncent 'un gangstérisme aux dimensions de la
planète,' " *Le Monde*, January 13, 1970, 4.
2   This shift would later be cemented in 1988 by the creation, under Socialist Prime
Minister Michel Rocard, of the position of secretary of state for humanitarian action—a
position filled by none other than Kouchner.
3   *Le Monde*, "Des personnalités de gauche dénoncent 'un gangstérisme aux dimensions de la planète.' " See also Richard Marienstras's similar condemnation of the lack of
intervention by capable powers (the UN, Great Britain, the USSR, Egypt) in *Les Temps
Modernes*'s special section on Biafra. Richard Marienstras, "Biafra: La fin d'une nation," *Les
Temps Modernes* 283 (February 1970), 1169.

to keep in mind previous discussions of *gauchiste* support for worker immigrants from the former colonies and regionalist movements in France. The key
concern of Sartre and others on the noncommunist Left in taking up their
causes had been the promotion of freedom—whether it be social, economic,
political, or cultural. The concept of freedom provided *both* an important
continuity for and a rupture with arguments in favor of French socialism, and
also the late-1970s critique of Third Worldism on humanitarian grounds. In
terms of continuity, the mistrust of the state as necessarily repressive—a
mistrust that grew out of left-wing analyses of the Soviet Union under Stalin, of
which Sartre's *Critique of Dialectical Reason* was among the earliest and best
known in France—blossomed during the 1970s into broad support on the Left
for reconciling socialism with the basic liberties guaranteed in Western democ-
racies. Appeals to decentralization and popular democracy were staples of
radical left-wing attempts to defend the individual. Railing against the
Communist Party and Soviet repression, *gauchistes* would feel much more at
home among the French Socialist Party.

Yet some claims to freedom—in particular, those based on culture—
proved far more difficult for the Left to defend with vigor. In spite of left-wing
interest in the early 1970s in anti-racist and regionalist movements—both of
which insisted in some way upon culture as an important variable in claims for
autonomy or political representation—by the end of the 1970s one of the
central tenets of the anticolonial era, the right of self-determination of peoples,
had been rejected by large segments of the intellectual Left (except, perhaps
paradoxically, when it came to European countries such as Poland).

Both such continuity and rupture with *gauchiste* interpretations of freedom
were directly related to a rise in fortunes of the critique of "totalitarianism"
(pursuant to the publication of Alexander Solzhenitsyn's *The Gulag Archipelago*
in France in 1974), which, aside from being applied to Nazi fascism and Soviet
communism, came to be associated with all manner of undemocratic regimes
that emerged in the wake of decolonization. As Michael Scott Christofferson
has shown, the emergence of "totalitarianism" as a key term of political debate
in France was intimately tied to the battle between communists and anticommunist socialists for hegemony on the Left; ultimately, it was the socialists who
won, putting their leader François Mitterrand into power in 1981.[4]

The ideological war these two sides waged gathered the Third Worldist
critique of colonialism and neocolonialism in its wake. Although the very

---

4   See Michael Scott Christofferson, *French Intellectuals Against the Left: The Antitotalitarian Moment of the 1970s* (New York: Berghahn Books, 2004).

definition of *Third* Worldism had entailed nonalignment with either of the two superpower blocs, the undemocratic outcomes of many Third World revolutions made them easy targets for the "totalitarianism" label—which the noncommunist Left was quick to hang on them, thus associating them with the totalitarian regimes in Eastern Europe and their French representative, the Communist Party. In a complex and often confused debate that took place under the auspices of left-leaning *Le Nouvel Observateur* in the late 1970s, noncommunist intellectuals renounced the hopes many of them had placed in the Third World. Calling for the protection of the rights of individuals against predatory, "totalitarian" Third World governments, these intellectuals breathed new life into the rhetoric of the polemical opposition of European civilization to non-European barbarism, effectively reanimating the moral discourse of France's *mission civilisatrice*, according to the debate's observers.

Through the debate on these vexing subjects, intellectuals on the Left ultimately sat in judgment on the process of decolonization itself, I argue, discrediting and reversing many of the key claims of anticolonialists. I wish to show how, once again, Jean-Paul Sartre played a role in all of these debates, sometimes as an activist, but also as an increasingly discredited symbol of the a fallen Third Worldism. His health failing by the early 1970s (he became blind enough in 1973 that he could not read), Sartre was no longer a master polemicist who could move debate on his own; at the same time, he was still France's biggest intellectual "star," whose presence at any event or participation in any project generated spontaneous media coverage—a fact that those who used him (and he was happy to be used) knew well.

FROM ANTICOLONIALISM TO A "DUTY TO INTERVENE"?

In June 1978, Parti Socialiste (PS) supporter and longtime *Esprit* collaborator Jacques Julliard published a scathing polemic in *Le Nouvel Observateur* condemning the confidence many on the Left had given to Third World revolutions, particularly in the 1960s, which he judged to have been misplaced. His essay, "The Third World and the Left," sparked immediate controversy. In it, he made his infamous claim, "There will be no African socialism that is not totalitarian," stressing that there was at that moment an impossible choice between "a corrupt, unjust, repressive [*policière*], and often bloody capitalist Africa and a 'socialist' Africa that is simultaneously anarchic and tyrannical, and no less bloody."[5]

---

5   Jacques Julliard, "Le tiers monde et la gauche," in Samir Amin et al., *Le tiers monde et la gauche* (Paris: Editions du Seuil, 1979), 38. As an indication of the international stakes of

In Julliard's rendering of Africa, it seems that not only socialist regimes in Africa were "totalitarian," but regimes of all political stripes were. The reason, he judged, was Europeans' export of their own "ideologies," above all the dogma of the right of self-determination. "The right of peoples," he averred, "has become the principal instrument for strangling the rights of man." The result was that Third World states everywhere were using that right as a shield to repress their citizenry with impunity. The United Nations, meanwhile, had "sacrificed its liberal ideals to the principle of nonintervention," thus becoming "the docile instrument of the bloodiest of religions, the religion of the state, legitimated by national sovereignty." For Julliard, "No, nation-states are not the expression of the freedom of peoples. Yes, there are indeed two camps in the Third World. But these two camps are not American and Soviet. They are torturing states and martyred peoples." The only solution Julliard saw to this deplorable situation was to integrate citizens of the world irrespective of the political regime they lived under into an "International of the Rights of Man, which is the only response to the International of the States."[6]

Julliard's essay marked an important moment in left-wing debate on the Third World for two reasons, both recognized and hotly contested at the time. First, it set the debate firmly within the horizon of contemporary discussions on totalitarianism, which had emerged as a crucial term of political contest with the appearance in France of Alexander Solzhenitsyn's *The Gulag Archipelago*. Second, it cast decolonization, especially in Africa, as an enormous and almost unimaginable catastrophe. These two reasons were intimately linked: it was the strong, repressive, "totalitarian" state that was at the root of the postcolonial horror. Decolonization had failed—failed deeply—to change anything for the suffering citizens of the Third World; colonialism was gone, but repression remained: "Free just so long as they were fighting for their

---

Julliard's claims, the first sentence in Article 1 of the International Covenant on Economic, Social and Cultural Rights reads: "All peoples have the right of self-determination." Center for the Study of Human Rights, *Twenty-Five Human Rights Documents* (New York: Center for the Study of Human Rights, Columbia University, 1994), 10.

6   Julliard, "Le tiers monde et la gauche," 38–40. More up-to-date sociological litera-ture suggests that Julliard's implicit comparison of the African *post*colonial state to the "totalitarianism" of Stalin's Soviet Union was inapt. In their comparison of postcolonial states in Africa with post-Soviet states in Eurasia, Mark R. Beissinger and Crawford Young argue that the dysfunction and crisis of these "post-" regimes stem from the fact that they are heirs to the two most transformative and authoritarian state models of the twentieth century: the Stalinist state and the African *colonial* state. See Mark R. Beissinger and Crawford Young, "Introduction: Comparing State Crises across Two Continents," in Beissinger and Young, eds, *Beyond State Crisis: Postcolonial Africa and Post-Soviet Eurasia in Comparative Perspective* (Washington, D.C.: Woodrow Wilson Center Press, 2002), 11.

national emancipation, the peoples of the Third World fall immediately, once this is obtained, into the hands of pitiless dictatorships."[7]

Julliard's assertions were bold and sweeping—and also controversial, so much so that the editors of *Le Nouvel Observateur* decided to organize a debate in its pages assessing the merit of Julliard's position. Had many of the core beliefs held by many leftists concerning colonialism, neocolonialism, economic dependency, and the desirability of immediate political independence and sovereignty been mistaken? And, if so, why? Were repressive states, rather than international economic and political arrangements, or domestic social conditions, truly to blame for the lack of development in many Third World countries? Had culture-based claims for defining rights had the effect of repressing individual freedom in a severely detrimental way, or the freedom of members of other minority groups? Was the power of the postcolonial state so robust that its repressive aspects outweighed and outdid the lingering effects of the violent social reconfiguration that the old colonial power had imposed through force? Or was the much-decried postcolonial state in fact just a continuation of the state apparatus invented by the colonial power?

Few of these questions were discussed with much seriousness by those criticizing the Third World. What was discussed instead, by the likes of Bernard Kouchner, Jean-Pierre Le Dantec, Régis Debray, Jean Lacouture, Jean Ziegler, Maxime Rodinson, Gérard Chaliand, Samir Amin, and others, was largely the "illusions," "fantasies," "desires," and current "guilt" of the so-called Third Worldists, by this time rendered as a unified group of people sharing a rather vague—yet dogmatically and perhaps fanatically held—ideology that was based on a blind faith in the redemptive power of Third World liberation movements. That is, the *Nouvel Observateur*'s debate on "The Third World and the Left" was self-consciously about the Left's own instrumentalization of the Third World, an instrumentalization that the debate itself often appeared to reenact and continue. One of the main assumptions of the critics of Third Worldism appears to have been that, as an ideology, Third Worldism did not merely undermine the concern for human rights, but was fundamentally incompatible with it.

What prompted Julliard's essay? In the preface to the essays collected in *Le tiers monde et la gauche*, published in 1979 in the series "*Le Nouvel Observateur présente*" for Editions du Seuil, Jean Daniel averred that it was an effect of the disillusionment of the Left with the outcome of revolutions in the Third World. Or, as the editor of the volume, André Burguière, claimed, "To be

---

7   Ibid., 39.

honest, the subject of this debate is not the Third World, but Third Worldism."[8] Like many of the participants in the debate, he appealed explicitly to the psychology and the personal histories of left-wing intellectuals, whose youthful idealism had led them to the error of utopianism. What some of the critics of Third Worldism—Julliard, and especially Kouchner and Le Dantec— argued was that their earlier commitments concerning decolonization should be viewed not as *political* in nature, but rather as a matter of personal desire or a fascination with the exotic. This depoliticization was somewhat at odds with the alternative claim that Third Worldism had been too political—in effect, elevating politics above the universalist (and, hence, apolitical) commitment to human rights. In any case, Kouchner even went so far as to claim that support for revolutionary movements had come from a "masculine taste for violence-spectacle," thereby emptying these engagements of all meaningful political content.[9] In so doing, critics made the implicit claim that their current judgments on issues concerning the Third World were based on a more informed, clear-eyed realism.

The frequent appeal to totalitarianism in the debate suggests, however, that more was at stake than simply coming to terms with youthful error. Instead, I argue that what motivated this move was an attempt on the part of intellectuals sympathetic to the PS to build its support against the PCF. In this, I follow the arguments of Michael Scott Christofferson in *French Intellectuals Against the Left: The Antitotalitarian Moment of the 1970s*, though I might give more weight to the interrelationship of foreign and domestic concerns than he does in his book.[10]

According to Christofferson, the emergence among French intellectuals in the mid 1970s of an interest in totalitarianism was not, as is often claimed by both historians and the intellectuals themselves, the effect of the "shock" of finding out the "real" nature of the repressive Soviet regime under Stalin by reading Solzhenitsyn's *The Gulag Archipelago*. French intellectuals already knew about the gulag system (largely dismantled by the 1970s) and had openly criticized it—Sartre and Merleau-Ponty among them—in the late 1940s and after. Rather, the publishing of *The Gulag Archipelago* was used as an occasion for the noncommunist Left to shore up its political position against the PCF, which had adopted a Common Program in a "Union of the Left" with the PS in

---

8   André Burguière, "Introduction," in Amin et al., *Le tiers monde et la gauche*, 14.

9   Bernard Kouchner, "Les bons et les mauvais morts," in Amin et al., *Le tiers monde et la gauche*, 45–6.

10   Michael Scott Christofferson, *French Intellectuals Against the Left: The Antitotalitarian Moment of the 1970s* (New York: Berghahn Books, 2004).

1972 in an effort to bring a unified left-wing government to power. When, even before its publication, the PCF started to attack Solzhenitsyn's book, noncommunist intellectuals took this as a sign that the PCF was still up to its old Stalinist tricks of terrorizing and dissimulating, and was not only an undesirable political partner, but perhaps a dangerous one. According to Christofferson, socialist intellectuals actually feared the loss of basic civil liberties in France should the PCF come to power in a Union of the Left, and the critique of totalitarianism was thus a strategy they used primarily to discredit the Communist Party in France, rather than the Soviet Union.[11]

Christofferson's argument is persuasive, and the evidence he marshals impressive. Though he might have extended it to the debate on Third Worldism in *Le Nouvel Observateur*, he does not do so in any substantial way, mentioning it only briefly in his conclusion.[12] It is clear, however, that the terms "totalitarianism," "Solzhenitsyn," and "gulag" were all key to the participants' depictions of and arguments concerning the Third World. Aside from Julliard's conclusion that totalitarianism was the dominant political fact of African nations, Le Dantec, for example, wrote that postcolonial leaders in the Third World who had been educated "in the same universities as us [were] naturally ready to place themselves under the protective wing of the first totalitarianism to come along, provided that it was 'progressive.'"[13] Kouchner referred twice to "the gulag" in his plea for viewing "oppression as *one* ... no one can any longer distinguish whether the Left—socialism—or the Right—capitalism —holds the record for it."[14] Maxime Rodinson, the great ethnologist of Islam and the Arab world, also made the debate on revolution and the gulag a central theme of his contribution, writing that many still had not absorbed the lesson to be learned from the "belated discovery" of the gulag system's existence.[15]

Not all of the participants were comfortable with these references, however. Claude Bourdet, the former editor of *Combat* (after Camus) and *L'Observateur* (later *France Observateur*) and a stalwart anticolonialist from the

---

11   Christofferson does not discuss in detail the strategy, articulated by the PS faction closest in ideology to the PCF, called the Centre d'Etudes et de Recherches Socialistes (CERES), of criticizing communism as a way to help the anti-Stalinist forces within the PCF to assert themselves. On this point, see David Hanley, "CERES—An Open Conspiracy?" in D.S. Bell and Eric Shaw, eds, *The Left in France: Towards the Socialist Republic* (Nottingham, UK: Spokesman, 1983), 112–13.

12   Christofferson, *French Intellectuals Against the Left*, 267.

13   Jean-Pierre Le Dantec, "Une barbarie peut en cacher une autre," in Amin et al., *Le tiers monde et la gauche*, 42.

14   Kouchner, "Les bons et les mauvais morts," 47.

15   Maxime Rodinson, "La fin des 'compagnons de route,'" in Amin, et al., *Le tiers monde et la gauche*, 54.

1950s, outlined the division among participants, writing that he felt closer to "Jean Ziegler, Maxime Rodinson, Guy Sitbon, Jean Rous, Jean Lacouture, Ahmed Baba Miské, and Thomas Sisowath than to Jacques Julliard, Bernard Kouchner, and Jean-Pierre Le Dantec."[16] The former group still believed that Third World countries were of political interest, that the distinction between progressive and nonprogressive governments might be maintained in some cases, and that it was worthwhile for Europeans to support some causes rather than others on political grounds. They also continued to hold the "Third Worldist" view that neocolonialism was a fact of international economic and political arrangements. None of these men were members of the PCF (Rodinson, a member until 1958, was a fellow-traveler), and many of them, such as Bourdet and Rous, were active and important members of the PS.[17]

As for the latter group, though Julliard, Kouchner, and Le Dantec took pains to say that Third World countries had certainly been hamstrung by the legacy of colonialism, the lion's share of the blame for the disastrous outcome of decolonization in Third World countries was, they said, to be laid at the feet of repressive states. "Authoritarian socialism" and "bureaucratic machines modeled on Eastern European countries" were the terms Le Dantec used; colonial historian René Gallisot described the phenomenon as "state nationalism."[18] Some, such as Le Dantec, still believed that their positions in the 1950s and 1960s had been correct, even if the outcomes had not been what were imagined. Le Dantec wished to be "understood correctly, in particular by those who suffer and struggle against hunger, racism, humiliation … I will—we will—always be at their side against our own military."[19] Nonetheless, paradoxically, earlier support for anticolonial and revolutionary movements had been based on mere "imaginary territories" invented in the minds of Europeans.

Those participants who wished to defend the records of at least some postcolonial states, and also to reject the collapse of distinctions among them, took dead aim at the term "totalitarianism" and, as Ahmed Baba Miské put it, "the democratic friends of the Anti-Gulag International."[20] Miské, who was a

---

16   Claude Bourdet, "La gauche mélancolique," in Amin, et al., *Le tiers monde et la gauche*, 127.

17   Rous, a former companion of Trotsky, had also been a significant anticolonialist figure in the 1940s and 1950s. On Bourdet and Rous, see Paul Clay Sorum, *Intellectuals and Decolonization in France* (Chapel Hill: University of North Carolina Press, 1977), 17, 49, 51.

18   Le Dantec, "Une barbarie peut en cacher une autre," 42, 43; René Gallisot, "Les empires se portent bien," in Amin et al., *Le tiers monde et la gauche*, 57.

19   Jean-Pierre Le Dantec, "Une barbarie peut en cacher une autre," 41.

20   Ahmed Baba Miské, "Les nouveaux civilisateurs," in Amin et al., *Le tiers monde et la gauche*, 72.

member of Mauritania's Front Polisario, and Sitbon, reporter at *Le Nouvel Observateur*, pleaded for nuance in the discussion. "Each country is different," Sitbon pointed out. And though it was not forbidden for French intellectuals to see the world in a Manichean vein—"On one side, those who don't live like us: the gulag. On the other, civilization, us."—he added, "Isn't this a little simple to 'gulagize' two-thirds of humanity with a single teardrop?"[21] Miské similarly complained that "it is not fair to put in the same sack, *including when it comes to human rights*, Tanzania and Morocco, Madagascar and Uganda, Algeria and Zaïre, Guinea-Bissau and the Central African Empire (and, moreover, Vietnam and the Philippines, etc.)." Moreover,

> in those countries that appear to you [the critics] to be fixed, blocked in authoritarian—you employ the word "totalitarian" which ought to be used, I think, with more rigor—systems, a hard, permanent struggle is unfolding at all levels, including at the heart of power, for the institution of a more just society.[22]

For his part, Régis Debray objected that the discourse on totalitarianism was not applicable in any coherent way to states in the Third World. If violent repression and civil war were constant features of the Third World political landscape, it was because too many states in the Third World were *weak*, rather than strong—perhaps prefiguring the post–Cold War focus on the "failed state" and the necessity of "nation-building." He also made the case that Julliard and others, against their own better judgment, wished to aid objectively the forces of neocolonialism that they continued to decry:

> Everyone knows that the Cambodian people do not suffer from an excess of state but rather, and to the point of martyrdom, from the absence of a state— juridically and practically independent from the arbitrary [power] of the party. For, instead of helping promote states ruled by law [*Etats de droit*], whose existence is the first condition of the exercise of individual rights, instead of accompanying the movement of submitting backward civil societies (with their religious, social, or racial discrimination) to the formal authority of the public power, the ideology of human rights sacrifices [itself] to the present interests of the Western bourgeoisies: weaken to the maximum the sovereign states of the periphery in order to extend itself directly into the riches and the labor forces of the country, without an intermediary "bureaucracy," without juridical controls or national barriers.[23]

---

21   Martine Sitbon, "Le temps des méprises," in Amin et al., *Le tiers monde et la gauche*, 75.

22   Miské, "Les nouveaux civilisateurs," 71.

23   Régis Debray, "Il faut des esclaves aux hommes libres," in Amin et al., *Le tiers monde et la gauche*, 91.

Though Debray did not specify how the interests of the Western bourgeoisie were being gratified by mass killing in Cambodia, he put his finger on one of the least convincing elements of the totalitarianism moniker as applied to the Third World: Did these often cash-strapped and aid-dependent governments —especially by the late 1970s, after the first oil shock and the collapse of many commodities' prices meant that many Third World countries were massively in debt—have sufficient resources to reach into and to command all areas of social life in comparison with, say, Nazi Germany or the Soviet Union?

Thus, on the level of internal coherence, there is something puzzling about the transference of the totalitarian discourse to the Third World as a whole. On the level of domestic political contest, however, the transfer made a great deal of sense. Kouchner excoriated the PS's lack of a foreign policy; indeed, he wrote, "The PS is abandoning this terrain to its great rival, the PCF, which remains the principal provider of ready-to-wear [ideas] in the matter of international opinion."[24] *Le Nouvel Observateur*'s debate on the Third World was an attempt to correct this lack by consciously attacking both the PCF and Soviet-aided causes.

Thus, although "totalitarianism" may have been applied to regimes of both the Right and the Left, when Julliard did mention *specific* countries and struggles, they tended to be those that had made claims to being "progressive." Hence he and others wrote of Cambodia, Vietnam, and Guinea as countries that had instituted "totalitarian" regimes; and they also wrote of the Cuban- and USSR-supported conflicts in Angola and Eritrea that were then ongoing. These latter conflicts were key references in the debate. All of the "denouncers" of Third Worldism—Julliard, Kouchner, Le Dantec, Gallisot, and Rodinson—wrote about at least one of them.[25] Kouchner's take on Africa was typical: he condemned Cuban intervention in Angola and Eritrea, as well as those on the French "Left" who supported it. The focus on these conflicts was an important signal that the debate was not only, or even primarily, about the "fantasies" of 1960s-era Third Worldism, but rather about *contemporary communist support* for intervention.

Moreover, discussions of Angola and Eritrea enabled the introduction of a useful confusion into the debate: on the one hand, "Third Worldism" as defined in the Bandung era meant nonalignment with *either* superpower—and the Soviet Union had been skeptical of or even hostile to many revolutionary movements in the Third World, especially those led by "adventurists" such as

---

24   Kouchner, "Les bons et les mauvais morts," 49.
25   These five comprised the section of *Le tiers monde et la gauche* entitled "Third Worldism Denounced."

Che Guevara; on the other, noncommunist French intellectuals in the debate wanted to associate the Soviet Union and its PCF allies with the abuses of Third World revolutionaries and regimes. Kouchner in particular made great use of this confusion. "On the Left," he wrote, "we try to forget that Africa, following Asia, now sees the … extension of massacres. We condemn all the Western interventions, approving by this fact of all the Soviet deployments and the Cuban troops."[26] Though Kouchner did not specify who was included in the "we" of these claims, clearly it was the communist, and not the noncommunist, Left that was targeted, since most on the noncommunist Left had lost their confidence in either Cuba or the Soviet Union years before. The fact is, many so-called Third Worldists, Sartre chief among them, were strongly critical of the Soviet Union, particularly in the 1970s, and certainly did not support the export of the Soviet model to Third World countries. The claim, then, that Third Worldists hypocritically criticized US imperialism while supporting Soviet imperialism seems implausible when applied generally.

In short, participants in the debate on Third Worldism chose their examples strategically. In some sense, even Burguière's claim in his introduction that the debate was about "Third Worldism," and not the "Third World," is unconvincing. Three of the denouncers—Le Dantec, Kouchner, and Gallisot—cited Che Guevara's famous speech in which he called for the creation of "two, three … many Vietnams"—Gallisot even opens with that famous phrase—as a kind of foundational moment for *all* regimes to have come after. Guevara could certainly have been classed as a Third Worldist, precisely *because* the Soviet Union's position on his activity was not just ambiguous, but even hostile— especially after his famed "disappearance" in order to create clandestine armed rebellions around the world that this speech had announced. The assimilation of Third Worldism to Soviet communism abruptly denuded Third Worldism of its central claim of neutrality with respect to Soviet communism—thus dissolving its particular force. This Third Worldism that the late-1970s French intellectual Left wished to evoke was not exactly the Third Worldism of the era of decolonization.

TOWARD A JUSTIFICATION FOR INTERVENTION

Pointing out the political instrumentalization of the critique of Third Worldism is not to make a judgment about whether certain criticisms were right or wrong. Nor do I wish to suggest that participants were not serious about what

---

26   Kouchner, "Les bons et les mauvais morts," 48.

they were saying. Rather, my aim is to show that, in addition helping accrue political benefit to the noncommunist Left, the debate appears to have been about an issue larger than the critique of Third Worldism. That issue was decolonization—and, more precisely, the contemporary relationship between France and its former colonies—which encompassed Third Worldism as only one aspect of its process.

This claim is borne out by taking a closer look at the specific political context of Julliard's essay. Though in his introduction to *Le tiers monde et la gauche*, Burguière tried to cast the essay as an attack on left-wing Third Worldists, even a quick glance at the contents of the *Nouvel Observateur* edition in which Julliard's essay actually appeared points to a provocation of the *opposite* kind. The most significant story for the magazine in May–June 1978 was President Valéry Giscard d'Estaing's decision to conduct a military and humanitarian intervention in Zaïre, and it was *this* story that provided the direct context for Julliard's article. Giscard had intervened on behalf of the corrupt, pro-Western Mobutu government, which had lost control of part of the strategically valued mining region of Shaba (formerly Katanga—the secessionist region from the early independence days) to rebels who sought not just control of the region but also the overthrow of Mobutu. It came to be known as the Second Shaba War,[27] although it was a short-lived one, as the deployment of French and Belgian forces immediately restored control of the region to Mobutu. This was, Daniel noted, the fourth such intervention since Giscard had taken office in 1974 (the other three taking place in Chad, Mauritania, and Lebanon). "In short," he wrote, "Valéry Giscard d'Estaing wishes for France a certain form of presence outside of its borders that makes us appear in the eyes of the world—and the Third World—interventionists."[28]

In addition to being an attack on misguided leftists, Julliard's claim that the "right of peoples has become the principal instrument for strangling the rights of man" should be viewed as a condemnation, perhaps first and foremost, of the Mobutu regime that Giscard had just sent troops to support. This was precisely how Jean Daniel read Julliard's essay. Daniel argued that, since the Shaba rebels had essentially "offered Giscard a humanitarian pretext for his intervention," now the Left merely had to "denounce his crusade in the very name of the arguments developed in this issue by Jacques Julliard, and which I consider to be irrefutable."[29] Thus, Julliard was not giving primary attention to

---

27   For details, see Winsome J. Leslie, *Zaire: Continuity and Political Change in an Oppressive State* (Boulder, Colo.: Westview Press, 1993), 138–9.

28   Jean Daniel, "Giscard l'Africain," *Le Nouvel Observateur* 704, (May 8–14, 1978), 38.

29   Daniel then footnoted the article "Le tiers monde et la gauche." Jean Daniel,

a state that had been overtaken by a Third Worldist revolution, or that was supported by the so-called Third Worldists. Quite the contrary. This was why the concept of totalitarianism was such a convenient tool—it could be, and was, applied to regimes of the Right and the Left, and used to criticize French supporters of either type of regime.

It is thus important to view Julliard's own "intervention" against the backdrop of President Giscard d'Estaing's activist foreign policy, and as a critique of policy toward Third World nations of Giscard's conservative Independent Republicans. I argue in this section that Julliard—along with many on the Left—was attempting to re-establish the noncommunist Left's *own* criteria for the legitimate reasons, rules, and goals for intervention, and to do so in such a way as to marginalize and even attack the positions not just of political competitors on the Left, as we have seen, but also of those on the Right, such as Giscard.

Decolonization, according to the left-wing critics, had gone wrong; but where, exactly? As Julliard claimed, and almost everyone agreed (Régis Debray and Ahmed Baba Miské being strong exceptions), the problem had been with the emphasis on the right of self-determination of peoples—one of the fundamental principles of the liberal postwar world order and the moral lynchpin of claims for decolonization. There were two arguments made for reconsidering and even rejecting this principle. First, as I have already noted, Julliard and his supporters argued that it was all too often used as a shield behind which regimes might commit human rights abuses. The second argument—paradoxical, given the first—was that belief in the possibility of self-determination was absurd, since Third World countries were not autonomous at all, but rather subjects of US, Soviet, and Chinese empires. "Does the Third World still exist?" asked Julliard. "In terms of poverty and underdevelopment, more than ever. In terms of nonalignment, less and less. Already, all of Asia has been divided into spheres of influence: Soviet, American, and Chinese."[30]

Kristin Ross has made the astute observation of the late-1970s left-wing critique of Third Worldism that it represented an evisceration of the 1960s image of Third World people(s) as individual or collective political agents, replacing that image with one of Third World people(s) as agency-less victims.

"L'affaire Erulin," *Le Nouvel Observateur* 707 (June 5–11, 1978), 32. Daniel's article is about the discovery that one of the military leaders of the intervention, Colonel Erulin, who had been declared the "hero of Kolwezi," had been recognized that spring by Henri Alleg as one of his torturers during the French-Algerian War. Daniel was thus able to depict the links between colonialism and neocolonialism using more than just analogies, but with reference to particular continuities.

30   Julliard, "Le tiers monde et la gauche," 36.

"Fanon's 'wretched of the earth' as the name for an emergent political agency," she claims,

> has been essentially reinvented: the new third world is still wretched, but its agency has disappeared, leaving only the misery of a collective victim of famine, flood, or authoritarian state apparatuses. The whole political subjectivation that took shape among some French over the War in Algeria is annihilated.[31]

Though her generalization in compelling, Ross could have linked it more directly to the political context for this shift. She links it instead (and with some reason) to broader processes, such as "the conversion of some ex-*gauchistes* to the values of the market" and the "retreat" of French intellectuals from politics into ethics.[32]

But there is stronger reason to see the denigration of Third Worldism as an early and formative expression of a fundamental rethinking on the French socialist Left's relationship to the Third World, and especially to its former colonies. The perceived failure of decolonization either to produce "progressive" regimes or to break the bonds of imperialism (US or Soviet) meant that the commitment to and engagement with Third World countries had to be retooled—and not, as a Cartierist might argue, abandoned in favor of aiding French compatriots first. Indeed, many of the commentators argued that criticism of Third Worldism ought not to be read as a plea for the French government's back to be turned on Third World countries. As Burguière noted of contributors Lacouture, Chaliand, Rous, Bourdet, and Sisowath, they feared "a Cartierism of the Left that would have catastrophic effects on aid."[33] By the same token, Giscardian-style intervention to prop up corrupt pro-Western regimes must also be rejected as an extension of US foreign policy—and hence imperialist—aims. Thus, the moral claims to support for and involvement with independence movements developed in the course of decolonization were not to be jettisoned, but rather reformulated in the discourse on the protection of human rights.

New ends also had to be developed along with this reformulation. Those ends were to include development aid, which the PS had promised to raise to the 0.7 percent of GDP recommended by the United Nations, as well as the will

---

31   Ross, *May '68 and Its Afterlives*, 156–7.
32   Ibid., 180, 168.
33   André Burguière, "Du tiers-mondisme au tiers monde," in Amin et al., *Le tiers monde et la gauche*, 97. These writers appeared in the section Burguière entitled "From Third Worldism to the Third World."

to stand up for the interests of Third World countries against US and Soviet imperialisms. Each of these can be interpreted as strongly in line with anti-colonialist principles, in that development aid might help Third World countries achieve the economic independence they lacked, and nonalignment with either of the superpowers was a staple of much noncommunist anti-colonialist discourse. By making human rights, and not self-determination and autonomy of peoples, the centerpiece of this reformulation, the socialist Left put itself in a position to effect a startling reversal of anticolonial principles: a move toward a left-wing justification of intervention on humanitarian grounds. Whereas radicals' support for revolutionary movements in the 1960s might have entailed a personal engagement with revolutionaries—as in the case of Sartre's ethics of personal responsibility for the least favored, regardless of nationality—here the ground was laid for the argument that a *state* has the right to intervene in the affairs of another when the protection of human rights is at stake, regardless of nationality.[34]

None of the participants in *Le Nouvel Observateur*'s debate went so far as to argue immediately for state intervention to protect human rights. Indeed, Julliard seems to have rejected this idea out of hand, writing, "A French government, no matter its politics, can do practically nothing for the Czechs. Nor for the Cambodians nor the Vietnamese nor the Argentineans. Nor for the Ethiopians nor the people of Zaïre."[35] Nonetheless, one can see in these texts, and particularly in Kouchner's contribution, the beginnings of what by the late 1980s and early 1990s would come to be known as the *droit d'ingérence*—a "right," based ultimately in international law and principles, to intervene in another state on humanitarian grounds. One of the original proponents of this right was Kouchner, who edited the seminal volume *Le Devoir d'ingérence: peut-on les laisser mourir?* with Mario Bettati in 1987 under the auspices of his foundation Médecins du Monde, launching the career of an idea that gained a considerable amount of force in international affairs in the post–Cold War era.[36]

---

34   This marked a direct contrast with Giscard's official justification for intervening in the Second Shaba War, which was to protect French citizens threatened with violence in that part of Zaïre.

35   Julliard, "Le tiers monde et la gauche," 40. He argued instead that left-wing intellectuals had the responsibility of protesting equally all human rights abuses, whether the perpetrator was "progressive" or not—again, an attack on the communists.

36   Mario Bettati and Bernard Kouchner, eds, *Le Devoir d'ingérence: peut-on les laisser mourir?* (Paris: Denoël, 1987). Kouchner had broken with Médecins Sans Frontières in the late 1970s.

The germ of this idea was generated from the French Left's questioning of the right of self-determination of peoples in the late 1970s. If it was true, as Julliard had argued on the basis of the cases he identified, that "nation-states are not the expression of the freedom of peoples," then those entities would lose their legitimate claim to sovereignty.

RECASTING SARTRE

By the late 1970s, Sartre was too ill to participate meaningfully in these debates;[37] yet his presence in them was still palpable. Not only had Sartre been a world-famous representative of Third Worldism, however it was defined—he had actually launched the phrase in his preface to Fanon's *Wretched of the Earth*. It is difficult not to view the Left's recasting of its relations with the Third World as a simultaneous recasting of the Third Worldist version of Sartre: the staunch defender of the FLN in Algeria; the enthusiastic supporter of Cuba in the "honeymoon" of its revolution; the melancholy observer of the failed revolution in the Congo (later Zaïre); and the denouncer of US actions in Vietnam as genocide.

Sartre was not frequently mentioned by the participants in *Le Nouvel Observateur*'s debate. When putting together the essays for *Le tiers monde et la gauche*, however, Burguière sneaked Sartre in as one of the main symbols of the Third Worldism he claimed many of the essayists to be denouncing. The book included an appendix, entitled "Some Signposts of an Itinerary," three items of which are directly related to Sartre. The first, "Polemic between *Les Temps Modernes* and Jean Daniel," was from the spring of 1960. At issue was whether or not the Left in France ought to support the FLN; *Les Temps Modernes* argued that it should, as the only method of forcing de Gaulle to grant full independence. Daniel countered that the Left should not abandon its principles by aiding a group that "is marked by Arab-Islamism." Even though it was "without a doubt the most progressive [movement] among the Arab nationalisms … the very conditions of its struggle direct it toward Arabism and by this token it is not yet the carrier of universality."[38] Daniel worried that non-Muslim minorities, who had prospered under the colonial system, would be punished were the FLN to come to power.

The second text was the Manifesto of the 121, which Burguière characterized as a document that "illustrates well the ambivalence of Third Worldism,

---

37   For a description of Sartre's slow physical deterioration, see Beauvoir, *Adieux*.

38   Jean Daniel, "Socialisme et anti-colonialisme," in Amin et al., *Le tiers monde et la gauche*, 169.

which was able to give rise to an effective and just political mobilization on the Left from the starting point of a partially phantasmatic analysis."[39] The third was an extract from Fanon's *The Wretched of the Earth*. Though Burguière found the book to be "powerful and inspired," he concluded that its "messianic and universalist escapism (Third World peoples have to resolve the problems in front of which Europe had demonstrated itself as impotent)," made it the most important indicator of the state of the young, rebellious French Left in the 1960s.[40]

Sartre was thus in play as a paradigmatic representative of the presumed excesses of French Third Worldists who, according to the their denouncers, simply substituted the Third World peasantry for the proletariat in their messianic historical schema after having become disillusioned with the Soviet Union in 1956. (Of course, once again, this would seem to have contradicted some of the denouncers' identifications of Third Worldism with the communists and the Soviet Union.)

Although Sartre's symbolic function in *Le Nouvel Observateur*'s debate was largely hidden, Pascal Bruckner was to amplify and solidify this function a few years later in his controversial and much-publicized anti-Third Worldist book, *The Tears of the White Man*. Writing in a polemical style worthy of Sartre himself, Bruckner aimed "to uncover the devious bad faith of the virtue professed by self-appointed partisans of the Third World, their self-admiring sophistry, their selfish alibis, and their dishonest bombast."[41]

Bruckner—a novelist, essayist, and professor of politics who had studied with Roland Barthes in the 1960s—took special aim at Sartre in this look at how the "self-hatred [that] became a central dogma of our culture" had, in his view, fed many left-wing French intellectuals' support for anticolonial, anti-neocolonial, and anti-imperialist views in the 1960s. Even though these intellectuals represented but a small minority of the French population (and even of French intellectuals), Bruckner thought the time was ripe for setting up a "balance sheet of what in France has been called 'Third Worldism.' " For, according to Bruckner, in spite of the "placid indifference, if not hostility, of

---

39   André Burguière, "Manifeste des 121 (septembre 1960)," in Amin et al., *Le tiers monde et la gauche*, 171.

40   André Burguière, "Extrait de l'ouvrage de Frantz Fanon, *les Damnés de la terre*," in Amin et al., *Le tiers monde et la gauche*, 174.

41   Pascal Bruckner, *The Tears of the White Man: Compassion as Contempt*, trans. William R. Beer (New York: The Free Press, 1986), 6 (translation modified). The translator had rendered "mauvaise foi"—a possible dig at Sartre—not as "bad faith," but as "chicanery." In general, this poor translation misconstrues most of the phenomenological terms that Bruckner uses.

most people toward so-called underdeveloped countries," Third Worldist
ideas ran deep in the public consciousness:

> In fact, every Westerner is presumed guilty until proven innocent. We Euro-
> peans have been raised to detest ourselves, certain that, within our world, there
> is a certain essential evil that must be relentlessly atoned for. This evil is known
> by two terms—colonialism and imperialism—tens of millions of Indians [*sic*]
> wiped out by the conquistadores, two hundred million Africans deported or
> dead in the slave trade, and the millions of Asians, Arabs, and Africans killed
> during colonial wars and wars of liberation.
>
> Crushed under the weight of this shameful memory, we have been led to
> believe that the weight of the very Western civilization our fathers thought was
> the greatest on earth is, in fact, the worst.[42]

Bruckner's ultimate goal in the book paralleled the goals of many of the participants in *Le Nouvel Observateur*'s debate: to jettison the outdated fantasies
and illusions of Third Worldism as a method of devising positions and policies
that might better help people in the Third World. To this end, the book was
organized around describing and criticizing three forms of the "look" (*regard*)
that Westerners turned toward the Third World: "(1) Solidarity, the 'being-
together' stance; (2) compassion, the 'being-in-the-place-of' position; and (3)
imitation, the 'being-like' attitude."[43] In his conclusion, Bruckner then
proposed an alternative attitude for friends of the Third World to adopt—one
of "love," which he did not define, but which he described as a nonexclusive
love for both the West and for the Third World. Adopting ideas that appear to
have been influenced by the philosophy of Emmanuel Levinas, Bruckner urged
people to travel to non-Western lands and to take a position of openness
toward and "faith in 'others' " living there. "The faraway peoples, the beyond-
the-seas, the tropics tell us with their myriad voices, their illusions, their
mirages: Come," he wrote in the final sentences of the book. "Come to what?
They do not say. The stranger out there is neither a promise, nor an oath
[*serment*]: only a call."[44]

   In the prologue, Bruckner singled out Sartre as the "magisterial" representative of left-wing intellectuals' "dogma of self-hatred." It was Sartre's refusal of
God, authority, and obedience to accepted values that had set the stage for a
"taste for suffering, for the image of the oppressed."[45] Bruckner continued this

---

42   Ibid., 5, 6, 4.
43   Ibid., 7 (translation modified).
44   Ibid., 172 (translation modified).
45   Ibid., 5 (translation modified).

line of argument in the main body of the book by naming Sartre as the Third Worldist best suited for and most convincing at triggering the "feeling of a debt that can never be repaid"—that is, a kind of original Western sin. The text? Sartre's preface to Fanon's *The Wretched of the Earth*, "about which one can never say enough times that it remains a treasure-trove of theoretical nothingness."[46] Bruckner condemned Sartre's attempt to make the French feel personal complicity in the crimes committed in their name during the French-Algerian War. Although he did not produce any counterarguments, his disagreement was implicit in his characterization of the claim of personal complicity under the psychological rubric of "masochism." For Bruckner, as a direct effect of Sartre's preface,

> Many "progressive" Europeans became living torches of self-punishment, ready to immolate themselves to redeem the debts incurred by their fathers. Miraculously, hostility to "Father," far from being a fault that would burden his offspring, as the Freudian vision would have it, was one and the same as justice. This explains why the support of progressive Europeans went only to those regimes that openly proclaimed their disgust for white civilization.[47]

Bruckner thus extended one of the central trends of *Le Nouvel Observateur*'s debate: the depoliticization of engagements in favor of Third World liberation movements and their recasting as determined upon purely psychological lines. He then relied on Sartre's infamous castigation of the United States in 1953— "Beware! America is a mad dog!"—to argue that leftists channeled their self-hatred toward a demonization of the United States that had no justification outside of psychology. "Parasitical, murderous, and sick, America was the ideal scapegoat," Bruckner averred.

> The existence of a total, absolute, perfect enemy bestowed on us a free hand for hating with serenity, hating with legitimacy, and even hating with high moral purpose ... Suddenly, the internalized hatred of the European was directed at another party, one that was a symbol of absolute crime.[48]

Having explained Europeans' solidarity with Third World liberation movements in terms of a psychology of frustration, resentment, and hatred, Bruckner turned to an examination of the two attitudes to which Sartre, *tiers-mondiste* par excellence, fell prey: masochism and indifference. Summarizing all of Sartre's statements and actions concerning the Third World in a two-page

---

46   Ibid., 14, 185.
47   Ibid., 14.
48   Ibid., 17.

box entitled "Sartre, Third Worldist?" Bruckner questioned whether Sartre's support for liberation movements after the French-Algerian War had had any real teeth.[49] He noted that, after the war in Algeria (during which Sartre had shown "real courage," in Bruckner's estimation), Sartre sat around "polishing his *Flaubert*" and ignoring any civilization other than his own. "He whose ambition was to engage the whole of humanity in his smallest gestures," Bruckner claimed of Sartre, "remained the least critical, the most naïve Euro-centrist."[50] As proof, Bruckner cited what he termed Sartre's moral "abdications"—in particular, to revolutionary regimes ("Let us remember his quasi-apology for the massacre of Israeli athletes by members of the PLO in 1972"); to the Maoists ("giving his name to ideas and actions that went against his innermost convictions"); and to violence and "Stalinism." In the end, said Bruckner, far from lending real support to the Third World, Sartre mocked it with his indifference. "This follower of the Third World did not accept it unless it fulfilled the familiar role of the victim from whom he had nothing to learn."[51]

Thus, in a stark reversal, Sartre was recast in the narrative of decoloniza-tion in the antithesis of his former role. No longer the friend who sought to use his pen and his prestige to shore up the political and economic claims of non-European peoples, Sartre was now, for Bruckner at least, the enemy who had held those same people in contempt; the philosopher who, in his calls for recognizing particularity, had never seen that particularity himself; the ethicist who had abdicated his principles in the face of revolutionary regimes; and the observer whose position was, in the end, not engaged, but wholly narcissistic. This symbolic burial of Sartre the Third Worldist continued among left-wing intellectuals. For a colloquium sponsored by Liberté Sans Frontières in 1985 entitled, "Third Worldism in Question," Médecins Sans Frontières president Rony Brauman invited participants to comment on the ills of Third World-ism—by that time surely already well publicized. When Sartre's name came up—as it did with Brauman, Bruckner, and Socialisme ou Barbarie founder Cornélius Castoriadis—the judgment on him was bluntly negative. Castoriodis, for example, reproduced the idea that Sartre's anticolonialism should be reduced to the "political confusionism" he expressed in his preface to *The Wretched of*

---

49   In the French edition, these comments appear in a special box devoted to Bruckner's condemnation of Sartre; in the English edition, the full text of the box is relegated to a long footnote oddly placed at the end of a chapter that is not clearly related to Sartre. See the original in Pascal Bruckner, *Le sanglot de l'homme blanc: Tiers-Monde, culpabilité, haine de soi* (Paris: Editions du Seuil, 1983), 72–3.   .

50   Bruckner, *Tears of the White Man*, 185 (translation modified).

51   Ibid. (translation modified).

the Earth, in which Sartre had supposedly simply switched the Third World peasantry for the industrial proletariat in an orthodox Marxist schema.[52]

The debate on the Third World and the Left, whose main themes were established by *Le Nouvel Observateur* in the late 1970s, set the stage for this re-evaluation of the role of the Third Worldist intellectual—Sartre chief among them, as Bruckner's book demonstrated. Thus, when Sartre famously attended a press conference in 1979 in support of Kouchner's initiative to give aid to the Vietnamese "boat people," many interpreted this action as Sartre's own auto-critique of his now discarded Third Worldist positions and, as a corollary, his move rightward toward the "correct" positions of old foe Raymond Aron. While others may have found a deep symbolism in the brief Sartre-Aron encounter, Beauvoir recounted that Sartre did not and, indeed, left before Aron's speech. "Sartre attributed no importance to this meeting with Aron," she pointed out, "although some journalists went on and on about it." Bernard-Henri Lévy went so far as to coin the term "Sartron" in his lamenta-tion of post–Sartre/Aron encounter intellectuals who thought it was the role of intellectuals to "get along" in a "religion of consensus" as "Sartrons" rather than to disagree fundamentally.[53]

This will to recast Sartre's politics in the postcolonial era overshadowed what Sartre's presence at Kouchner's press conference more plausibly symbol-ized: the end of radical anticolonialism and the collapse of the idea that colonialism and imperialism were a self-sufficient theory of patterns of global domination—a collapse that had been brewing for Sartre as it had for others since the Biafran war, or even earlier. According to Nourredine Lamouchi, "Beginning in the 1970s, Sartre no longer defends the Third World or colonized countries above all others, but especially the poor and the weak of all kinds and, above all, oppressed ethnic minorities: Basques, Corsicans, Bretons, Occitans."[54] Sartre's development of an ethics of the least favored in the mid 1960s would seem to put this shift at a rather earlier date. Theories of colo-nialism and imperialism may still have had importance, but only when the particularities of diverse cases were taken into account, and with the recogni-tion that other forces might be at work. In the wake of this collapse of theories of colonialism and imperialism as all-encompassing explanations of patterns of domination, certainly complete by the late 1970s for most left-wing intellec-tuals, what was to take its place?

---

52 Cornélius Castoriadis, "Démocratie et développement (suite)," in Rony Brauman, ed., *Le tiers mondisme en question* (Paris: Oliver Orban, 1986), 214.

53 Bernard-Henri Lévy, *Eloge des intellectuels* (Paris: Grasset, 1987), 32–3.

54 Lamouchi, *Jean-Paul Sartre et le tiers monde,* 173.

SINGULAR OR SINGLE? THE NEW/OLD UNIVERSALISM OF THE LEFT

By the late 1970s, the critique of Third Worldism and corresponding de-legiti-
mation of the right of peoples as a preliminary condition to guaranteeing
human rights led to a move toward elevating humanitarian claims—thought of
as universal—above all others. Jean Daniel described this shift on the Left,
which included an apparent jibe at Sartre's notion of the singular universal, as
well as a comment upon the resurgence of the language of civilization and
barbarism, in the opening sentences of his preface to *Le tiers monde et la gauche*:

> How to rediscover the Enlightenment in the night of barbarian revolts? How to
> pass from the contempt of "prelogical mentality" to the exaltation of "savage
> thought"? How to discover the revolutionary universal in the ethnic-religious
> singular and the national particular? These three questions summarize the
> history of the relations between the Western Left and the Third World.[55]

Universalism was dangerous, Daniel argued—even in "progressive" forms
such as Third Worldism. He thought that the late 1970s represented a "crisis of
the universal" brought on by the collapse of faith in Third World revolution. In
the place of a homogenizing Third Worldism must be placed a "respect for the
Other" and a genuine "right to difference."[56]

For Daniel, the universalism of the Left had blinded it to the fact that
certain movements did not represent universal claims: specifically, those
movements that integrated Islam. Thus, in spite of his own calls for a "right to
difference," he came to criticize movements that had integrated Islam for their
false pretensions to universality. Daniel's misgivings fit well with the growing
anxiety in France over assimilating non-European, non-Christian populations
that ultimately fed into the debate on Third Worldism. By the late 1970s, political Islam had begun to figure prominently in left-wing debate on the Third
World. The critique of Third Worldism as totalitarianism often broke down
into criticisms of and anxieties over the rise of Islamism.[57] Critics of Third
Worldism invoked Islamism as a sign of Third Worldism gone awry—in effect,
of escaping the boundaries of what French Third World supporters *thought*
would happen in the aftermath of independence. Jean Daniel, for one, claimed
to have avoided falling into the trap of exoticism, of supporting this falsely
revolutionary movement, but only because of his personal experience:

---

55   Daniel, "L'universel, le tiers monde, la gauche," in Amin et al., *Le tiers monde et la gauche*, 7.
56   Ibid., 7–8.
57   For a succinct history of political Islam, see Gilles Kepel, *Jihad: The Trail of Political Islam*, trans. Anthony F. Roberts (Cambridge: Harvard University Press, 2002).

These efforts and this temptation [of the extreme Left to think that there was no difference between themselves and Algerian revolutionaries] could have been mine if I had not lived my childhood and my adolescence in this Algeria where opposition to injustice and humiliation sought refuge in a religion that functioned less as a return to spirituality than as a recourse to ideology.[58]

Islamism, as the unforeseen outcome for those without the experience of Daniel, could not be judged progressive. Both Burguière and Le Dantec echoed these sentiments in *Le Nouvel Observateur*'s debate, noting that part of the French Left's disillusionment with the Third World came with the recognition that a number of regimes were not socialist, but Islamist—Le Dantec implicitly compared them to Stalinist totalitarianism.[59]

That Islamism, in particular, became a target in the late-1970s critique of totalitarianism (even before the revolution in Iran, but especially afterward) is noteworthy. On the one hand, French observers evinced genuine concern about individual freedom under fundamentalist regimes. On the other, the choice of this target seemed to be motivated by more than just the sincere desire to protect human rights; indeed, its selection may have had much to do with domestic French politics, and the continuing battles over French identity in the face of an "onslaught" of seemingly inassimilable people—namely, Muslims.

Along with these worries about the role of Islam in some Third World regimes, intellectuals began to revive the civilization/barbarism distinction, which had been so effectively countered as imperialist mystification by anti-colonialists in the 1950s and 1960s, as well as by anthropologists as different as Leiris, Lévi-Strauss, and Balandier. In that era, the distinction remained a staple of right-wing discourse justifying continued French control of the colonies, but was largely rejected on the radical and moderate Left. By the mid 1970s, the revisionist view of Third World independence movements, coupled with the fashionable usage of the word "totalitarian," spurred a resurgence of talk of non-European barbarity, typically defined by those regimes that (to varying degrees) repressed rather than protected what French observers considered to be the most important human rights.

Aside from Daniel's own evocation of this language in the opening sentences of his preface, this resurgence is demonstrated throughout the contents of *Le tiers monde et la gauche*. The resurrection of these terms on the

---

58   Daniel, "L'universel, le tiers monde, la gauche," 9.
59   See Burguière, "Introduction," in Amin et al., *Le tiers monde et la gauche*, 21; and Le Dantec, "Une barbarie peut cacher une autre," in Amin, et al., *Le tiers monde et la gauche*, 43.

Left ought to be traced at least to the 1977 publication of Bernard-Henri Lévy's antitotalitarian tract, *Barbarism with a Human Face*, whose subject is Soviet communism.[60] The transfer of this terminology to the context of the decolonized states was, however, particularly powerful (and for some, objectionable): it simultaneously re-emphasized the supposed link between Third Worldism and barbarous, totalitarian communism, while reintroducing the old trope of civilized Europe's mission to help the savages in the non-European world. For Miské, this language was nothing short of scandalous, as the mocking title of his essay—"The New Civilizers"—underlined.

If Daniel had evinced disquiet about the perils of universalism, other left-wing intellectuals sought to embrace it, in the form of human rights, as the solution to the problem of endemic violence in the Third World, and also as the best path to ensuring respect for "difference" at home. For the defenders of human rights, in short, universals ought not to be discarded—rather, they ought to be understood as single, not singular; they were to apply to all equally, without respect for history, situation, or politics; they were to be what "everyone" could agree upon regardless of their position. This was a profound shift away from the basic anticolonialist, not to mention Third Worldist, arguments for recognition of national particularity, for relativist criticism of Eurocentrism, and for the claim that human rights were best guaranteed by nation-states independent of external rule.

Thus, over the course of the 1970s, a new universalism—one founded on human rights—ultimately won out in debates among left-wing intellectuals in the 1970s on how best to guarantee freedom both within and beyond France. In this chapter, I have discussed intellectuals' engagements with colonialism in the postcolonial era—specifically, with reference to a recasting of relations with the Third World along humanitarian, rather than political, lines. The left-wing use and reassessment of the utility of the colonial model in their engagements was, I have argued, directly related to *gauchiste* activism and the rise of a new left-wing, noncommunist force in electoral politics, the Parti Socialiste. That socialists, in particular, should have adopted the themes and rhetoric of anticolonialism can come as no surprise: it had been the war in Algeria that had literally broken apart the party's earlier incarnation, the SFIO, and had helped shape the careers of anticolonialists such as Daniel, Bourdet, Rous, and many others. "Magazines like ours were born with anticolonialism," Daniel wrote of *Le Nouvel Observateur*. "What the renaissance of the Left in France owes to the

---

60   Bernard-Henri Lévy, *Barbarism with a Human Face*, trans. George Holoch (New York: Harper & Row, 1979).

solidarity with colonized peoples struggling for their freedom is considerable."[61] Many on the Left now felt they owed it to those peoples to continue the struggle against imperialism by demanding the protection of human rights.

What was to become of the ill, blinded Sartre in this shifting intellectual terrain? Though he was a pioneering anti-racist, staunch anticolonialist, and tireless defender of individual freedom, he was in the process of being reduced to his most infamous and Manichean text: the preface to *The Wretched of the Earth*—a text that many interpreted him as having symbolically repudiated by appearing with Aron at the 1979 "boat people" press conference. Whereas Guadeloupan poet Daniel Maximin had admired Sartre's will and capacity to "listen to the savages"[62] as evidence of a respect for their autonomy, critics such as Bruckner recast him as a Eurocentric naïf who was directly responsible for the blinding of a generation. Sartre, in the end, was held to account, was put to judgment and judged guilty, for the undesirable outcomes of the decolonization process he had fought to bring about.

61   Daniel, "L'universel, le tiers monde, la gauche," 11.
62   Daniel Maximin, "Sartre à l'écoute des sauvages," *Le Nouvel Observateur*, May 5, 1980, 63—quoted in Chapter 2, fn. 3, above.

Conclusion: "He Ran While Dead" —Afterlives of Colonialism and Jean-Paul Sartre

In his contribution to a special edition of *Les Temps Modernes* marking its fiftieth anniversary in 1995, Jacques Derrida reminisced about his own ambivalent and deliberately distant stand with respect to Sartre's journal. Just as Sartre had said of Camus after their break that their relationship did not end, but rather that the two had found "another way of living together," Derrida seemed to indicate here a similar kind of negative affiliation, or, as he called it, a "permanent altercation":

> Everything that I have lived, read, tried to think, write, and teach for nearly fifty years (since, as an adolescent in Algiers before having ever visited the Metropole, I read Sartre and *Les Temps Modernes* or admired *No Exit* ...), everything, really everything will have been "oriented" by *Les Temps Modernes*, configured at bottom by *Les Temps Modernes*, a title under which one must designate both the journal and that which is inseparable from it, the "milieu," the "movement," the quasi-institution thus named, the constantly moving boundaries, the breaks (interior and exterior), especially, yes especially the breaks that marked its history and sculpted the landscape.

Thus, as for Deleuze, what seemed most important to Derrida was both what Sartre and *Les Temps Modernes* were and what they were *not*. By the latter, he meant, first, that process by which they broke successively with Aron, Camus, Merleau-Ponty, and the psychoanalysts Bernard Pingaud and Jean-Bertrand Pontalis[1]—"structuring" breaks, in Derrida's eyes, for both his development and the development of the postwar era. Second, he meant writers and thinkers to whom Sartre and the journal had introduced him—Bataille, Blanchot, Ponge, Hegel, Husserl, and Heidegger—and who had effectively turned him away from Sartre's style of thinking, writing, and doing, while also keeping the problems he posed within Sartre's orbit.[2]

---

1   For this last "rupture," see the debate surrounding "L'homme au magnétophone," *Les Temps Modernes* 274 (April 1969), reprinted as "The Man with the Taperecorder," in Jean-Paul Sartre, *Modern Times: Selected Non-Fiction*, trans. Robin Bass (New York: Penguin, 2000).

2   Jacques Derrida, " 'Il courait mort': Salut, salut: Notes pour un courrier aux *Temps Modernes*," *Les Temps Modernes* 587 (March/April/May 1996), 33, 34, 40, 44.

Derrida's musings focus on the Sartrean notion of engagement, of what it means "to write for one's own time," as Sartre called on his fellow writers to do in a 1948 essay.[3] In that text, Sartre wrote of a story that the messenger from Marathon had died while running to deliver his message of victory to the Athenians. "It's a beautiful myth," Sartre wrote,

> it shows that the dead still act for a little while as if they were alive. A little while, ten years, fifty years ... and then they are buried a second time. This is the measure we propose to the writer: as long as his books provoke anger, annoyance, shame, hatred, love ... he will live.

This idea, for Derrida, supplied the perfect entry point into the meaning of Sartre for him and, more broadly, for his generation, and it was fortuitous that the text itself cited the fifty-year anniversary as the mark of a "second burial."

Derrida, for one, was ready to bury *Les Temps Modernes* a second time, but only by looking forward to doing it a third: "The essential thing is that 'the second time' not be the last." The open-ended period of time that *Les Temps Modernes* announced through its consistent presence and the fact that, as its title indicated, it wished to comprehend "modern times," indicated that it was still running while dead, and Sartre alongside it. The unfinished nature of the period and the project was, in turn, reflected in Derrida's text, which was itself unfinished: a long set of notes for an article he claimed to be "incapable of writing," because of the "impossibility of delimiting my 'subject,' space, and time ... The limits are lost, and even the horizon. I wonder how the others have managed it."[4]

As I hope to have shown in this book, the legacy of intellectual anticolonial protest lived on into the postcolonial era, and tracing its history gives a compelling alternative to a story of postwar French politics that focuses on the divisions of the Cold War. Without attending to the dilemmas of decolonization, historians are ill prepared to address the cultural cleavages that appeared particularly forcefully from the 1980s onward, and they have few tools with which to grasp the complex, often contradictory assertions of the Left concerning French universalism (itself an oxymoron), cultural difference, the appearance of a diplomatic-cultural bloc of "Francophone" nations, and

---

3 Jean-Paul Sartre, "Ecrire pour son époque," *Les Temps Modernes* 33 (June 1948), 2113–21, part of which is reprinted as "We Write for Our Own Time," in Michel Contat and Michel Rybalka, eds, *The Writings of Jean-Paul Sartre, Vol. II: Selected Prose*, trans. Richard McCleary (Evanston, Ill.: Northwestern University Press, 1974).

4 Ibid., 36, 33, 34.

the role of the state in creating a modus vivendi.[5] Moreover, the demographic, cultural, economic, and social shifts engendered by decolonization are, of course, still evolving issues—or "unfinished projects"—that are now subsumed under the rubric of "globalization." Again, historians will be ill prepared to tackle that phenomenon if sufficient consideration is not given to the ways it is intimately related to the struggles and the outcomes of decolonization. Indeed, there are direct affiliations between the anticolonialist and anti-imperialist protest movements of the 1950s, '60s, and '70s and the alterglobalization movements of the current era—affiliations that are themselves shaped by the international economic and institutional arrangements resulting from both the end of European empires and the global hegemony of the United States, which some observers are increasingly willing to call "imperial."[6]

Thus, questions of how and when decolonization will "end"—or if it will[7]—and what path should be traveled in order to enter the network of global markets, institutions, media, and so forth, are still being debated. Perhaps this is also a reason why the legacy of Jean-Paul Sartre was and still is being debated in France by the likes of Derrida, Lévy, and others after his death. What is noteworthy, however, in contrast to this persistently ambivalent attitude among French intellectuals toward Sartre, is the almost complete absence of discussion about his work or significance in the Indian-Anglo-American tradition known as "postcolonial studies." This absence is remarkable for four reasons

---

5   This latter point is best illustrated by the law banning the wearing of obvious religious symbols—Muslim headscarves, large crosses, and Jewish skullcaps—in public schools. The law was passed under a broad consensus of Right and Left. For a discussion of the influence of American ideas on debates about "identity politics" in France, see Jean-Philippe Mathy, *French Resistance: The French-American Culture Wars* (Minneapolis: University of Minnesota Press, 2000), esp. Chs 4 and 5.

6   The literature on this theme has exploded, with the term "empire" often taking on new meanings. See, for example, Michael Hardt and Antonio Negri, *Empire* (Cambridge: Harvard University Press, 2000); Alain Joxe, *The Empire of Disorder*, trans. Ames Hodges (New York: Semiotext(e), 2002); Paul Marie de La Gorce, *Le Dernier empire: Le XXIe siècle sera-t-il américain?* (Paris: Grasset, 1996). For a dissenting view, which announces the demise of American empire, see Emmanuel Todd, *After the Empire: The Breakdown of the American Order*, trans. C. Jon Delogu (New York: Columbia University Press, 2003).

7   On the fate of decolonization in such places as New Caledonia and Guadeloupe, see the works on the French overseas departments and territories (the DOM-TOM)—Dominique Ghisoni, Wassissi Iopué, and Camille Rabin, eds, *Ces îles que l'on dit françaises* (Paris: L'Harmattan, 1988); Jean-Luc Mathieu, *L'Outre-Mer français* (Paris: Presses Universitaires de France, 1994); Fabienne Federini, *La France d'Outre-Mer: Critique d'une volonté française* (Paris: L'Harmattan, 1996); Ernest Moutoussamy, *L'Outre-Mer sous la présidence de François Mitterrand* (Paris: L'Harmattan, 1996); and Jean-Marc Regnault, ed., *François Mitterrand et les territoires français du Pacifique (1981–1988)* (Paris: Les Indes Savantes, 2003).

which would seem to make Sartre pertinent: the radical anti-essentialism of Sartre's philosophy; his direct relationship with (and sometimes influence on) foundational thinkers such as Frantz Fanon and Albert Memmi, and foundational institutions such as *Présence Africaine*; his attempt, like that of so many in the field of postcolonial studies, to theorize individual agency in some productive relationship with Marxism; and the fact that he was, at one time, the world's most famous intellectual supporter of movements in the non-European world.

Vilified by French poststructuralist thinkers as a "philosopher of the subject"—practically an epithet—Sartre has been written out of the foundational story that postcolonial studies tells about itself.[8] I hope this book may serve to modify that story, and that, like Derrida, those who do postcolonial studies may re-examine their discipline's history to find that Sartre is running while dead, perhaps in a state of permanent altercation with them, inside the story itself.

---

8   Two exceptions to this trend—both relatively recent—are Robert J.C. Young, *Postcolonialism: An Historical Introduction* (Malden, Mass.: Blackwell, 2001); and Ranjana Khanna, *Dark Continents: Psychoanalysis and Colonialism* (Durham, N.C.: Duke University Press, 2003). For a sample of founding texts, see Bill Ashcroft, Gareth Griffiths, and Helen Tiffin, eds, *The Post-Colonial Studies Reader* (New York: Routledge, 1995); Padmini Mongia, *Contemporary Postcolonial Theory: A Reader* (New York: Oxford University Press, 1996); and Reina Lewis and Sara Mills, *Feminist Postcolonial Theory: A Reader* (Edinburgh: Edinburgh University Press, 2003).

Index

.